Holk Master-class

ABC of Strategy, Marketing & Communications

Table of contents.

Introduction.

Holk Master-class is the result of 4 years work, researching, interviewing, editing and writing. A book and film project that could not have been made without the help of all the amazing interviewees to whom I am most grateful.

In my position as professor and lecturer at academic institutions, I have experienced and acknowledged a need for more practical learning. Academic business institutions in general, are designed to foster a high academic level but lack the tools that prepare and enable students to succeed in practice.

Over the past 10 years I have authored, directed and produced a total of 126 academic film episodes featuring CEO's of fortune 500 companies, acclaimed entrepreneurs, professors etc. in order to bring more practice in to the learning experience.

93% said video has had a positive impact on student satisfaction
Kaltura's annual State of Video in Education report:

77% of U.S. companies offer online training as a way to improve their employee's professional development.
Elogiclearning.com

I have authored, produced and directed the acclaimed international project "The mind of a leader", including a best-selling book and four film series (78 episodes). The mind of a leader is based on

Machiavelli's The Prince and Sun Tzu's The art of war, and includes legendary leaders such as Philippe Starck, Artistic Director, Stan Shih, founder & fmr. Chairman Acaer Inc., Philip Kotler, Professor and best-selling author, Jørgen Vig Knudstorp, Chairman and Fmr. CEO LEGO group, Late Dame Anita Roddick, founder of The Body Shop, Bjorn Borg, tennis legend and many more.

Besides my teaching experience, I hold an MBA, a Master of law and a certificate in directing from UCLA. My professional work titles include: Sales manager at Berghaus, and Steilmann GmbH & Co., Account Manager with Kunde & Co. advertising agency, Senior Trade Officer - Entertainment at Trade Commission of Denmark Los Angeles, Head of Trade Department at The Danish Embassy in Singapore and Founder of Astromax Entertainment. Experience I have carefully used when developing the foundation for Holk Master-class.

Holk Master-class is divided into 8 parts. It presents elements and workflow from strategic planning to campaign development, including the creative brief and Holk's communication platform model defining the brand coms or value words. It features graphic strategic models and academic descriptions, followed by interviews with acclaimed entrepreneurs, CEO's, industry professionals and professors. Learn from companies like IKEA, Carlsberg, Trustpilot, Joe & The juice, Mikkeller, Ole Henriksen skincare, David & Goliath advertising, Red Cross and many more.

In respect of the interviewees, interview statements are kept in the original grammatical format. The figures featured in the book serves to connect the book with the film series. As some images are small, all important text parts are listed explicitly in the book text.

Read the book or watch the short film episodes before class as flip-the-class-room, in class as basis for discussion, or simply as inspiration. Bring your class book to life. Connect business models with real life experience. Each chapter topic is based on the film episodes (approx. 15 min. in duration). Tailor made for individual learning or classroom interaction. I hope you will enjoy the concept.

Part I. Strategic planning and branding.

Mission & Vision.

Mission and vision are a set of guidelines that indicates what an organization wants to do and be.[1] In the entrepreneurial startup phases it's often dreams and desires that motivate a team. Smaller organizations are flexible and adaptable, and there are many examples of very successful companies that started out doing one thing and ended up in a different direction. However, as the company grows it becomes increasingly important to have a specific vision and mission that guides and motivates the employees.

A Mission frequently defines what the company or organisation aims "to do", whereas a Vision is a state of being, "to be".

If we look at Nike. Their Mission is:

"To bring inspiration and innovation to every athlete in the world. If you have a body, you are an athlete."
Bill Bowerman.

And their Vision:

---

[1] Campbell, A., Yeung, S. (1991). Brief case: Mission, vision and strategic intent. Pergamon Press plc.

"To carry on his legacy of innovative thinking, whether to develop products that help athletes of every level of ability reach their potential, or to create business opportunities that set Nike apart from the competition and provide value for our shareholders."

Another strong example is Coca Cola. Their mission is:

"To refresh the world..."
"To inspire moments of optimism and happiness..."
"To create value and make a difference."

Their vision is divided into areas:

"People: Be a great place to work where people are inspired to be the best they can be."
"Portfolio: Bring to the world a portfolio of quality beverage brands that anticipate and satisfy people's desires and needs."
"Partners: Nurture a winning network of customers and suppliers, together we create mutual, enduring value."
"Planet: Be a responsible citizen who makes a difference by helping build and support sustainable communities."
"Profit: Maximize long-term return to shareowners while being mindful of our overall responsibilities."
"Productivity: Be a highly effective, lean and fast-moving organization."

Over the years their communication platform and slogan has adapted to the changing environment but stayed true to their Mission. Here are a few selected examples of slogans that appear very much in sync with the mission "to refresh the world" and "inspire moments of optimism and happiness":

1904 Delicious and refreshing.

1945 Passport to refreshment.

1979 Have a Coke and a smile.

1985 America's Real Choice.

1991 Can't Beat the Real Thing.

1993 Always Coca-Cola.

2000 Enjoy.

2005 Make It Real.

2006 The Coke Side of Life.

2010 Twist The Cap To Refreshment.

2011 Life Begins Here.

2012 Open Happiness.

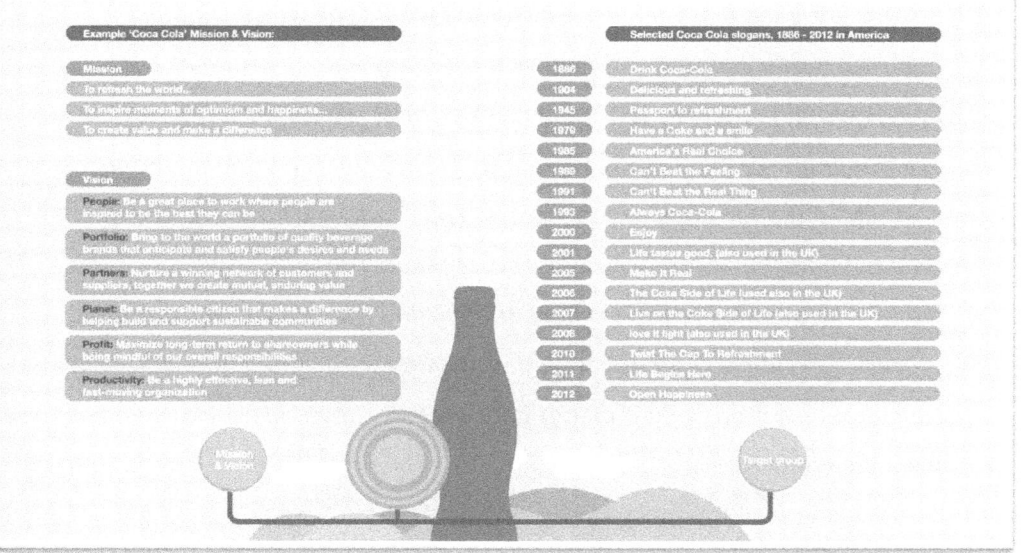

Figure 1.

In recent years more companies have added a motivational 'ethical' purpose to the Mission & Vision. Something that makes employees and other stakeholders feel that they are part of something bigger. Something that makes a difference.

Interviewees.

Dennis Balslev, CEO IKEA Germany. Fmr. CEO IKEA Denmark.

"The IKEA vision, missions, business idea is that's what we live for. So IKEA is very, very strong. We talk about, "create a better everyday life for the many people" witch is our vision and make all our decision based on the vision of the company. I think also with the business idea, that we focus on home furnishing, that's what we should do and nothing else. And

11

with the founder, Ingvar Kamprad, 90 years old this year. He has put the history into Ikea in a very strong way so I would say we are not just a home furnishing company. We have a company with a strong history, have a vision in life why we are here. We are very long term the way we are thinking. We want to create a better life for our coworkers, for our customers and for people in the world. That's why we have created this Ikea Foundation, where we support more than 100 million people in the world with support to their school, to their life where they live, different places. It's really a company with a vision and with values and culture we talk about everyday and it means a lot for us to have this background as we have today, yes."

Kaspar Basse, Founder, CEO Joe & The Juice.

"There definitely to start out with was, you'd call it a vision, whatever. Mine was probably Starbucks to some extent. I wanted to tweak it with the dramatizing the health and expanding the experience. It was never something I sat down and wrote on a paper. I didn't, interestingly enough, as I came from advertising and a marketing degree, I didn't take that very planned, organized approach. I didn't do a segmentation. I didn't really do a very strong conceptualization. I just had some ideas of what it was I wanted to deliver. I was always very focused on doing something that I would be proud about, that I would want to indulge in and that ... The vanity around that has been a very strong direction for me.

I think you said it correctly. Over the years, if you're gifted by development and building a company, at some point you start to, perhaps, feel the necessity to formulate whatever it is that you have going. I think that's a very challenging exercise. For our sake it was a necessity when our private equity partner went in and said, "Listen we can feel that you have a thing going. We know it's something you don't have to talk about, because you and the top management, you all have it in your stomach. Whether you can really pronounce it or not."

But for them and for their boards to understand it a little better, we were required to somehow formulate it. Which is an interesting exercise. I think it's a two edged sword or whatever you say. Partly you can kill something by formulating it, writing it down. When you talk about visions and missions, the most ridiculous thing is seeing the visions and missions of greater companies. Which are absolutely the same. Imagining a company formulating their mission or vision or whatever they want to call it, as being the strongest, most profitable, recognized retail concept in the world. Something that any one of us would never be able to argue, but which has absolutely no soul and identity and nerve to it."

Anders Kryger, Senior Business Strategist, Industrial PhD Fellow at MAN Diesel & Turbo.

"For some organizations, it's extremely important. For others, it isn't so important. It depends a little bit on what kind of a company it is. I think if it's a very old company, people will have a very good understanding, a very good idea of what this company does so with a mission. That's why I think in that sort of company, it's not that important to voice, articulate and describe the mission statement because people will have a pretty good sense of it.

On the other hand, if you do it, it might drive them to solve their jobs with excellence so that's the whole point of having a mission statement. On the other hand, if you have a very new company, I think its extremely important that they have a vision. Something that they can aspire to so having a stretch goal that they can work hard and drive themselves to reach. In the strategic planning process, which I think has an internal focus for the company's management, I think it is the easiest if they have both a mission and a vision."

Dennis Balslev, CEO IKEA Germany. Fmr. CEO IKEA Denmark.
"The vision and mission is where we start. When I start to talk about Ikea, if I start to make my strategy, for the many years ahead, I start with the vision and the mission of the company. That's very important for us and for all new coworkers, we have trainings in understanding the vision, the mission and our values and culture. We said we want to be company who have a reason to exist and not just a company who make profit. For us, it's still very important when we make long-term decisions."

Benjamin Holk Henriksen, Strategic planning & branding.
Lecturer DIS and Copenhagen Business School, Author, Filmmaker
"The Mind of a Leader", "Holk Master-class".
"Mission and vision, are an important part of the organization as they describe the purpose of the organization "what we do". And formulate some kind of vision or goal... "what we want to be". And as we have witnesses some organizations stick so closely to their mission that it has a strong influence on both organization and brand image.

As described by Andrew Campell and Sally Yeung in their article "Mission, Vision and Strategic intent", organizational have to be careful about how they define their vision. On the one hand the desired future state cannot be too specific or easy to accomplish since it would then loose it's purpose. I mean… Ideally you would be able to strive for it forever. However on the other hand, if the desired future state is too far away it looses its motivational and guiding purpose. So it's a delicate balance."

Peter Holten Mühlmann, Founder and CEO, Trustpilot.
"I think whether you call it a mission, or vision or something else is less important. I do think it's very important that you are stating how do you want to change the world? How would you like the world to be? I think that's important because it sets a guideline in terms of "what's our values?"

It can… If you want to scale a business, the most important thing is that people can make the right call without asking me. However, I don't think it's enough to have a vision or a mission. I think you need to translate that into long term and short term goals. Also, because it's in that translation that decisions are made and that the vision becomes real."

Kaspar Basse, Founder, CEO Joe & The Juice.
"I think it's very important when you do this, that you keep your creativity and you keep the edge in it, and you're very focused on being a little radical in defining it. You can't be worried about everybody understanding it. Everybody agreeing to it. You need to really have the guts to pronounce what your stomach feeling is telling you.

On the other side, it's also a healthy exercise, because having to formulate it fairly briefly, or even illustrate it briefly forces you to be precise. Some of the things you thought were precise inside yourself, suddenly, when you have to really choose that one word, or that one illustration, you have to actually let something go. Which you didn't have to do as long as everything was just one big direction, journey. It becomes more and more necessary over time. I agree to that.

One thing is formulating it. Another thing is preaching it, teaching it. At a very ambitious, but not instructional level. Getting people to feel it instead of just learn it. There is a big difference between actually buying into stuff and being ... People always say, "You have to be able to quote it when you wake up at four in the morning." No. You actually don't. That's like rehearsing for an exam. What happens there? The second you're done with it, you let it go. You need to have it inside yourself, so it's just a natural journey for you. The storyline needs to be very natural, this happened, this happened, that's why we are what we are today, and we see it this way."

Benjamin Holk Henriksen, Strategic planning & branding.
Lecturer DIS and Copenhagen Business School, Author, Filmmaker
"The Mind of a Leader", "Holk Master-class".
"Two concepts that overlaps with mission and vision, are the strategic intent and the mission statement.

The strategic intent encompasses criteria. It encompasses an active management process that includes: focusing the organization's attention on the essence of winning, motivating people by communicating the value of the target, hereby leaving room for individual and team contributions. Known examples are: Canon sought to "beat Xerox". Or Honda strove to become a second Ford, an automotive pioneer.

The Mission statement involves an analysis of employee values and organizational behavior. Like described in the short animated film, it encourages discussion of who we are and adds some kind of greater purpose to the organization's. Why do we go to work? Do we go to work to produce cellphones or do we go to work to make people come closer together. So adding an emotional value that is rooted in your organizational behavior can be a strong motivational factor in terms of the mission statement."

Target group.

A target market is a group of customers towards which a *business* has decided to aim its marketing efforts and products.[2] The target group is often defined as Primary target group and Secondary target group. A well-defined target market is the first element of a marketing strategy.

The marketing mix variables: price, product, promotion and place, determine the success of a product in the marketplace. Target markets are groups of individuals that are separated by aspects.[3]

Traditional segmentation includes:

• Their location or region.

• Demographic and Socioeconomic segmentation such as gender, age, income, occupation, education, household size, and stage in the family life cycle.

• Psychographic segmentation meaning similar attitudes, values, and lifestyles.

• Behavioural segmentation such as occasions and degree of loyalty.

• Product-related segmentation referring to their relationship to a product.

In addition to these segmentations, market researchers have advocated for a needs-based market segmentation, to identify smaller or better defined target groups. Or segmentation based on lifestyle in

[2] Simons, R. (2014). Choosing the Right Customer Harvard Business review, March issue.
[3] Avery, J., & Steenburgh, T. (2012). Target the Right Market. Harvard Business review, October issue.

specific social media communities. People of different ages may still have the same lifestyle or preferences.[4]

Interviewees.

David Angelo, Founder & Chairman, David & Goliath advertising agency.

"...You start with the authentic core of the brand, first and foremost, right? It's like you don't sell feminine hygiene products to men. You go to the core of who you are as a brand, what you stand for, what you believe in, right? Then you look at like-minded people that believe in that as well, and you target those people. You don't try to sell to other people, you target the people that believe in the same things that you believe in. By doing so they become your base, your core audience, your core fans, your core ambassadors. From there you develop a relationship between you and this core. You know what? That audience is as much part of the brand as the product itself. It becomes one giant sort of mindset experience, product and people together. You could dissect that today into a million different pieces. You could, because of all of the technology that we have, in regards to segmentation and be able to pin point, really just go after a person who just left-handed people. We have the ability now to target them like that.

I believe that will always exist, but I think that the challenge there is that it's kind of a Pandora's box for the most part, because where does that

---

[4] Caffarella, R. S. (1982). Identifying client needs. *Journal of Extension, 20* (July -August), 5-11.

19

end? It just keeps going and going and going. It's like, people with big noses, people who skip, people who dribble at basketball on Fridays. It just becomes so niche, to the point where I just believe that at the end of the day, that if you target a belief system, a like-minded belief system, then chances are you're going to grow a more authentic audience, and the right type of audience for you, as opposed to niche marketing."

Kaspar Basse, Founder, CEO Joe & The Juice.

"No. We never did. We never segmented ... This is a very peculiar and funny thing, because even though I came from advertising, which lives off segmentation. For some reason there was just, as I started saying earlier, for me it was doing something that I would be proud about. I didn't consider whether that was men or women from nineteen to twenty-five. We really just did something that we wanted to be proud about, and wanted to enjoy ourselves.

The interesting thing is that I think I can argue that we ended up appealing more widely than most other concepts. If you go into Joe & the Juice today, you'll see anything from mothers with newborn kids, to young kids, eight, ten years old, having fun with music. The new funky thing with juices or shakes. To teenagers and even their parents. You take many concepts. The problem with teenagers and parents are nobody wants to go where mom and dad goes. Somehow we managed to transcend those barriers. We'll have business people having a double espresso, in and out fast. Even, perhaps, two seventy-five year old female friends sitting there enjoying fun times for a few minutes until they can't stand the loud music anymore. It has become much wider in it's appeal than we would ever have dreamed of or been able to define starting out.

You got to watch out being too traditional in your approach when you build businesses."

Lars Liebst, CEO Tivoli.

"Since we are a program park, there is one more time, he helped us quite a lot, because the way we have to plan our program is done in a way that it can target different target groups. For instance when we do Friday night rock, it's funny enough Friday night at 10:00 so it won't disturb elderly people having a walk in the park. When we do classical music it's 7:30 or 7:00. When we do theater productions it's a different time. Our programming is different throughout the week and throughout the day and throughout the season. That's, I think, the sole reason why we can have that many visitors. We have 4.7 million visitors on an annual basis, and it's from the newborn to the 99 year old. They come from different aspect of the society. We try to target each of them in a different way and we are very much aware of it."

Malin Gardeström, International Marketing Manager, Carlsberg & Tuborg.

"It is very important but very difficult to define the target group in terms of segmentation. Tuborg has I would say the broadest target group in Denmark. Our target group is 18 plus. It's basically everybody above the legal drinking age. We acknowledge the differences within this group, but for us, it's important to reach everybody and not to be appalling to anyone. It is very difficult because you need to try to target some people and we do this in ways we're trying to segment, not so much based on age anymore like we used to do. Like the saying goes, the 40 is the new 30, and the 30 is the new 20s. This is very much true also in terms of how

people purchase. You can target in terms of festival goers, or how you buy or how you spend your life if you're a young family, if you're an older couple. That's how we try to think when targeting."

Asger Leth, Director & Screenwriter, DGA award winner. (Ghosts of Cité Soleil, Man on a Ledge, Five Obstructions, Move on (Telekom)).

"I have a target group example that I want to share with you. I did one commercial spot for a clothing company where clothing companies are usually, especially this brand is a very urban, young, male, hip hipster type. That's the target group. What we did was, me and the owners of the brand and the agency decided that that doesn't matter. If we focus on maybe the craziest cool movies, little movie spots, then that's the way to reach our target. If we decide to do that, why don't we flip it around and not cast beautiful young or hip quirky urbanites, but let's cast these old geezers that we just find on the street? Drunks and people with other problems, but with great faces and character. Let's put these guys into these outfits, this hip clothing and make movies with these old guys wearing this stuff and see what happens. I think all kinds of magic happened, and the brand became a massive international brand, or it's becoming that. Sometimes, you can flip it completely upside-down and hit your target group even more directly, because your target group, especially when you're talking about urban hipster-nites in their 20's and so on, they're so sick and tired of being target group, target-it, that they actually appreciate that you flip it upside-down."

Birgitte Mabeck, Head of fundraising and marketing Red Cross.

"When there is a disaster we get a lot of funds coming in, when there is no disaster, the funds kind of dry out and we get a fluctuation in our income. How do we get that steady? What do we start communicating in order for people to find this interesting and getting an attraction to us? In order to figure this out, we also have to figure out who are the people who are interested in donating to the Red Cross. We started looking into our original database. Who has been supporting us? Who are they? We did look at the basics around what is the age group? Where are they living? What are they reading, blah, blah, blah. We started the combination of, what is it actually that they would like to be part of? What is the feel good feeling that they would like to take away from us? What is the product that we are selling to the donor, so to speak?"

Fumiko Kano Glückstad, Assistant Prof. PhD in Cross-Cultural Communication & Cognition.

"Previously, yes, gender or the age, education, background, this typical segment has been used as a segment in each countries. I'm actually supporting value based segmentation, so if I can talk about current research for example, I'm analyzing for example World Value Surveys. You can access to the almost five, almost half billion people's database from a hundred countries. You can see what kind of value patterns people have, express or prioritized. These kind of database can be really useful segmenting consumers type across cultures, then you can really see what type of people is actually sharing values across cultures, what type of people is actually having culture specific values, and this kind of segmentation, or segments, group, can be used for global marketing. Not global marketing actually, intercultural marketing in a way.

23

Benjamin Holk Henriksen, Strategic planning & branding.

Lecturer DIS and Copenhagen Business School, Author, Filmmaker "The Mind of a Leader", "Holk Master-class".

"You need to analyze the whole distribution system, distributers, importers, retailers etc. and not just the end user. Depending on your strategy and whether you are using a push or pull strategy it's important to know the different influencers and decision makers. You need to study their values, preferences and buying habits. In many cases the buyer and the user are not the same person... You know, moms buying cloth for their kids, husbands etc."

Petter A. Stordalen, Founder and owner of Nordic Choice Hotels.

"I think it's more important than ever to understand your guests of today, but even more important to understand the guests of tomorrow. What will they ask for? What do they want? And you need to be open-minded and you need to understand that the future for the hotel industry will not be made by a guy like me at 54. So when I open, the last concept was a hipster concept in Stockholm, AAA location, it's called Hobo. The GM is 26. Nobody working there is probably more than 30. I can't even see the difference between the people working there and hanging in the bar. It's been a huge success since day one. They didn't even do marketing the traditional way. They do everything different, but for that group, that society, it's unique. It's something new in the hotel industry. When I'm coming in there, I know I'm too old to stay there. And I don't feel at home. But it's not for me and it could never be done by me or people like me, because it was only a guy under 30 that could do it.

It's the same with food concepts, new chefs. You need to have people that are different, that think different, that challenge you. In everything from concept to digital guest journey, to everything. Be bold. Have a bad ass determination. And be willing to put together people that are different from yourself and give them the space to develop the product or the hotel for the future. I did. And it was a huge success. And that's the future of my company, to find the right people because it's not about the cash. It's about finding the right people and give them the opportunity to do something that's not been done before. And sometimes you will fail. But that's a part of the game. Just do it different next time."

Stakeholder - & Issue management.

Issue Management involves a certain foresight. It's the art of recognizing problems that might occur and affect companies, government, or consumers and then planning ways to solve them. Some marketing and communications professionals implement routines or set up warning systems that enables them to monitor stakeholders.[5]

A stakeholder is any individual, group or organisation that can affect or is affected by the achievement of the organization's objectives. Stakeholder management is a critical component to the successful delivery of any product, service, activity or communication campaign.[6] The discipline involves understanding, prioritising, engaging and communicating with stakeholders. Who are our stakeholders? What are their stakes? What opportunities do our stakeholders present to the firm? What information do they want from us and what are our responsibilities?

Examples of stakeholders are:

Customers.

Customer advocate groups.

Unions.

Employees.

Trade organisations.

---

[5] Dougall, E. (2008). Issues Management. Institute for Public Relations, December 12.
[6] Freeman R. Edward and Evan William M. (1990). Corporate governance: A stakeholder interpretation. Journal of Behavioral Economics, vol. 19, issue 4, 337-359.

Competitors.

Suppliers.

Government.

Political or activist groups.

Owners.

Financial community.

Media.

Figure 2.

There are different ways to organize and prioritise stakeholders. Some use the term Primary and Secondary Stakeholders or Direct and Indirect, as a measurement of how much they are affected. Others like to address them as Internal and External Stakeholders depending on their relation to the organization. Effective Stakeholder Management

27

creates positive relationships with stakeholders and manages their expectations and objectives.

Interviewees.

Andreas Rasche, Professor at Copenhagen Business School. Department of Management, Society and Communication.

"Issue management systems are usually used to deliberately manage social and political issues. For instance, the sweat shop scandal, which can appear in relation to corporations. The biggest advantage with regard to PR is that a corporation can sense weak signals. Whenever weak signals appear, whenever the corporations exposed to risk or can potentially be exposed to risk, corporations are knowledgeable about this. One the other hand of course, you can also turn it around. You can say such issue managements systems can also be tremendously helpful in order to get to know about certain PR opportunities. For instance, if a company is engaged in developing a new technology, a very eco-friendly technology and then this can be something that it goes into issue management and then, also be of course, used for PR effects."

Benjamin Holk Henriksen, Strategic planning & branding. Lecturer DIS and Copenhagen Business School, Author, Filmmaker "The Mind of a Leader", "Holk Master-class".

"Both stakeholder - & Issue management requires a certain foresight. But while issue management focuses on turning the development of a given situation or issue into your favor, Stakeholder management focuses more on the players that may affect your business.

28

In marketing and communications that means creating content that informs or in other ways meet stakeholder expectations. But it also means thinking about how your actions and campaigns affect your surrounds and vice versa.

An example of issue management is when the council of fashion designers in 2012 released model health guidelines for New York Fashion Week. An effort from the industry to help them self – not only by eliminating eating disorders and negative press stories but also by preventing forced government regulations."

Andreas Rasche, Professor at Copenhagen Business School. Department of Management, Society and Communication.
"Obviously, the classical definition of stakeholder is very broad. That would be any individual or organization who can be affected or can affect the achievements of corporations objectives. This is very often sided as the classroom definition of it and it comes from Edward Freeman and his book on Strategic Management: The Stakeholder Approach, which is seminal work in this area."

Leif Rasmussen. Strategic Branding. Lecturer, DIS – Study Abroad in Scandinavia.
"When you are having stakeholders, you first of all should start defining them. If you don't define your stakeholders, you might be lucky to handle it properly, or you might be more, realistically, you might be unlucky doing the wrong things. So what is very important is to keep in mind who are your actual stakeholders and then whenever you communicate to

them, you should start thinking about how do they perceive my message. It is not so much about how you think of yourself, it is about how it is being perceived by your stakeholders and that's the essence of how you manage your stakeholders."

Andreas Rasche, Professor at Copenhagen Business School. Department of Management, Society and Communication.

"One of the key reasons for this is to simply legitimacy. Legitimacy reasons, organizations need to legitimize themselves. I wouldn't say the only way. One important way to legitimize yourself as an organization is to talk to others, to talk to others and to be answerable to others. That means dialog and it means engaging with others, engaging with those which normally you would not engage with them. Companies very often engage with their shareholders, with their investors. Of course, also other parties also have important stakes in the corporation. In this sense it is quite important to have this communicative channel from the corporation towards it's stakeholders.

This is true of course, for the corporation at different levels. For instance, I also believe the Board of Directors needs to have some consultative forums, where stakeholders can raise concerns, where stakeholders can also comment on corporate policies on corporate risks and corporate strategic ambitions. I believe these kinds of channels are important for corporations, for legitimacy reasons, but also to learn. Because corporations of course, they don't exist in a vacuum and they need to learn. They only learn of course, by talking to others and getting their perspective."

Peter Giacomello, Sponsorship and Reputation Director, Marketing Carlsberg.

"Yes, of course we do. For instance, the area we're in right now is a hospitality zone which is made for our biggest customers, and it's a networking place. All the musicians come here, all the press come here, and of course all of our customers. We have 2,000 guests over 4 days. They can come in here, relax, enjoy a cold beer, and just rest their legs before they go out to see another concert."

Malene Torp. Executive Director, DIS – Study Abroad in Scandinavia.

"Managing stakeholders is a perhaps the most important thing of being a successful leader and I think one advice that I would give to future leaders would be not to define their stakeholders in a very narrow sense. I think as a young leader you could be very tempted to only think of your stakeholders as your key customers and as your, say, executive board or something like that, but I think to think widely about stakeholders and defining your stakeholders in the widest possible sense and then managing them and being in close communication with them is something that I would advise people to do."

Andreas Rasche, Professor at Copenhagen Business School. Department of Management, Society and Communication.

"I would suggest it's also based on academic literature. They are three criteria to prioritize stakeholders. The first one is power. How much does a certain stakeholder an individual or a group influence a corporation? The second one would be legitimacy. How legitimate is the claim is the stakeholder towards the corporation? Legitimacy here would be judged

as whether a claims appropriate in a given social context. In the context of course, that the corporation operates in. Last but not least, it's all about the urgency of the claim. How urgent is this claim being framed? Do corporations need immediate attention towards that claim?"

Lars Liebst, CEO Tivoli.

"Since we are what we are, there is a lot of stakeholders. I think that we shouldn't forget that many of our stakeholders are actually citizens of Copenhagen. It goes from Mr and Mrs. Hansen to the Lord Mayor. It goes from Mr and Mrs. Peterson to the Prime Minister of Denmark. It is a wide range. In one way, of course, we do list them as such, but it's a huge target group, and we have to see if we can bear in mind that all of them are very important for us."

Christina Bilde, Spokes person Roskilde Festival.

"The advice is to be very specific on what you yourself represent and what you want with whatever you are... I think authenticity is a word that maybe helps. Being very clear of what you expect and want from your partners, the artists, and the audience and where you are prepared to be moved and where you're not prepared to be moved. You can't do that without knowing what you yourself stands for, you could say."

Peter Holten Mühlmann, Founder and CEO, Trustpilot.

"Initially, if you're starting a business; per definition, there's not going to be a lot of people. You'll tend to manage most of them. Then, I think the key here is to hire people that you feel are comfortable in managing these stakeholder relationships. Then, only picking a few of the very most important ones. Then, manage those yourself."

Benjamin Holk Henriksen, Strategic planning & branding.

Lecturer DIS and Copenhagen Business School, Author, Filmmaker

"The Mind of a Leader", "Holk Master-class".

"There are two interesting and complicated cases that involve the toy maker Lego. The first one was the 'everything is not awesome' viral video launched by Greenpeace. Playing on a sad version of the Lego movie theme song, the film featured an oil-stricken Arctic built from around 120 kg of Lego bricks.

Accusing Lego of "letting children down" Greenpeace pressure Lego in to dropping a partnership that distributes toys at Shell petrol stations. The video broke 1 million views a day after it was launched... more than 1 million people signed the campaign petition urging the company to "stop playing" with Shell. You may argue that Lego was working with the wrong partner or taken hostage by Greenpeace. I mean... Greenpeace was dicking into to almost sacred ground... associating our future, meaning our children and their creative development, with the ruin of our planet.... A smart move by Greenpeace. Nevertheless the case is an example of how major issues can arise from distant stakeholders.

The second Lego case involves Ai Weiwei, the Chinese Contemporary artist and activist. A very difficult case since creativity is part of the Lego DNA you could say. Apparently Weiwei has previously been able to get about 1.2 million Lego bricks for his portraits of 176 prisoners of conscience. But in this case Lego refused to sell him bricks for a planned installation in Australia, as they "cannot approve the use of Legos for political works". Before long the case went viral on the social media... offers came from admirers and fellow artists around the world to donate their own blocks, their own bricks. Cars were parked outside art museums to collect bricks etc. The Danish Minister of foreign affairs Kristian Jensen came to the rescue saying that Ai Weiwei was welcome to buy the brick in any Lego store and that he respected Lego's decision as a company decision. Others harshly criticized Lego for cocooning themselves in a modern world where it's impossible not to take a political stand."

Klaus Nørskov, Head of communication Red Cross.

"That's a complicated question because I think it changes over time very much. I've been in this business for quite a number of years, and I wouldn't have answered this the same way five or ten years ago. Not ten years ago, at least because our environment has changed so much since then. I would find it hard to tell whoever is going to have my job in five or ten years, how he has to or she has to go about because I'm pretty sure it's going to be changing rapidly further on as we progress. That's a difficult question, possibly not even wise to answer. I think what you can say about stakeholders is, as the situation is right now, that it's very volatile. You have to be very careful how you deal with them. Stakeholders, in general, are very demanding, so you can't just declare a target group and say this is our friends. They're only our friends for as long as we manage to maintain their interest, maintain our relation, and avoid positioning ourselves in places that they don't want to be persistent themselves.'

Positioning.

Brand positioning is the process by which marketers create an identity or image of their product or service. The objective is to benchmark, identify a market niche and utilize traditional marketing placement strategies, such as price, promotion, distribution, packaging etc. to create the position.

One of the most common models for positioning is the price/quality model. For example: low price/low quality or high price/high quality.[7]

Figure 3.

---

[7] D'Aveni, R. A. (2007). Mapping Your Competitive Position. Harvard Business review, November issue.

Models can be tailored to fit specific industries. For example, if you are in the car industry you might want to take fuel economy into consideration.

There are many different ways to develop a position. Some of the most important elements are:

1. Identify your direct competition.
Players that offer the same product or service.

2. Understand how your competitor is positioning their business.
What defines their communication platform? For example do they claim to be: original, innovative, the safest, the fastest, cheapest, largest etc.

3. Define your own current position or desired position.

4. Understand your primary and secondary target market and their preferences.

5. Compare your company's position relative to its competitors.
Compare your company's position relative to its competitors and try to identify areas for differentiation.

It's been argued that it is not wise to differentiate on price alone since the concept is easy to copy. Therefore, if you want to build your business and position on cheap prices, it's advisable to differentiate on the system that enables you to offer low prices. For example a special distribution or manufacturing business model.

6. Develop a differentiated value-based positioning concept.
What image and identity are we aiming for, what are the values, and how do we get there?

Some people mistakenly believe that the ideal product portfolio contains products from different segments, in order to tap into more target groups. However this is not always the truth. Some organizations may be better off being dominant in one segment where they have the needed know-how and expertise.

Interviewees.

Matthew Bagwell, Managing Director Naked Communications Europe.
"We've been involved in a lot of brand positioning work, and we also receive a lot of briefs that are a consequence of other agencies or organizations having already determined their brand positioning. I think that when I've been involved in helping clients determine where they should position themselves against a competitor. Some of the complexes I see are about... the positioning may be slightly different from market to market. Does that create a sort of a schizophrenic brand where the central marketing organizations are trying to drive out consistency, but actually it's not just the marketing execution in local markets that needs to be different, but that its positioning may be different.

A sort of a well known example of this might be something like Mercedes-Benz. Here in the UK a Mercedes-Benz is positioned as a sort of a premium, an upper premium product, and yet when I fly to Germany, almost every taxi is a dependable E-class Mercedes-Benz. The positioning is subtly different in some of the products across a range, and can be different for a brand across multiple markets."

Dennis Balslev, CEO IKEA Germany. Fmr. CEO IKEA Denmark.

"I think Ikea has a very good standpoint on price and quality. Ikea produce our own products. We design them, we produce them. Ikea have decided to work with what we call democratic design. In democratic design, we have five, you can say, legs we stand on, which one of them is form, design, sustainability, quality and then the low price. We've really tried to build in a way of thinking in each product.

I think, I must, Ikea is very strong in selling solutions. We are not only selling products and price. We try really to spend a lot of efforts to give customers inspiration, to find good solutions for their homes and not only selling a chair for a low price. We have put our positions very clear and invested, I think, a lot of money in our big stores around the world to really show customers how they can live and give them good solutions for their needs they have at home. We have taken a quite different approach to the home furnishing market you see in most countries in the world.

I talk a lot about in Denmark that our competitors, they have a product and then they have a slash price because the home furnishing market is very much about prices up and down and we have a different point. Again, we have 12-month prices in our catalog, which is outstanding in retail so we promise you a fixed price for the next 12 months. There's not many companies who can do that. We don't talk about slash prices. We talk about home furnishing, life at home. There a quite big difference to the approach to other companies we have taken. We believe this the right way for us to work because life at home is the most important for the most of us. This is our castle when we come home. This is where we have to relax and we live with our families. Ikea wants to really be part of that and not only selling products. That's a big focus for us."

Fumiko Kano Glückstad, Assistant Prof. PhD in Cross-Cultural Communication & Cognition.

"Brand positioning and also making positioning map, that is of course important in a way, because we have to communicate to the right target segment. We also need to know other competitors, how do they target the segment, are they targeting the same segment? How do they communicate, you need to understand first, then you have to really, afterwards you have to develop communications strategy for example, or marketing strategy. Positioning map is quite useful in a way that you really have to overview how the competitor is approaching which segment and targeting what kind of customers, how do they communicate, and then how your company has to actually sell to which target group. For finding out that kind of stuff I think positioning map could be useful."

Malin Gardeström, International Marketing Manager, Carlsberg & Tuborg.

"Tuborg and Carlsberg can appear to be very similar brands. Of course it's important to try and position them differently. In the Danish market

it's kind of blurry because they've both been there more or less at the same time. They are in more or less the same outlets. However, Carlsberg brand has always been about quality. The Carlsberg brand is always about what's inside the bottle, about the liquid, about always having a bit better at product. Not saying that Tuborg is not a good product because it is, but the main focus of Tuborg has been what's around it. It's been about making iconic marketing about having humor, because of course it's very difficult to have a very high quality product and to speak very funny about it or to have a lot of humor. Tuborg is about what's around and the lifestyle, and Carlsberg is very much about the quality of what's inside."

Matthew Bagwell, Managing Director Naked Communications Europe.

"It's a complex piece of work to do, to sort of exactly say, "How do you differentiate yourself from other brands which may be in a similar position?"

I've experienced it, where brands have come to us with brand positioning work, and we haven't necessarily agreed that they are positioned, or should be positioned where they are being told they should be positioned. Then it's a very careful negotiation with the client, to sort of say, "Okay, how did we arrive at this point? What evidence is there? Has a sufficient analysis been done? Are we absolutely confident?" Because you're going to then build everything around where you are positioned in a particular market, against your competitors. If that first step is wrong, then everything that follows could be by degrees increasingly incorrect.

It's absolutely true that we help clients understand their position. I think it's also about testing and learning, not to commit your entire global strategy as you're trying to move a position, but sort of see if there is appetite and permission for you to move. Also, when we receive briefs, are we absolutely sure that the created brief is correct for the positioning, and is the positioning correct for the brand?"

Klaus Nørskov, Head of communication Red Cross.

"I think everybody needs a home pitch in which they are fairly alone. This is our stronghold. At the Red Cross, our stronghold is our legal right, obligation, to be at the battlefield. We are born at the battlefield, and we have a unique right to help humanitarianly at the battlefield, so that's one thing. The other thing is that out of this, we have a very, very strong position on the entire humanitarian issue. This is what we declare our home pitch. That's the Red Cross home pitch. We're active in a lot of other areas, but this is out stronghold. Obviously when we talk about competitors or competition, we look at organizations who are also active in this area. From that perspective, obviously, Doctors Without Borders is a very, very strong competitor."

Lars Liebst, CEO Tivoli.

"Well we do follow up quite a lot, but who are our competitors actually? Will it be Bakken, an amusement park just north of Copenhagen. Is it Legoland in Jutland? Or is it actually the city? Or is it your mobile phone? Or what is it? I think you have to have a broader view on what is really... Who are you competing with and it can be narrowed down to time. It is time consuming going into Tivoli, so that is maybe one of the roads that you have to follow up. Do you have a product that can compete with the

time that people want to spend? If so, yes, I think we do follow up quite a lot, but we have a broader view than just our simple competitors."

Malin Gardeström, International Marketing Manager, Carlsberg & Tuborg.

"In terms of Carlsberg and Tuborg, when we are positioning in other markets as very much as an international premium beer, like Heineken for example would be in the Danish market, and it's a good segment but it's still very small compared to the full market. So it's easy but it's still difficult depending on what you are aiming for."

Christina Bilde, Spokes person Roskilde Festival.

"Being a non-profit festival and being an independent, non-profit festival is a very clear position that divides us from most other festivals in the world actually. Then, the way we work with our content trying to cross the borders between arts and music and different kinds of ethical issues or topics, our non-profit values actually, is also very specific or special for us and for the way we work. Of course, then that's also what we're trying to stress. Another thing that is quite important is also that we have nine stages. This year we presented one hundred and eighty-three bands in a very large diversity focusing also on up-coming music and talents in different parts, not just the music, also in arts, also in food, for instance, also in trades and start-ups and that is also very special for us.

As I said, we're a city so there are many things that are quite special about the way we work, sustainability is another part of it. Something that for us is taken, not for granted, but it's natural for us to work with it. Often I'm being asked whether it's something new that we're using to brand ourselves with, but being non-profit also means that you have an ambition to make a mark on the world and make a change in the world not just through donations but by the way you work and that means that sustainability is something that we've always concerned ourselves with and actually worked with as well."

Reflection on the Marketing Mix.

The marketing mix is a business tool used in marketing to determine a product or brand's offering.[8]

The term is attributed to Neil Borden who wrote an article called "The Concept of the Marketing Mix", and James Culliton, who in 1948 described the job of the marketing manager as a "mixer of ingredients".[9]

It refers to the set of actions, or tactics, that a company uses to promote its brand or product in the market and is often synonymous with the four P's: Product, price, promotion, and place.[10]

1. Product.
An item that satisfies what a consumer needs or wants. Intangible products are service-based. Tangible products have an independent physical existence.

2. Price.
The price is the amount a customer pays for the product.

3. Promotion.

---

[8] McCarthy, E. J. (1971). Basic marketing; a managerial approach. Homewood, Ill, R.D. Irwin.
[9] Borden, N. H. (1964). The Concept of the Marketing Mix, J. of Advertising Research, 2, 7-12.
[10] Kotler, P., Armstrong, G., Cunningham, P.H. (2005). Principles of Marketing. Toronto: Pearson Education Canada. pp. 67-70.

The methods of communication your may use to provide information about your product or service, such as advertising, public relations, personal selling and sales promotion.

4. Place.
The importance of providing the product at a place that is convenient for consumers to access. Place is synonymous with distribution.

These are the 4 P's. Other supplementary factors that may be included in the term 'marketing mix' are:

5. Physical evidence in relation to the store, such as storefront, uniforms, signboards, etc.

6. People meaning the employees the consumers interact with.

7. Process meaning systems within the organization that affect the marketing process.

Interviewees.

Peter Holten Mühlmann, Founder and CEO, Trustpilot.
"When you're starting a company, I fundamentally believe, it's all about the product. If you don't have a product, I don't really think you have anything. In the startup phase, I really recommend you invest all your time in figuring out what is it that you're taking to the marketplace. Then, once you figure that out, I think the others are becoming equally

important to figure out. They're the things that allow you to scale. If you don't figure out price, place and promotion; then how are you going to become a big business. Just take it in that order."

Henrik Fisker, Automotive designer and entrepreneur (BMW Z8, Aston Martin DB9, V8 Vantage, Fisker Karma, Mustang Rocket, VLF Force 1, Destino V8).

"Well, for me, I think when it comes to marketing, for me, the product is always comes first. You got to have a good product, in my opinion. I'm not a marketeer, where I can say, "I can sell anything you make as long as we make a good ad campaign." I'm sure there is some examples where that has worked and maybe it worked even more in the past.

I think today, what has changed dramatically in marketing is social media. We used to use words like word of mouth. Word of mouth come from the old days where truly somebody in the village had to tell somebody else. It would maybe take ten years until it reached the next village and another ten years until it reached another country. Today, you say something and within a second, it's reached the entire world. I think there is more emphasis on the product today. If it's a product that is in a slightly higher price range, then your authenticity of the product is very important. The story behind the product, as we get even into the higher premium segment, and luxury segment, the story of this product is extremely important."

David Angelo, Founder & Chairman, David & Goliath advertising agency.

"It's so hard to tell these days. Somebody once said, "Hey the true measure of great advertising is when people are buying the product off the shelves." I believe at the end of the day, that's the desired effect, but advertising is just one part of the whole equation. There's the on-premise experience of a dealership, a car dealership, to a customer sort of experience at a fast food restaurant. There's all these things, these sort of other touch-points that help define the success of a brand.

For me to say that... is one piece successful or one piece, should I give more credit to just being able to sort of target something specifically, is that going to ensure success for the brand? I'd say no, it's just one piece of it, but it's one piece of many pieces that you have to get right. The way I look at it is, what is the overarching idea that you're looking for? What is that common belief that we need to get, we need to make sure all of those touch-points are aligned with that common belief. Whether it's your media segmentation, or on-premise showroom traffic, to your broadcast TV, to digital efforts."

Dennis Balslev, CEO IKEA Germany. Fmr. CEO IKEA Denmark.

"If you looking into the future retailing, it's very modern to talk about multi-channel, omni-channel but we're trying to say it's about retailing. It's not about any smart words. It's about what does the customer want. They customer should be in the middle of everything we do. When we talk about the whole retailing, we talk about, of course, the product should be right product at the right price otherwise, we have no customers but then how do we show the product to the customer? How does the customer meet the company? It can be from home, on e-commerce. It can just be on the website. It can be in the physical store so we strongly believe that the

combination of all the different medias with the strong product in the middle, with the selling the solution for the customer, we believe the mix is the right one.

Ikea is one of the companies who talk about e-commerce and we will do that and we already do it quite successfully but the main focus for us is the physical store, the meeting with the customer, the day out for the family. That's why we invest in quite big stores, a bit opposite of the business today, where everybody believes the e-commerce will take the future. We believe the customer will still visit the stores. We can see that. We still have more and more visitors to our stores. We're still opening new stores because we believe the mix is important but the physical meeting with home furnishing has to happen in a physical store. I will not say that one part is more important than the other part. It's the customer who decides. They are in the middle. They decide how they want to meet us. They decide where they want to buy and how they want to buy so that's quite important in our focus.

As a company, we spend a lot of time to know our customers well. We visit our customer in their home. We have a lot of surveys. We have work groups. We really want to know our customers and understand what do they want and then we try to adapt as much as possible to that. That's really another angle from our point. It's... we decide not what the customer wants. We listen to them."

Seidi Suurmets, PhD Fellow at the department of Marketing, Copenhagen Business School.

"Marketing mix, it comprises the price, the product, the promotion, and the place. Yes there have been developed many frameworks of how to look at the marketing mix from the product management perspective and regardless of how many different aspects that could be defined it always comes down to these four aspects. Each of them can really be extended. For example, promotion could be divided into PR or direct selling or retailer mix and so on and so forth. At the end of the day, this model of four P's still applies to all possible producers and brand owners in that sense.

And it also applies to services because the service can also be perceived as a product that is sold to the market. So therefore the different characteristics that relate to service management and service marketing, this can also be viewed from the perspective of these four P's. So I think that it's value, it's simplicity is easy to remember and it always assured that all the relevant aspects are taken into account. For example, some CEOs and some managers may only focus on one P. For example, they only focus on price and that is not a sustainable or a good strategy because all the other important elements are left out of the equation. So that can really have a bad impact long term. For example, if the promotion or product and product innovation does not receive enough attention. So in the long term, it doesn't pay off to focus only horizontally on one aspect."

Leif Rasmussen. Strategic Branding. Lecturer, DIS – Study Abroad in Scandinavia.

"Yes, the Four Ps are very traditional, have been used for many, many years as one of the basics within marketing, which is true. If you're

looking into the real world, the real business world and how it works, it's difficult to say what is the most important. It depends on which line of business you are in, at which stage your product or products or brands are in and so on. There's only, I would say, one general thing that real life, real business life has proven to me and that is something which not everybody actually thinks about. It is so that if you should make this work with the Four Ps, you've got to apply them simultaneously and that is the important word, simultaneously, meaning that you cannot run a very good promotion if your price is wrong. So, you need to have both things in place simultaneously and that's how it goes with all the Four Ps, which is very often forgotten."

Henrik Fisker, Automotive designer and entrepreneur (BMW Z8, Aston Martin DB9, V8 Vantage, Fisker Karma, Mustang Rocket, VLF Force 1, Destino V8).

"For me, when it comes to marketing, it really is about marking an amazing product that has a pretty clear statement. Of course, it comes a little bit back to who do you make this product for. In this case, let's say if it's a car, who do you make it for? It's good to know that at least you have some strong group of people who truly appreciates certain aspects about what you're doing. I think in the higher end spectrum of products, that is very important because they will lead the introduction of this product.

Now, of course, if you go down market and you're talking about making a toothbrush or a cup, a takeaway plastic cup, at that point, it maybe that price is one of the more important things because you're looking at saying, "I just need a toothbrush. I'm just going to get the cheapest one"."

Kaspar Basse, Founder, CEO Joe & The Juice.

"My first answer would be that I would rule them all out and choose the P one as people. As I explained earlier, that's the fundamental thing that everybody else does wrong. The lack of honesty in creating a people company.

To be very concrete, for us, in the game we're in, with our existing category of business right now, place is tremendously important and challenging. That is the place where we compete with everybody else. If you ask, "Kasper, what are your competitors?" It depends on how you define it. There's nobody who does what we do, so there's none, or there's a lot of lunch places, so there's a lot. The fact is that all of these branded food and beverage places look for a hundred and twenty square meters at the exact right corner in the exact right city. The landlords know this, so you need to b ... That brings all the there P's in place with the price and the product.

You need to become tremendously precise and solid to pay the ridiculous rent levels around the world. That is the fundamental, the place is what we fight for. This is also what makes it difficult to engage on this journey, because it takes a lot of experience and to create the self confidence it is to take on the big rents and to be able to negotiate the right contracts and really turn up your level of expansion."

Fast Moving Consumer Goods.

Fast Moving Consumer Goods or ' FMCG' are products that are sold quickly and at a relatively low cost. Products such as soft drinks, coffee, bread, butter, cheese, soaps and other grocery items.[11]

Profit on FMCG is generally low, but due to high volumes, the cumulative profit can be substantial. Major global players are; Procter & Gamble, Unilever and ITC Limited.

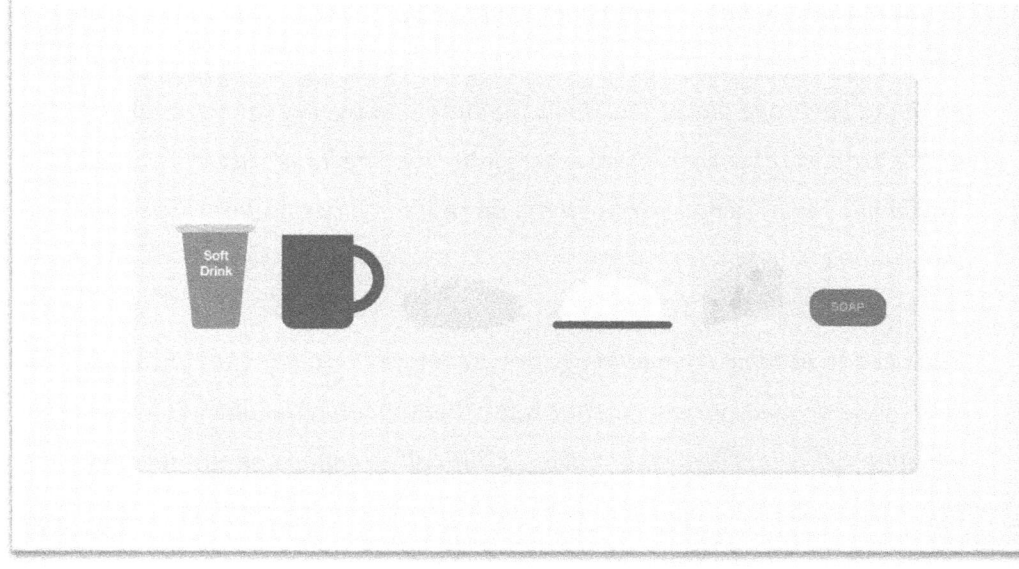

Figure 4.

---

[11] Leahy, Rose (2011). "Relationships in fast moving consumer goods markets: The consumers' perspective", European Journal of Marketing, Vol. 45 Issue: 4, pp.651-672.

From a consumer perspective, the main FMCG characteristics include:[12]

1. Frequent purchase.
2. Low involvement.
3. Low price.

Interviewees.

Malin Gardeström, International Marketing Manager, Carlsberg & Tuborg.

"As fast-moving consumer goods, it's a very fun business to work with. You need to be very flexible because the market is changing all the time. The entry barriers are very low. Pricing becomes very important. You need to add value to your product, in order to not just lose your profit, and you need to be top of mind at the consumers all the time. Of course we spend a lot of money and we use a lot of resources in marketing above the line and close to where the consumers are in the moment of truth, and to be very visible in order for them to make the right choice."

David Angelo, Founder & Chairman, David & Goliath advertising agency.

"Interesting. We're talking about like deodorant, right? Things that you consume on a daily basis. It's so tough in today's day and age, because everything is parody for the most part. You look at deodorant, you look

[12] Steenkamp, J.B.E.M. & Dekimpe M.G. (2009). Marketing strategies for fast-moving consumer goods. Financial Times, February.

at eggs, I mean it all kind of, all the things that we consume, and it very little, minor differences between them all.

Because those experiences are immediate, fast, it behooves a brand to make sure that the experience of that product, there's an old saying that great advertising makes a bad product fail faster. You've got to make sure that the product is great to begin with, or else people are going to find out so much faster how much you suck. Make sure that the product experience is amazing and consistent across every single sample, every single experience. That's number one.

Number two, make sure that the marketing experience is just as impactful. You have those two things sort of like, they need to live in the same world. If you're going to have a product that is a parody product, then you better damn well make sure that it's a great experience for that consumer. The conversation that's wrapped around it, through marketing, needs to be just as impactful and experiential. That's kind of how I see it, it's consumer goods are CPG for the most part, are consumed so fast that they never ... They'll remember how well you made them feel, but they'll never forget if you ever made them sick."

Dennis Balslev, CEO IKEA Germany. Fmr. CEO IKEA Denmark.
"First of all, we work with what we call a price ladder. We should have something, you can say, the cheapest price in the function and then we should go up in the price ladder, depending on your needs, where you are in your life. Then we have the fast moving, consumer goods like napkins and candles and so on but we believe so much in the combination of furniture and all the accessories make a fantastic opportunity for the

customer. Of course, from our concept point of view, it means a lot for the customer. Sometimes you come and look for a new kitchen but you don't buy a kitchen today but then you buy something else to your kitchen at home.

The mix, and we spend more of less 50/50 percent of the space in our stores to secure both areas so we believe if you have a fun day out, it's not only furniture, it's also the accessories to your house and of course you can renew money with a few money if you buy accessories and that's a big difference in they way of thinking again for us. We are quite strong in accessories today and have high quality to low prices which means we see that part growing in the company in total."

Seidi Suurmets, PhD Fellow at the department of Marketing, Copenhagen Business School.

"Well, I would split it into separate parts. First of all when talking about consumer decision making, the most important aspect of it is that it's low involvement purchase. Meaning that people don't think too much about it when choosing the product. So, for example, if the preferred product is out of stock, then they simply substitute it with another one. That is maybe the main characteristic.

These are often bought on impulse, based on impulse motivations. So there isn't too much deliberate processing behind choosing this product. When people see the risk is really low because the price is not high, they just take it, put it in their basket, and buy it.

In general, these products have short shelf life. That means that the turnover is fast. Either it is because the demand is high, or because simply they are none durable. For example food and dairy, they get old fast. Therefore, they don't stay on the shelf long. In general, there are branded consumer goods as well as private label, which are more generic, value brands for example."

Matthew Bagwell, Managing Director Naked Communications Europe.

"We work with a number of FMCG brands. One of the trends that I think we see increasingly is brands working with us to understand what relationships they can have with customers, above and beyond the sort of rational product relationship. Coca-cola, Danone across all of its products, where we are helping those clients explore what their brand means. Within the permission space for their customers, how else can they contribute, above and beyond the utility of a tub of yogurt or a can of refreshing drink? What does that brand mean? What permission does it have to create content and add over and above product plus the service around that product. Is there a permission space, such that it's not just a price-based engagement?

That there is a sort of an impression being built up in the mind, so that as I walk into an environment where I am going to consume an FMCG product, some of the things that are sort of talking to me in the shelves actually have a meaning above and beyond. It might be a nostalgic memory, it might that there's content that I understand comes from an organization, it may be some values that they represent in a particular way, because of the things that they've involved themselves in, and there's some content that they've created, or some engagement that I've been involved in. The trend really is sort of, this is my product, and if I don't want to compete on price, then I need to compete on meaning."

Seidi Suurmets, PhD Fellow at the department of Marketing, Copenhagen Business School.

"The space is allocated to each of the variance of the fast moving consumer goods. It depends on how profitable they are for the retailer. The more margin the retailer can earn from this product, the more space they want to allocate for it. When the consumer goes to the store, generally he or she looks at the height from the eye level to hand level. So this is the area where the consumer normally or most frequently choose the product because that is the area that is first noticed. So therefore, the least profitable products or the cheapest products are placed in the bottom. And nich products or products that meet some different type of a need are placed upper part. The most expensive slots for the producers are the ones that are between the eye and the hand level.

And when talking about consumer goods, another important distinction is between the buying motivations. For example, whether the person buying it wants to solve a problem of some kind, meaning that there is a negative motivation. So the product is consumed in order to avoid some negative consequence. So that would be, for example, washing powder just to avoid having dirty clothes. Whereas the experiential motivation is based on pleasure. For example, a chocolate bar that's when the person or the consumer wants to experience some pleasure. That's a different motivation there, that's a positive motivation."

Benjamin Holk Henriksen, Strategic planning & branding.

Lecturer DIS and Copenhagen Business School, Author, Filmmaker "The Mind of a Leader", "Holk Master-class".

"Fast Moving consumer goods is a thriving industry and a competitive one too. Consumers prefer to buy these products when required and without doing much of a comparative study. As a result, the decision making process is really short and purchase decisions primarily influenced by brand loyalty. Recommendations from a reliable retailer or friends or it's also... heavy advertisement also has a major impact. Innovation is key. In fact according to the Telegraph, 40% of brands on the top 100 list twenty years ago have already been replaced by new names today.

The consumer is king and FMCG has a history of delivering what consumers want. To quote Sam Walton, founder of Wal-Mart: "High expectations are the key to everything"."

Part II. Strategic planning and branding.

Reflection on product portfolio management and the Boston Consulting Group Matrix.

The Boston Matrix is a marketing tool used for project or product portfolio analysis and management. The objectives are to evaluate performances of each product, Including development, distribution and sale. And schedule activities that enable the organisation to reach its goals. The Boston Matrix is a highly used chart created by Bruce Henderson for the Boston Consulting Group in 1970 to help corporations analyse the performance of their business units or product lines.[13] What is the product or service's current market share? What is the market growth potential?

Dogs.

Dogs are confronted with low market share and low market growth problems. They tend to absorb cash rather than generate it and are developing in a slow-growing industry.

Question marks.

Question marks often consume large amounts of cash, due to a rapid market growth and competition. A question mark has the potential to gain market share and become a star, and eventually a cash cow.

---

[13] Henderson, B.D. (1970). "The Product Portfolio". The Boston Consulting Group.

Stars.

Stars are products with a high market share in a fast-growing industry. The organisational goal is to turn these stars into Cash cows.

Cash cows.

Cash cows are units with high market share in a mature or slow-growing industry. Some argue that they are to be "milked" continuously with as little investment as possible, since it would be a waste of resources to advertise in a mature market. However one should always consider the situation and what it takes to maintain market shares and profit.

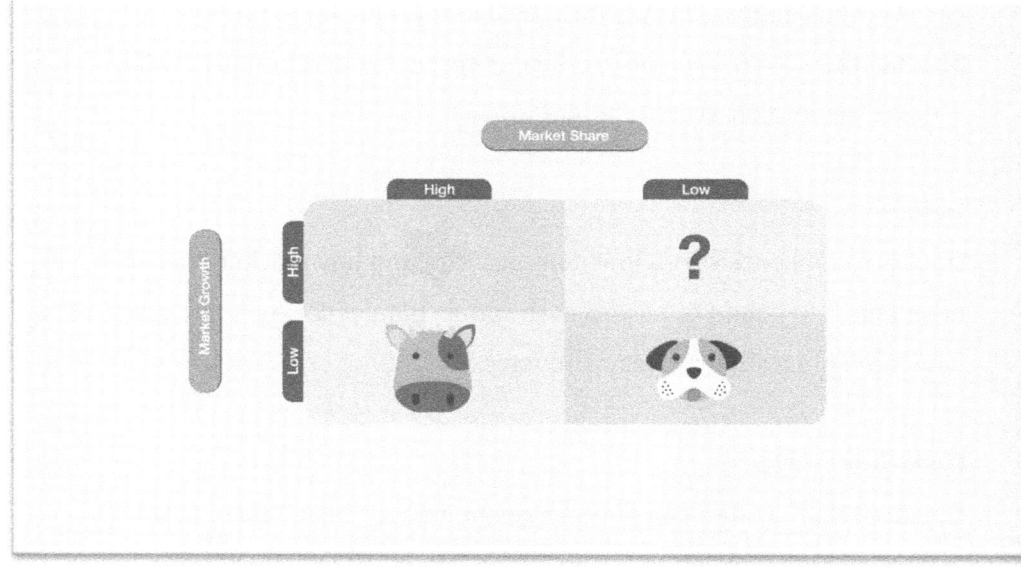

Figure 5.

The purpose of this matrix is to help companies decide which of their units they should keep, where they should invest further and which ones they should consider getting rid of.

This work presents marketing & communication abstracts. For more details about the theory please view the authors' own works.

Interviewees.

Lars Liebst, CEO Tivoli.

"Well we try to do our homework, but I will say, we are human all of us, and in this kind of business that we are in, you do failures. I won't say all the time, but you do failures. Many of those things that we will present will be in the theater, it will be music, it will be concerts, and you are never sure about if it works. If you were, you would be a multi-billionaire, probably not sitting in this office but somewhere else. The recipe for that is just hard work."

Ole Henriksen, Founder and Creative Director, Ole Henriksen Skin Care Brand.

"Well, developing products for me is like my love affair. Honestly, I'm a lousy cook in the kitchen for a regular dinner, but, boy, can I cook up a storm when it comes to products. I started cosmetic chemistry in London, and the fact I got that background, of course, gave me wonderful insight to the excitement of cosmetic chemistry. And so for product, they actually have evolved very organically for me, because my background was, first and foremost, way back in 1975, treating skin at my first facility called

61

Ole Henriksen of Denmark Skin Care Center. Proud of being a Dane and Scandinavian. And I would make the products in my own kitchen those days, bring them on my bicycle to work in Tupperware containers, and actually the media loved it. I remember Barbra Streisand when she first became my client was in awe of the fact that, "Wow, he makes his own products in the kitchen".

But, of course, there was more to it when I moved on, wrote my first American book that became a best-seller. I went on Oprah, and Oprah being the powerhouse of icons and TV, helped bring a profile to my brand that I'd never thought would happen. And that ignited the fire for me, too. We put a little bit more focus around the product I developed. But I first and foremost develop product based on the concerns that I know my clients would have. So when I've had that dialogue over the years, I clearly understood what their needs were, and that's how I began developing products. And then you put them to market, and you really don't know. It's like putting a feature film out there. You have the highest hopes and it fails. And that may be the case for the product.

I would say a big turning point for me was when I put together the Three Little Wonders kit. That kit was one that addressed every concern from hyper-pigmentation, open pores, clogged pores, lines and wrinkles, textural imperfections. And I did it because many clients would say, "I'm frustrated with my skin. I've tried this and that, I'm getting nowhere fast". And I thought if I can develop three products that works synergistically to address all these concerns, that feel good, that smell good, and most importantly transform and elevate skin every day. So initially I called it the Seven Day Transformation kit. And then when the response was so extraordinary, it became the Three Little Wonders. That Three Little Wonders kit put me on the map in a big way, and this very day is the number one selling kit in the world of Sephora Canada, in the USA and Australia, five years in a row now. And that's an example of how products, when they perform well, and they are easy and accessible to use, can pave the way for something very successful."

Peter Ålbæk Jensen, Producer, Founder & fmr. CEO, Zentropa.

"There's around two years from the first idea to ... The earliest that we've ever finished film, which means that we shoot that as all choosers of products, try to foresee what people want to see in two years from now. So, it's very much a question for the creators to read a lot of newspapers to really try to have some kind of organic feeling of where is the audience heading now. The moment somebody has a success in a new type of story, in a new environment, strangely enough ten, fifteen others have the same ideas at the same time. So, there's a question about some movement and streams of information that gathers together in the head of the creators and then more simultaneously everybody wants to make a film about the second world war or the hippy times in Copenhagen and late 60s. We are part of a bigger movement than we sometimes realize."

Malin Gardeström, International Marketing Manager, Carlsberg & Tuborg.

"Carlsberg as a company has a very long history. Carlsberg dates back from 1847, so it's the earliest. Tuborg comes shortly after. They are both very old and brands to be very proud of, but we don't really take that into consideration thinking about marketing split, etc. It's very much based

on the market share. Where Tuborg as such is the biggest brand in Denmark."

Birgitte Mabeck, Head of fundraising and marketing Red Cross.

"Yes, we use the Boston Matrix as an appendix to other information sources. What happens is the organizations we are competing against are not only within our own area. They are also health organizations, cancer foundations, heart foundations and so forth. Therefore it's important for us to constantly look at, where does our campaign fit into this picture? In order to do that, we use some Boston Matrix to see what is performing well and what is not performing well. In some of our campaigns we have decided that we are actually continuing year on year because they have kind of become our cash cow if you like. We can see we can differentiate ourselves here and we can see that our competitors, they cannot enter this area. We have other areas where we've decided we are never going to enter. Yeah, so we use it but we are never using it as a standalone. We use it in combination with other tools."

Malin Gardeström, International Marketing Manager, Carlsberg & Tuborg.

"We have a very broad portfolio at the moment, and of course in order not to D-list anyone, you need to of course to make sure each of these different products play a role in the portfolio. Yes, there are a lot of brands that we don't really support with marketing and spending. You could call them a cash cow, I suppose. Yes, everyone has its own different positioning within the portfolio."

Peter Ålbæk Jensen, Producer, Founder & fmr. CEO, Zentropa.

"The lucky or happy thing that our best intellectual performers are also the best commercial performers. That's strange, but whenever films try to be too stupid they are normally also very local. Our type of film has to be, again back to our target audience, which are women in between thirty and sixty that are educated. That put a certain demand on the quality of elements of the films, if we shall sell them."

Lars Liebst, CEO Tivoli.

"We are the only listed company in the world with our own symphony orchestra. It probably tells the whole story. For us, it's not only a question about a plus on the bottom line, it's a question about the branding effect of what we do. In some areas, we gain, in some areas we know that we are going to lose. When the day is done and we finalize, it seems like we are on the right track. We will keep our symphony orchestra, we will keep our pantomime theater, the ballet, the music school and all of that. We have to be much more professional in where we are earning our money so this is very important for us to remember each and every day."

Ole Henriksen, Founder and Creative Director, Ole Henriksen Skin Care Brand.

"But there's no doubt as my business has grown, I think a lot about what white spaces to fill. But I don't want to just fill it because it could maybe even be a trend. I want to create my own trends. I want to do what I feel is right in that moment, and then I love the gambling part. One of my newest products that are coming out this Spring is called Power Bright. And the Power Bright ... I love the word "power" and I love "bright" because it's so positive. But with the Power Bright it started out at this

one 25% stable form of vitamin C, no one has ever done before. So it's ground breaking in itself.

Of course, vitamin C is quite unstable, and vitamin C as an antioxidant is extraordinary at dealing with hyper-pigmentation, but also in reducing the depth of lines and wrinkles, and neutralizing free radical damage from the elements. So a lot of research has been done in that arena. But I also thought, that's a great product on its own, but what if I give it a prelude, and, again, that step number three, if you will- so one, two, three, it will be more intriguing, it will render even greater results, and, of course, again, at the end I'm breaking new grounds because it's the innovation piece. And I always liked to elevate the experience of product use to something exceptional. One thing is, you can do a one step, and that's great, but when you can make it more exciting and intriguing, and then, obviously render the results, it's even better.

So there is a lot of thought behind everything. But I can tell you in the world of Sephora, which is such a good role model to go by in retail today, you have a linear. And your linear allows you extra mile of square footage. And within that, you may have different franchises. So I have my Truth franchise, I have my Balance franchise, I have my Uplift franchise, I have my Nurture franchise. So, what happens is, Sephora measures the performance level. And if you don't deliver X amount per inch, forget it. And the beauty is that we live in a world today where literally you can get yesterday's sales in five seconds, and you can monitor everything. But I also believe that not everything can be a five star, performance level- wise. So there has to be room for the A and the B and the C level. It's just like a soccer team. There's some of the star players, but without the supporting cast, you can't win that game."

Benjamin Holk Henriksen, Strategic planning & branding.
Lecturer DIS and Copenhagen Business School, Author, Filmmaker
"The Mind of a Leader", "Holk Master-class".

"The Boston Matrix is a great toll for analyzing and prioritizing your product portfolio. Stars require relatively high funding to fight competitions and maintain a growth rate. However if you are able to keep the leadership position as the market matures, stars may be turned into cash cows. It's been argued that the idea is to invest money, generated by your Cash cows, in your Question marks, so that the Question marks can become Stars and generate money until then again the market matures and they become Cash cows.

Using the model implies having a lot of information.

1. Be aware of how narrowly you measure the current market share of the business. The result may look very different depending on whether you define the market by the exact same product or products that fulfills the same need.

2. Be aware of how you measure the growth potential of the business. It is not just about sales numbers... Look for movements in the society... Where is competition going, where is technology going, what are long term trends and indicators as opposed to sort term trends.

3. Make sure to draw your conclusions on long term studies and not just a single year.

4. Be ware of isolating a product.... A product may not be the biggest seller, but it can be important as a flag ship that draw attention to other products."

Product life cycle.

We have seen how successful products, brands, or trends disappear from the market only to re-emerge decades later.

The Product life cycle defines the stages a product or its category goes through.[14]

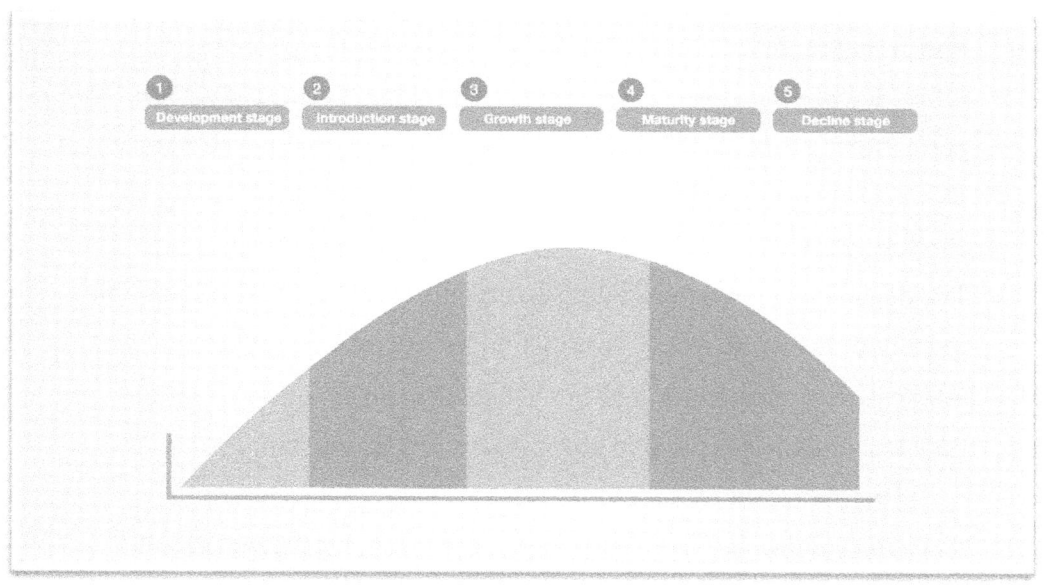

Figure 6.

Development Stage.

The development stage is where the product concept is conceived, developed, branded or tested before being introduced to the market.

---

[14] Kotler, P. (1967). "Marketing Management: Analysis, Planning, Implementation and Control", Prentice Hall, 12th edn, 2006.

Introduction Stage.

Brands and their product life cycle evolve in the public's eye during the introduction stage. During this stage, companies often advertise heavily in their brands and products.

Growth Stage.

The growth stage is when sales start growing.

Maturity Stage.

A brand will eventually reach the maturity stage of the product life cycle. During this stage, competition for market share may be fierce.

Decline Stage.

The decline stage is where sales start to fall. However it is still possible to extend the life of the product by finding new markets, like international markets, or additional uses. Not all products reach this final stage, some continue to grow and some rise and fall.

Since the condition in which a product is sold changes over time, it must be managed as it moves through its succession of stages.

Interviewees.

Peter Ålbæk Jensen, Producer, Founder & fmr. CEO, Zentropa.

"Film is particularly interesting because it can work quite many years after the first exposure. We are now sending a restored version of Lars

van Tiers first television series called "The Kingdom" on the market. This product is more than twenty years old. What other businesses, other than music and film, can take an old product and put it on new cans and seal it once again? This television show, "The Kingdom" , has sold continuously quite well for twenty years, each year. That's our hope for the future, that the more digital the whole world gets, the bigger the market the will be for older titles. When some of or talented directors are successful now, it will make the audience interested to see previous work of the same director. By that sense, we are lucky."

Malin Gardeström, International Marketing Manager, Carlsberg & Tuborg.

"I think the product life cycle in theory as such, is very much a aplicant also today, also with our products. In my current role as an international marketing manager, for Calrsberg and Tuborg, we have our brands in different positionings in different markets. We are entering the market in a lot of African markets and South American markets. Whereas in Western Europe for example, we are very mature and there's a very fine line between mature market and declining markets because of course there's a lot of different brands that want to fight our positioning. What we do for these markets is of course to kind of redefine ourselves maybe to make some product extensions to some line extensions which can also give a little CPR to the main brand, so we are very much working with that in our mature markets."

Kaspar Basse, Founder, CEO Joe & The Juice.

"I think on a general note we're not there yet. In that comparison we're a fairly young company. I also think that our category business, if that is

food and beverage, I think it's interesting to see that the very big companies, within food and beverage, actually remain. You're go to the medical companies or the tech companies or whatever, you will see from twenty years ago to today, they're different companies.

McDonalds, Starbucks, Coca Cola, they're still there. They will also still be there in twenty years. To the extent of Pizza Hut is maybe also an example of this, whether they're doing rice pudding or what. The companies that manage to reach that certain level seem actually to remain strong whether they feel they have issues with not developing enough certain years or whatever. They have strong positions. They have a fundamental thing that can not be exchanged by the internet. We typically see it as more of a risk that we won't get that far fast enough, than to remain being relevant if you're out there. The fact is the burgers, the pizzas, the coffees, even the Coca Colas, they keep being relevant. So will we when we reach that level of size."

Leif Rasmussen. Strategic Branding. Lecturer, DIS – Study Abroad in Scandinavia.

"If you want to have a long lifecycle, which, of course, many producers or brand owners want, you got to be very careful with the different stages, especially when you're coming to that stage which is called the mature stage because it might start declining when it becomes mature. What you can do there is that you can make a lot of new or some new activities, making interest on making your brand more interesting to the consumers than it would be if you just kept it as it has always been.

Could I make an example? Yes, I think that a brand like Heineken, the Heineken beer, is a very good example of a brand and a product, of course, which is able and has been able to have a very long lifecycle. I mean, it is not dead yet and I don't think it will die eventually, or at least for a very long period of time. They are very good at using different activities to extend their lifecycle."

Malene Torp. Executive Director, DIS – Study Abroad in Scandinavia.

"When I think of the product lifecycle. I actually think that it's a very old-fashioned and a very traditional approach. For my own work and with the product that I work with I don't recognize that traditional product lifecycle. Of course you can reinvent a product and of course you can over and over again develop, redevelop, redefine your product but still keep the same brand."

Lars Liebst, CEO Tivoli.

"Well I think this is why I'm here. We have to be aware that the next generation is just standing in front of our gates, and if they don't see something that they like and they can use then we have failed. I think the best example is probably our Friday night rock because when we started almost 20 years ago, there was a lot of people saying, "Hey, it's too much, you can't do that in such a wonderful park" and so on. What we did was actually we offered something to a group of people, guests, that we at that time didn't see. What we see now is it's over 20 years ago that we did it. Now we see the next generation that is coming because maybe some of those first comers they enjoyed it very much, maybe they even fell in love with another one, maybe they got children. Who knows? It's a life

span. We use a word in Tivoli that is called loyalty, loyalty to Tivoli. We have about 300,000 annual cardholders, and that is a lot of people in the area of Copenhagen, so keeping those guys loyal, year after year. That you can only do by offering new things each and every year, and being aware of that whoever is visiting Tivoli for a business lunch, the next night, he can be just dressed up casual, walking to a concert, so we have to have different offerings."

Benjamin Holk Henriksen, Strategic planning & branding. Lecturer DIS and Copenhagen Business School, Author, Filmmaker "The Mind of a Leader", "Holk Master-class".

"The goals of Product Life Cycle management are to reduce the time to market, improve product quality, reduce prototyping costs, and identify potential sales opportunities and revenue contributions. The model integrates people, data, processes and business systems and provides product information backbone for companies and their extended enterprise.

It's been argued that one of the limitations is, that its difficult to estimate accurately where a product is on its life cycle. For example, a rise in sales is not necessarily evidence of growth. And also that the duration of each PLC stage is unpredictable. There is a valid old article in Harvard business review by Theodore Levitt called "Exploit the Product Life Cycle". The article suggests ways of using the concept effectively. The chief discussion focus on "life extension" or "market stretching." It's gives the example of how nylon's booming sales life has been repeatedly and systematically extended and stretched and how it can serve as a model for other products."

Birgitte Mabeck, Head of fundraising and marketing Red Cross.

"The instant emergencies, those are where people would very much like to support, whereas the more long-term development projects, we can see a decline in that. What we are trying to do is, of course, to make sure the people understand that long-term development projects are actually not just long-term development projects. They are equally emergency projects because what happens is that people who are in the need of food are in a hunger situation, we would actually call that the biggest emergency of them all. We are now pushing or changing our communication model into explaining that this is not a long-term development thing, but it's actually an emergency situation and people have to support here. This is the way that we kind of changed our product lifecycle. Maybe the product is somehow the same but we are repackaging it and putting it into a new communication context."

Petter A. Stordalen, Founder and owner of Nordic Choice Hotels.

"I think the answer to that is a Japanese word called "kaizen." Continuously change. Do something better today than yesterday, but not as good as tomorrow. Because everything is changing you also need to change your hotels and if you're not a lucky one, having this super famous, world brand on the high street or the best location, you can still succeed. And that's the thing: very few are so lucky that they have this super famous hotel. I had nothing so why did I end up today having all these super famous hotels? The number one in Norway. You know? We did bold things. We opened a hotel in Oslo, the capital in Norway, and I named it The Thief. And people told me, "You can't name it The Thief? And do you know what they call the people working at Wall Street? The

thieves at Wall Street, and they are supposed to stay there. It's a hotel for bankers? For all these people." And I said, "But you don't see the irony in that?"

I want to rob them away from everyday life. And we have the story about, this was the last place in Norway where they hang people. Where they like... this was the place for prostitutes, robbers. This was called "the island of the thieves." So I had this story. And it's all about storytelling, but you need new stories. You need to reinvent yourself. You need to change, I changed literally a hotel every fifth year. Otherwise, one day you will find yourself out of business, because the world is changing. So you need to change. Technology-wise, everything with interior, everything. I think the reception is gone in ten years. I think brands in the future is less important. Not brands, but the big brands. I think Hilton is too boring. I think many of the big franchise hotels will think, "Why do I need to pay franchise fee to this hotel company when I can get all my guests from TripAdvisor?" And it's a good question.

So you need to start to think about where would my business be ten years from now? If you can see that, what do I need to do to change so I'm prepared for the future? And start now. Most people talk too much and it's too little execution. So remember: execution, never run out of cash. Two most important lessons. And the last one is this: if you're not happy with your job, quit. If you're not happy with your managers, quit. Quit more often. Follow your dream. Never give up."

Brand equity and Brand extension.

Brand equity is defined by the net worth and long-term sustainability.[15] A brand's power derives from the goodwill and name recognition it has earned over time. It's the value premium that a company realizes from a product with a recognizable name as compared to its generic equivalent.[16]

Some companies like Proctor & Gable often use *product branding*, meaning multiple brand names, to differentiate image and brand risk. Other companies build on one master brand, which is called *corporate branding*.

Brand extension is a marketing strategy and spin-off by which a company promotes a product with a well-developed image, using the same brand name in a different product category. Organisations use this strategy to increase and leverage brand equity.[17]

The use of core products or master brand, to reach new products new segments or to team up with partner products.

---

[15] De Mooij, M. (2014). Global Marketing and Advertising. Fourth edition. Sage publications. 30-31.
[16] Doorley, J. and Garcia, F. (2011). The key to successful Public Relations and Corporate Communication. 2nd edition, Routledge, London.
[17] Belsky, G. (2012). Business Time. The 10 Best Brand Extensions Ever. March 13.

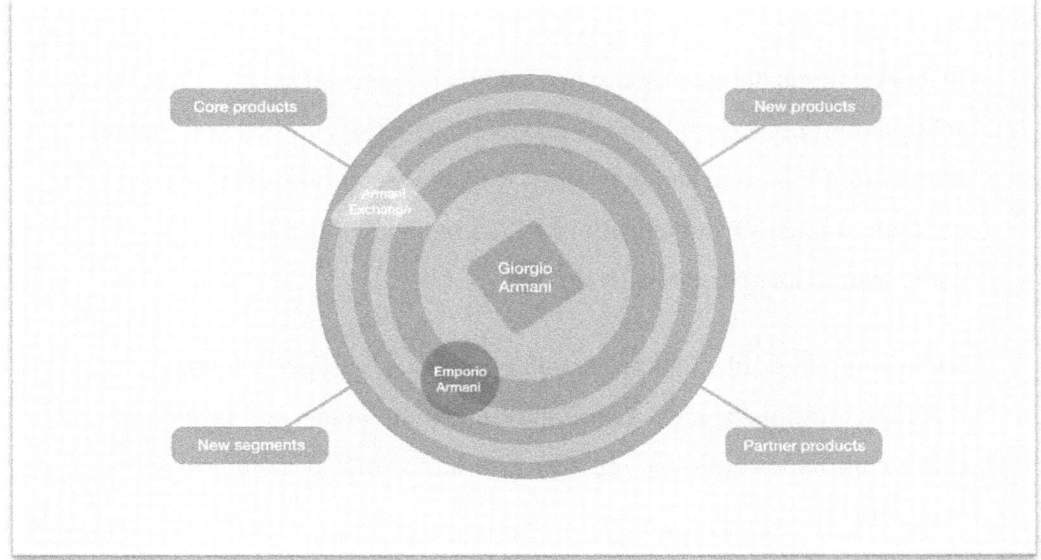

Figure 7.

The fashion company Armani is an example of an organisation that has build on its brand equity to reach more target groups within the clothing industry.

In 1991 The core brand of the fashion house 'Giorgio Armani', associated with the prêt-à-porter collection, introduced Emporio Armani, a young and trendy side of the fashion house and in 1991 Armani Exchange, which specialises in t-shirts, polo´s and tracksuits. As such the brand covers a much broader target group. And the brand now includes accessories such as sunglasses, perfume etc.

Another example of a company that practises brand extension to penetrate or develop new markets is Virgin. The master brand is

78

associated with a variety of industries such as the music business, airline industry and mobile market.[18]

Interviewees.

Matthew Bagwell, Managing Director Naked Communications Europe.

"I think there's a number of reasons why people will pay more for one product or a service than necessarily another. For example, the perception of premium, scarcity, if there's not enough of something then perhaps I'm prepared to pay far more for it. Maybe it is convenience, I love that idea that Amazon sort of said they don't know what business they'll be in in ten years time, but no one is ever going to ask for something to be less convenient. You might argue that there are brands that have been built about being less than convenient and difficult to source, difficult to find, difficult to buy, and actually that creates a premium that people are prepared to pay for.

Yeah, premium, scarcity. For me personally, it's about what does something mean? Is there something in this product or the service, or something around that, that means something to me, such as I am going to be incredibly loyal to it? Does it, as an organization, and manifest as a product or service, provides something that I truly value? Such as even if there was a little price increase, or a significant price increase, I would still seek it out.

---

[18] Lennox, A. (2014). Smart brand extension allows Virgin to keep up appearances., The Guardian., Thursday 23 October 10.42 BST.

Famously, I think Apple has done this. There are many ways that Apple retrain its customers, but I grew up and started with the very first Macintoshes. I owe my career to the entire, you know to the Steve Jobs revolution of digital desktop and digital publishing. It means so much to me that I'm almost blind to the price."

Seidi Suurmets, PhD Fellow at the department of Marketing, Copenhagen Business School.

"Brand equity, it can be viewed from different perspectives. One way is simply looking at the financial value of it, so it will be regarded as an intangible asset. What is of more importance is the equity of the brand that resides in the minds of the consumers. So that would mean the consumers awareness about the brand as well as the associations that they have towards it.

So in that way we can define brand equity as the differential affect that the consumer response has. When comparing the response that they would have towards a generic or unknown product or brand and compare that to the brand that brand product is. So that is where we see this difference and it can be positive but it can also be negative."

David Angelo, Founder & Chairman, David & Goliath advertising agency.

"I believe that our job as an agency partner, is to serve the brand first. What do I mean by that? It's looking at the brand and making sure that you help it succeed at any cost. That should be the main priority for

anyone, whether it's a marketing person or an agency owner, is to make sure, do everything in your power to help that brand succeed.

If you do that, if you are serving the brand first, it means that you really aren't looking at yourself as the agency and the client as the client. You're kind of looking at it like you are a collective, and you're responsibility is to help that brand succeed. If that brand succeeds, the marketing person is going to do well, and I have to believe that the agency is going to do well.

That's the way that we look at it. We look at if we can help the brand overcome whatever Goliath is in their way, and achieve greatness, then the by-product of that, if done well, would be awards. We never, we're not driven by the awards, we're driven by doing what's right for the brand, first and foremost."

Matthew Bagwell, Managing Director Naked Communications Europe.

"We have done this type of work creating brand equity, because that's what this is, for people like Coca-Cola. Now, of course, it's an incredibly powerful historic brand, where what it means is far more valuable necessarily, than what the product costs. 10, 15, 20 times fold, in terms of the total value of that organization.

We were involved in the 'Share a Coke' idea, where you could put somebody's name onto a can of Coke and share it. I think that was just another brilliant manifestation of the idea of sharing happiness. Incredibly appealing, incredibly engaging, and I think because it meant something above and beyond the simple ubiquity of a drink, or the utility of quenching thirst, that people sought it out and preferred it over other brands. That's creating brand preference through meaning, which was actually, I quite like sharing happiness, and I like the mechanic of doing this, it's fun, above and beyond what I'm actually going to get inside a can of pop, a can of soda. We've done that type of work."

Benjamin Holk Henriksen, Strategic planning & branding. Lecturer DIS and Copenhagen Business School, Author, Filmmaker "The Mind of a Leader", "Holk Master-class".

"I believe building on your master brand involves both business sense and involvement. Brand equity constitutes the basis for brand extension. But if the new line does not live up to the same quality, image or customer experience you risk devaluating the entire brand.

Take Virgin. Richard Branson started out in the media and entertainment business, basing his business and brand awareness on intuition, personal relations, his book publications and even his world record breaking attempts... – which by the way is quite interesting if you think about Red Bull and skydiver Felix Baumgartner recent free fall to earth. There are definitely some parallels in terms of the promotion and the adrenalin there.

Today Virgin's businesses consist of more than 400 companies worldwide. Its core business areas are travel, entertainment and lifestyle, but it also manages ventures in financial services, transport, healthcare, food and drink, media, even telecommunications etc.

The Virgin brand has implemented a uniform brand book laying out simple things, like how to display the logo, colors etc. And according to the Harvard business case Virgin.com, Richard Branson is extremely careful about the brand and customer experience he would call up his top managers 3-5 times a week. Just to here what their thoughts are, what is going on.

And yes have there been a few bad apples from Virgin, yes their have, like Virgin Cola launched in the beginning of the nineties and Virgin Trains in the late nineties but it's still incredible just how much Virgin has managed to "extend" their brand. To actually build on their equity."

Ole Henriksen, Founder and Creative Director, Ole Henriksen Skin Care Brand.

"Well, it's always tempting to possibly pursue other aspects. Extensions of your brand, no doubt. But for me, though, I've always been very tightly focused. I've always said "skin care is my expertise". That's what I'm best at. It's a world that offers a lot of opportunities for growth, and you should try, to your best ability, to stick with what you're best at and evolve that on a continuous basis. Because what I love about it, is that there's always something around the corner where you can up the antenna.

I love that challenge. You always think you have arrived, and then you have one of these brain-farts that pop, they don't smell, but they are magical in what they can do. And you say, "Wow, there's something I can do to make it even better". And what I have observed is that looking at some of the brands that have broadened their scope, many of them have failed. They have lost, so often, the essence of what they are and what they were respected for. And then often they pull back, they get back to where they came from. But there are some that have done it.

I just feel, for me, skin care is my thing and what I love about it is that I haven't just chosen to make it skin care, but I've made it a life-style brand. A brand where I've spread my wings across a broader territory. So I guess you can say I've extended myself on that level, but that part is not necessarily what brings money into the business. But it gives the brand a very strong identity, and it makes it very respected as a trusted brand: that I care beyond the product, which I care deeply about, the quality and obviously the integrity, but I also care about you the person. Your wellbeing, your happiness, and that you feel good about life."

Seidi Suurmets, PhD Fellow at the department of Marketing, Copenhagen Business School.

"That has a lot to do with associations that the consumers have with the parent brand. For example, if a brand is perceived as very safe, conservative, then there is not a good match if the parent brand would want to extend itself into some very innovative categories because the associations do not really match. When extending the brand into new categories, we would want the positive associations to be transferred to that extension. So that is where we would want to see this good match."

Peter Ålbæk Jensen, Producer, Founder & fmr. CEO, Zentropa.

"We have tried and we have lost so much money on it so don't ever do it. Unless you have a love affair with something else, this has to driven by

love not out of calculation. So, whenever we have tried to be too smart, it has not worked. So, be aware."

David Angelo, Founder & Chairman, David & Goliath advertising agency.

"I think it all comes down to a shared value system. When you create… first and foremost, you have to go to the core of what the brand stands for. If that brand stands for inspiration, like Nike does, or Apple, they both stand for inspiration. If you go to the core of that, and then you align that core with the values of the consumer, and they both sort of share the same belief system, then you have struck a very authentic chord, a relationship that is based on a shared interest, a shared value system.

From there you have this sort of amazing connection, from there, because of where we are today with technology and all the media vehicles that are available, then you have all of these other channels that you expand that relationship. You can take it, whether it's short-form, long-form, whatever it may be. Those are all just touch-points for that conversation. If you share that belief system, it doesn't matter what you make, it doesn't matter. Apple could create a car, because they've created this amazing connection through their ecosystem, amazing brand connection. Because they don't believe… people they don't buy what you make, they buy what you believe in. If you can get to that place, then it doesn't matter after that. People will buy whatever you make, because they believe in what you believe in."

Reflections on the SWOT analysis.

The SWOT analysis is a method used to evaluate the Strengths, Weaknesses, Opportunities, and Threats involved in a project or business venture.

The technique is credited to Albert Humphrey, who led a convention at the Stanford Research Institute in the 1960s and 1970s.[19]

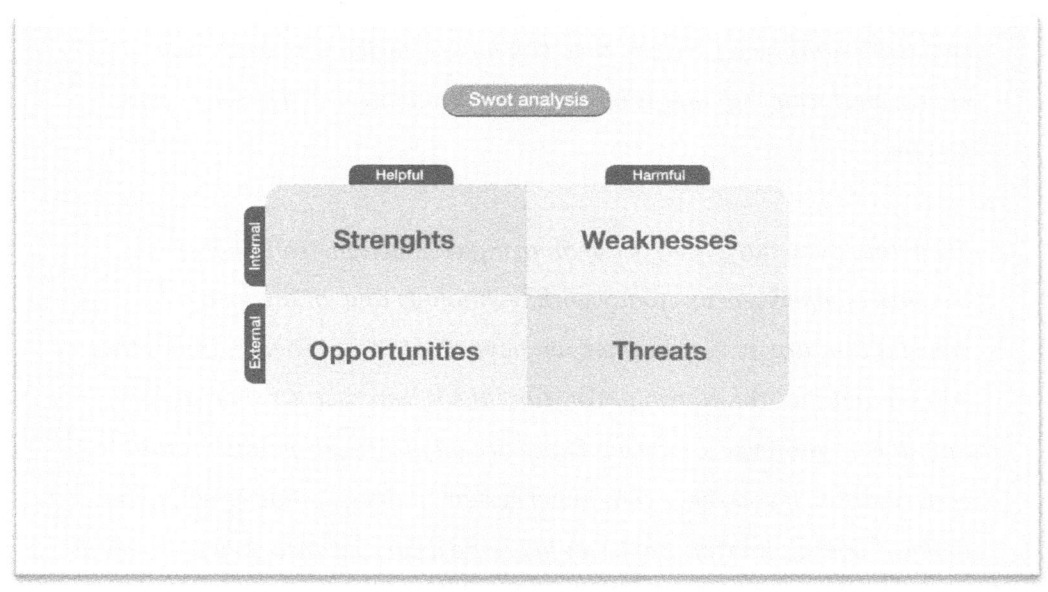

Figure 8.

Strengths:

Characteristics of the business that offer an advantage.

---

[19] Humphrey, A. (2005). "SWOT Analysis for Management Consulting".

Weaknesses:

Disadvantage relative to others.

Opportunities:

External opportunities or chances in the environment to improve the performance.

Threats:

External elements in the environment that could cause trouble for the business.

Strengths and weaknesses are characterised as internal factors, whereas opportunities and threats are external. The SWOT analysis serves as a helpful tool when evaluating or developing a business plan, product or communication campaign. Conduct your research list your strengths, weakness, opportunities and threats and take action to turn your disadvantages into advantages.[20]

This work presents marketing & communication abstracts. For more details about the theory please view the authors' own works.

<u>**Interviewees.**</u>

Andreas Rasche, Professor at Copenhagen Business School. Department of Management, Society and Communication.

---

[20] HBR Tools: SWOT Analysis. Tool by Harvard Business Review, 2015.

"I think The SWOT model is so widely used because it is simple. It is easy to understand for people. Of course, it provides a great analytical framework, and it covers the inside of the corporation, the strength and weaknesses and it covers the outside, the opportunities, and threats, and the mix and the interactions between inside and outside is what makes this a very strong tool for analysis."

Lars Liebst, CEO Tivoli.

Yes we do. If we are out and trying something very new where we... If it's a new field where we really haven't been before, we definitely do it because it's a very good instrument and we know... it force yourself to think what's up? What's down? What's the challenges? Yes, we do.

Peter Giacomello, Sponsorship and Reputation Director, Marketing Carlsberg.

"Yeah, we do. On every level, that means I can use it if I'm choosing between some different sponsorships, but we can also use it when we have an agreement, a partnership, and go in and see, does it work, doesn't it work? What's the good part, what's the bad part? Sure, we use it. Still a very simple and good model."

Klaus Riskaer Pedersen, Entrepreneur, Author, Founder of CyberCity and CopyGene. Fmr. member of the European Parliament (MEP).

"The basic of that kind of modeling is you have to work with some kind of known parameters. What about your unknown unknowns? To take the famous expression from the Ministry of Defense in the Bush Government, where he talked about, "We have known unknowns." Those we can plan

for with a SWOT model, but what do we do with the unknown unknowns? That's what innovation's all about. Every time we start up we say, "We understand where we are, let's get started. What is it we will we really face here when we are three months ahead, or six months ahead?" It will always be the unknown unknown. Consultancies that don't know anything about that. The SWOT model, I mean, put it aside. It's ridiculous. It is a completely different nature of being agile, quick response, integration of knowledge, distribution of experiences, and instant correction capabilities, and willingness to abandon strategies and replace them with new ways of doing stuff, that is how you do it."

Seidi Suurmets, PhD Fellow at the department of Marketing, Copenhagen Business School.

"SWOT stands for Strength, Weaknesses, Opportunities, and Threats. It's a really good model because it includes both the internal aspect of strengths and weaknesses. These are the aspects that are in the company as well as opportunities and threats, which are external. Therefore, it really matches the positives and negatives, both from the internal and the external perspective.

For example, when we talk about PEST or PESTLE, which stands for Political, Economic, Social, Technological, and possibly Legal and Environmental aspects, these are all external. So when use only that framework, we do not take into account the internal aspects. What could be done is that we use different models to look at the internal aspects and the external aspects separately. For example, when looking at the internal strengths and weaknesses, we could do it base on another model such as "Value chain" and there we can really look at all the possible aspects there are. We could use PEST or PESTLE or for external factors and then we can use SWOT as the conclusion actually. Which would make sense because then we still have a really good overview of all possible aspects and then in the SWOT analysis, which we will then use for building up a strategy that is a conclusion with only the most relevant aspects.

So that's where SWOT is really useful when making a grid... So that strength and weaknesses will be one axis and opportunities and threats on another axis, then we can actually build strategies of how we can use our strengths to combat the possible threats. For example, or how we can use the opportunities together with the weaknesses that we have so that we can maybe get over our weaknesses by building on the opportunities that are there in the external perspective."

Klaus Riskaer Pedersen, Entrepreneur, Author, Founder of CyberCity and CopyGene. Fmr. member of the European Parliament (MEP).

"No, well I mean you can make it, you can also make all sorts of mapping. You can map your competitive strengths and weaknesses. I mean there's a lot of techniques and tools. Have some fun with it, but if you want to run a company or build a company, you can't use it for much. Maybe down the line you have a middle manager, he may be very happy to do the SWOT, fine with me I don't give a shit, to be quite frank."

Christina Bilde, Spokes person Roskilde Festival.

"Yes, I find it useful whenever you're working with different kinds of tasks. Whenever you have to plan your projects, for instance, I find it

useful. Concerning the identity and the position of the festival, of course you have to be aware of it. There's so many other models you could use but it still comes back to the first thing I would say that you have to do is still, what is your own identity? Then you look out and see, are others trying to copy that? How are others threatening that? What are the strengths compared to others? The SWOT model won't work if you're not aware of your own identity. You have to know who you are, why you're doing what you're doing. You have to know how you'll do and what it is that you're presenting and then you can create or use the SWOT model. Maybe you have to look at yourself differently. Of course you always have to look also from the outside in whether the surroundings are looking at you the same way or are you getting through with the message, with who you are and the way you actually see yourself. Is there a correlation between those things? The SWOT analyst can help you do that. We are very aware of what is happening around us, of course. Really not just within music festivals but in festivals in general. There are so many other festivals, offers that people can enjoy, food festivals, art festivals, architecture, design, a lot of other things are happening. Pop-up events that are happening that are also something that we should look into and maybe even get inspiration from."

Klaus Riskaer Pedersen, Entrepreneur, Author, Founder of CyberCity and CopyGene. Fmr. member of the European Parliament (MEP).

"I'm completely sure if you said to Steve Jobs, "You ever done a SWOT?" He would look at you as you a completely idiot and he would say, "Business genius is being an agent of change, and it is change agents who

are creating these things." They do not look up SWOT models, they simply change reality as it is and that was basically his message as well."

Benjamin Holk Henriksen, Strategic planning & branding.
Lecturer DIS and Copenhagen Business School, Author, Filmmaker
"The Mind of a Leader", "Holk Master-class".

"The SWOT model is both useful and a very widely used tool as we have witnessed in this episode. From a strategy perspective it belongs to what Mintzberg's would classify as the Design school, as it takes both internal and external aspects into account and it has the leader in a thought of, you know, the strong leader in a kind of the center of the scheme.

It's been argued that it lacks a couple of aspects. First, some believe that it focuses too much on the current situation, instead of planning ahead. Which I seem to disagree with because again, it depends on what you plug into it. And if you have the ability to look ahead, and have a certain foresight, well you know that you can work with that in your model. It's also been argued that it's very difficult to compare or rank the different aspects of the SWOT model, well yes and no, but again that is the strength of the model that you yourself should know what to plug in and how to use it. So again, if you know what to plug in and how to use it, I believe that it's definitely there is a reason why it's so widely used and so efficient."

Reflection on leadership and Michael Porter's Value chain.

A value chain is a chain of activities that a corporation performs in order to deliver something valuable. The concept is first described by Michael Porter in his 1985 best-seller Competitive Advantage: Creating and Sustaining Superior Performance.[21]

The products or service pass through the activities of the value chain and adds value along the way. According to Michael Porter, a value chain consists of primary activities and support activities.

The primary activities include:

1. Inbound logistics.

2. Operations.

3. Outbound logistics.

4. Marketing and sales.

5. Service.

The support activities include:

1. Internal infrastructure.

2. Human Resource Management.

3. Technology development.

4. Procurement.

---

[21] Porter, M. E. (1985). The Competitive Advantage: Creating and Sustaining Superior Performance. NY: Free Press. (Republished with a new introduction, 1998.)

The idea is to optimize the chain, to maximise value while minimising cost.

This work presents marketing & communication abstracts. For more details about the theory please view the authors' own works.

Interviewees.

Christer Karlsson, Professor CBS, Stockholm School of Economics, EIASM Brussels Accredited "This is Lean: Resolving the Efficiency Paradox", N. Modig & P. Ahlstrom "Research Methods for Operations Management"

"I think the value chain as a whole is a key concept in this idea. And we know that, in the tools for assessing if you're Lean. The value chain, analyzing and assessing, that is a key theme. We know it from Michael Porter, his value chain. And he already has some very good ideas, that he separated the flow where you develop, you purchase, you manufactured, you have production, you have operation, you have services. And then he had the indirect things."

Dennis Balslev, CEO IKEA Germany. Fmr. CEO IKEA Denmark.

"Ikea works in a very interesting way with the whole value chain in the sense that we call something called a diamond. In the bottom, we have the raw material, in the top we have our customers and we are in the lucky position as a company. We can control more or less the whole journey in the value chain. That makes us very strong as a company.

Depending on where you work in the company, you influence the value chain in different places.

In retail, we can influence the range we are selling. We have opportunities to give input and work quite heavily with our range developers in what kind of range do we need and want and what kind of price level do we want. In distribution we also work what is the best way to get the products to Denmark and how much can we get directly from the suppliers and there, we are quite strong today, which means we can offer a lower price to our customers and we can take a lot of cost away in logistics."

Kaspar Basse, Founder, CEO Joe & The Juice.
"Yes. I have a very clear picture of every aspect of the organization. I'm, also very focused on the fact that leadership is not doing everything yourself. I definitely need on a very concrete note for myself, I have an impression of what areas are critical for me to manage, so the brand will develop. I defined them very clearly and I have people that I trust heading all these departments. Hopefully they feel that if they have challenges above what is usual, they can always discuss it with me. It's typically also the developments within each area that we go through in management meetings, etc.

I see my role very much as having these people perform and keep performing better and better on their own. Even to the extent where they may transcend traditional boundaries for their specific area. I definitely want to build a company where people who have ambition and enthusiasm and who wants to develop can do it. This also means that if

95

you're not that type of person, this organization is more difficult for you, because you may not be helped out that much. You need to have self confidence and be able to ignite, to perform well here. I think it's important to motivate and try and push these managers, so they can take their specific area to a different level."

Lars Liebst, CEO Tivoli.

"I think I'm pretty much involved in, I won't say all the aspects, because this company has grown immensely during the last 10 years but just, I was a little bit late this morning, because I was actually out in the garden walking with the head of the gardening and one of our architects, talking about grass, flowers and bees. Yes, I do care for, because the devil sits in the detail and as a CEO you have to know what is really happening. You also have to be aware that you can't look after everything. You have to have very good people and it's the people, our people that really drives this company. It is not me."

Mikkel Borg Bjergsø Founder and CEO Mikkeller brewery, bars and restaurants.

"I think it takes a leader who is always as motivated, or more, which again, is not something that I think about, but I'm pretty sure that my employees feel that I love doing what I do. I love making new beer, I love inventing new restaurants, or new ideas about restaurants, and I love working with bands and coffee roasters and stuff like that. If you kind of show yourself that way, I think it's hard not to follow. It's hard to not be inspired by that. The opposite way as well. I have employees that are extremely passionate about what they do, and I get inspired be that as well. One of our social media guy, or the guy who is working with that,

you can feel that when he talks to a heavy metal band about doing a beer together, you can feel that he loves his job. He loves working with people like that. He loves inventing new ideas, and I get inspired by that as well, as with all the other employees, as well.

I think the leader has to be the most motivated and be the one that shows up the earliest in the morning and go home latest and just show that he loves what he's doing, or she does."

Lars Seier Christensen, Founder and owner Seier Capital, Co-founder and fmr. CEO Saxo Bank.

"Sorry, are you actually asking about how to let go? I have never found that so difficult, because I think it's pretty evident that if you hire good people and they have the right attitude, and they focus 100% on one area, in all likelihood, they will do it better than if you spent 5% of your time on that area while you're dedicating 95% of your time for something else. Yes, particularly in the early years, we did follow quite closely the details of what was happening, but I still think that it's pretty evident that it'll be best for you also to let go and let other people do a lot of the innovation and heavy lifting on the projects that they happen to be assigned to."

Kaspar Basse, Founder, CEO Joe & The Juice.

"Then there's one specific thing which I have my focus on a lot, is that I want to do whatever I can to make sure we don't end up being a lunch sandwich. It's important that it doesn't end up being all about up selling and inelegant approach to product development and only being about expansion and how many stores. As long as I'm with us, and I hope that

will be many, many years it would be beautiful if we all aim at, perhaps even regarding your old school, if that was UCLA. Becoming a potential alternative to some of these management schools, where you have more practical approach. You put your twenty-two year old son or daughter into Joe & the Juice for three or four years. They get to travel the world. They may even finance it themselves. We have developed our campus to an extent where you get lessons in four different languages. Perhaps we have McKenzie coming in talking about this and this type of business, discipline, etc., etc. But a very focused, very practical institution. Developing abilities for people at the start of their twenties. That would be a beautiful thing. I believe as long as you keep that edge and you keep that interest, we will also make more of our stores more profitable than any of our competitors. The day that that becomes the ultimate goal, that's probably the day that I'm not around."

Christer Karlsson, Professor CBS, Stockholm School of Economics, EIASM Brussels Accredited "This is Lean: Resolving the Efficiency Paradox", N. Modig & P. Ahlstrom "Research Methods for Operations Management"

"So it's still very very valid, and I would say, every company I have visited or talked to, they do value chain analysis. Unfortunately I think it's still less understood in the business schools. They still teach the old sick stuff. But if I go up and look at the operation effectiveness or even efficiency, then value chain analysis, I would almost say the key concept. The only problem that occurs then is that there are consultants running around trying to sell tools because that's easier. So they sell tools like 5s or Kanbans or whatever. Starting at the wrong end of the process. Now you

must start with the flow analysis. Those who know it best they do it that way."

Dennis Balslev, CEO IKEA Germany. Fmr. CEO IKEA Denmark.
"I think we have a lot of influence in the whole value chain in the way of working but it feels quite comfortable as a company that we can control the whole chain from raw materials to meeting the customer. We take a lot of decisions with of course third part but we want to steer the process so we know there is no extra cost in the whole value chain. We have a very strong cooperation with our suppliers. Two-thirds of our suppliers and in Europe and one-third outside Europe. We have around 1000 suppliers in the Ikea world but what is most impressive from my point of view, that we have 11 years in average co-operation with our suppliers. It's not a one month or two year cooperation. It's 11 years in average with all our suppliers. We really make long term agreements and long term investments together with our suppliers, which make us quite strong in the way of thinking and can secure high quality to a low price so that's very important for us."

Christer Karlsson, Professor CBS, Stockholm School of Economics, EIASM Brussels Accredited "This is Lean: Resolving the Efficiency Paradox", N. Modig & P. Ahlstrom "Research Methods for Operations Management"
"What Michael Porter mainly talked about just internal chain, but that was not the whole Toyota approach, you know the whole idea of the Toyota supply system is that they also deliver zero-fault just in time. Well it really works, they do not have any inspection of incoming goods, in the Toyota plant. Because all the goods arrive zero-fault just in time, and

how do you do that? You have an example, normally at least two kinds of engineers, in each supplier. They work all the time, with developing their Lean system or TPS. So the suppliers are an integrated part and they are integrated both in manufacturing and in product development. So, the old value chain report, that was just internal. The Toyota system, that's the whole value chain, and it goes all the way out to the customer."

Benjamin Holk Henriksen, Strategic planning & branding.
Lecturer DIS and Copenhagen Business School, Author, Filmmaker
"The Mind of a Leader", "Holk Master-class".

"The word margin on the right side of Porter's figure indicates that firms achieve profit margins based on how the value chain is managed. The model offers a very systematic way of examining and evaluating all the different activities that goes on in a company in order to identify sources of competitive advantages. One important thing to keep in mind is the interaction between these internal aspects in a company. Having a very strong marketing team or sales force, is only strong if it's supported by an equally strong product development or production system. So again strategies are only as strong as their supporting activities."

Reflection on Lean.

Lean manufacturing is a systematic method for the elimination of waste "Muda" within a manufacturing system. Lean also takes into account waste created through overburden "Muri" and waste created through unevenness or variation in workloads "Mura".

The management philosophy takes the perspective of the consumer and defines "value" as any action or process that a customer would be willing to pay for.

The concept derives from the Toyota Production System, or TPS, and was identified as "lean" in the 1990s. It was first described by former Toyota-GM joint venture quality engineer, John Krafcik in his 1988 article, "Triumph of the Lean Production System."[22]

But the concept is also promoted by Toyota, called The Toyota Way. It focuses on improving the "flow" or smoothness of work, thereby eliminating unevenness through the system, and not upon 'waste reduction'.

The TPS has two pillar concepts:

1. Just-in-time or flow.
If production flows perfectly, meaning it is both "pull" and with no interruptions, then there is no inventory. If customer valued features

---

[22] Krafcik, John F. (1988). "Triumph of the Lean Production System." Sloan Management Review, 41–52.

are the only ones produced, then product design is simplified and focuses only on features that the customer values.

2. Autonomation.

The machines or systems are designed to aid humans in focusing on what humans do best.

The original seven muda, or wastes:

1. Transportation.

Moving products that are not actually required to perform the processing.

2. Inventory.

All components, work in process and finished products not being processed.

3. Motion.

People or equipment moving more than is required to perform the processing.

4. Waiting.

Waiting for the next production step, or interruptions of production during shift change.

5. Overproduction.

Over producing products beyond what the customer has ordered.

6. Over-processing or incorrect processing.

Resulting from poor tool or product design creating activity.

7. Defects.

Product rejects and rework within your processes.

In addition to the seven muda, an eighth has been proposed concerning skills.

Losing time, ideas, skills, improvements and learning opportunities by not engaging with or listening to your employees.

The role of the leaders is the fundamental element in sustaining the progress of lean thinking. It involves three basic principles based on continuous improvement:

1. Challenge: Having a long-term vision of the challenges one needs to face to realize one's ambition.

2. Kaizen: Good enough never is.

3. Genchi Genbutsu: Going to the source to see the facts for oneself and making the right decisions, creating consensus, and making sure goals are attained at the best possible speed.

And two principles concerning respect for people:

1. Respect: Taking every stakeholders' problems seriously, and making every effort to build mutual trust. Taking responsibility for other people reaching their objectives.

2. Teamwork: Developing individuals through team problem-solving.

This work presents marketing & communication abstracts. For more details about the theory please view the authors' own works.

Interviewees.

Christer Karlsson, Professor CBS, Stockholm School of Economics, EIASM Brussels Accredited "This is Lean: Resolving the Efficiency Paradox", N. Modig & P. Ahlstrom "Research Methods for Operations Management".

"Well, the whole thing started in the early 80s, when there was an observation that the Japanese auto industry took over from the American industry. Others also, but that was the concern. So there was a big project starting at MIT, where I was involved. It was about the future of the automobile from 80-84. We explained some of these driving forces, but also it would continue. It would happen also in Europe and so on. Everything would move away. That was an interesting way of getting in your research project from 86-90, which ended up as the international automotive program. I did some of those studies. I call it, we invented Lean.

Really what we did was, we were going inside the companies to explain this. I've done it especially of course in the Toyota Motor Corporation. Now we found something very spectacular. We found a couple of things. First of all, the explanation wasn't Japanese. It wasn't the Japanese production system, it was the Toyota production system. There were companies that worked also in Japan but they have developed a certain idea. It wasn't just about production. The whole system was about product development, relation with suppliers, production, distribution, everything. So we started studying that in quite a detail. And we were surprised, really surprised.

First of all, there was a focus on the flow instead of the utilization resources. I'll
come back to that later. They were so efficient that they didn't compare with anybody else. The assembly time for a car was down to 10-15 hours instead of 40, 50, 60, 70, 80, in Sweden and so on. It was just outstanding. We had this observation of course of zero-fault and a number of other things.

We started digging very, very deep into this, trying to measure everything. We left in a Ph.D. student from MIT in each plants, and he had a 80 pages question and he stayed there for one or two weeks helping them to fill it in.

I must tell you a very interesting story was when we got this response back from the Japanese company, saying we are please to participate in this world famous study, and we have done everything we can to fill in all the data.

We must point out that you have made one mistake in the questionnaire when translating between English and Japanese. Because you ask for the level of work in progress, that is how much the value is of the material you have in the plant, and you ask for the number of weeks. Normally, it was like 4-6 maybe up to 8 weeks or so, material you have in stock. And they wrote that 'We don't think you mean weeks, we think you mean minutes'. And we have a 120 minutes now, and we are trying to reduce it. And we said, what is this.

Dennis Balslev, CEO IKEA Germany. Fmr. CEO IKEA Denmark.

"I think Ikea's built on lean production. Our founder Ingvar Kamprad was very smart in the forties when he started the company and realized that if you don't have lean production then you have a lot of waste. Waste is money and what do we do with that? Already from the beginning I was a question about how are you using the raw material. The flat pack we have today, we were the first company to come with home furnishing in flat pack. How do you move goods from A to B in a different way?

The way we are using raw material today when we have a little bit of waste, then we always have a solution to use the waste for another product. The whole lean production is part of our DNA, the way we are thinking. That's very very important for Ikea and I think that's part of our culture and values. It fits so much with sustainability. I think in the forties, nobody thought about that but this meant a lot for the price tag on the products, if you can use all raw material and you can use a lean production and you optimize your production in a different way. We have

106

a flat pack you can send around the world with no big influence so that's a lot of steps in the past where maybe we were not aware of all the smart words of today but it was in the founder Ingvar Kamprad's way of thinking."

Christer Karlsson, Professor CBS, Stockholm School of Economics, EIASM Brussels Accredited "This is Lean: Resolving the Efficiency Paradox", N. Modig & P. Ahlstrom "Research Methods for Operations Management".

"The history in Japan is that, the grandson of the founder was sent to US to study automobile production because they were leaders, and he came back to his uncle and said "It's fascinating but we can't do it here. We don't have the volumes, we don't have the material, we don't have the raw material, we don't have the energy, we only have people. Lets built a system that's built on the competence of people". That's really how the whole thing started.

And then there are these famous stories about Mr. Ohno, who came in and studied the flow and why you had obstacles in that and so on. But that's what we can go on with. But that's really how it started.

So we wrote this book that's called "The Machine That Changed The World" and we realized we didn't understand anything so we didn't call it "Toyota Production System" at that time although it was. We call it "Lean Production". Why did we call it 'Lean' because we noticed they have relatively few resources in the whole system.

Now that is misunderstood sometimes trying to reduce workers and so on. That's very dangerous, it's actually opposite the idea. But in the whole system they didn't have so much, and then we noticed that like we would walk through along the assembly line and after assembly line, you normally come to a big area where they make adjustments. You know cars consist of 10,000 components. So, there are always some little faults. At that time, there was like 50% of the cars had to have at least one small correction afterwards, sometimes bigger. In "proto forty" and so, but I walk through this plant in Japan, came to the end of the final assembly. There was two cars standing along the wall. I said, "Why are they standing there?" And the guy flushed, got red, and said "Oh sorry, something wrong".

Something wrong? How many have you made today? 850. Okay. So it should be 400 with something wrong, no it was two. And they were so embarrassed because it normally didn't happen. So then we realized, there was no area for making adjustments. There were no rejections, there were no time to make corrections. So we were very happy to find something out about this, because the work pace was slower. The workload and workers were less. People think they worked harder, but that's not really the case. They need to have spare resources to be able to take care of any problem.

The thing was that there were no corrections, there were no middle levels of foreman and so on. So there were almost no indirect workers. They didn't have special quality control people. Why? Because they were no mistakes.

So, all these things started being understood to us as a very different system. And I still make people curious or doubtful if I know the system, when I say that the productivity on the assembly line about Toyota is low. What do I mean by that? I mean the workload on workers is low, but the flow is perfect."

Lars Seier Christensen, Founder and owner Seier Capital, Co-founder and fmr. CEO Saxo Bank.

"Not a lot, to be honest. We certainly never did it in a formal way using one of the consultancy services inside this. We've been blessed with a market where actually we make quite good money in spite of not being lean, which never really drove the same way as you would in certain industries, an absolute need to cut every cost down to the bone.

I would say of course we try to be efficient, of course we cut costs every now and again, but I wouldn't say that we have been very structured in that process, and potentially we should've been, but I think in a business like ours where we have relatively high value clients, you also want to make sure that there's adequate service to these clients and you certainly shouldn't make it so lean that the clients begin to feel that it's unpersonalized and that people don't have time for them. A good client for us can be very valuable and he expects to be looked after. It's not the same as having a mass production of an industrial product or something like that."

Christer Karlsson, Professor CBS, Stockholm School of Economics, EIASM Brussels Accredited "This is Lean: Resolving the Efficiency

Paradox", N. Modig & P. Ahlstrom "Research Methods for Operations Management".

"One special issue here is that we have the idea of flow, no mistakes and avoiding waste. So waste, was anything that didn't add value to the product. And then, there was seven Muda's and so on, then there have been added like Muda in product development and thinking and so on, made that available. The idea is the same, but you can say it has expanded.

So, there're different dimensions of not adding value to the product. Except for just not let it wait, or doing unnecessary things. Because that's also a thing, those who made corrections or so, they also didn't add value to the product. They worked, but they worked unnecessary you can say.

But then when the applications have developed, I think there's one interesting aspect especially when it has been applied to services and Lean services. Because then you don't really have a material thing like the car or something like that. But in most other situations you can use it, and I really like to use it in restaurants, or in hospitals, or so because then the raw material is the person.

I want to process that and so, and that's why we had the problems with the hospitals I talked about that, you don't focus on taking the material, the patient, through the system in the best way. You think of utilizing resources, but in some countries, they started with, especially one in Europe, they started connecting a nurse to a patient at the arrival to the hospital. And said, now I take you through the system."

Strategic Planning.

Strategic planning involves concepts and tools learned in other film episodes. If we look at Holk's Communication Platform left to right we have:

1. The organisation. The corporate DNA, including mission & vision, values, history and ideology. 2. The communication platform. The value words or brand coms the communication campaign builds on. 3. Media execution. 4. Target group.

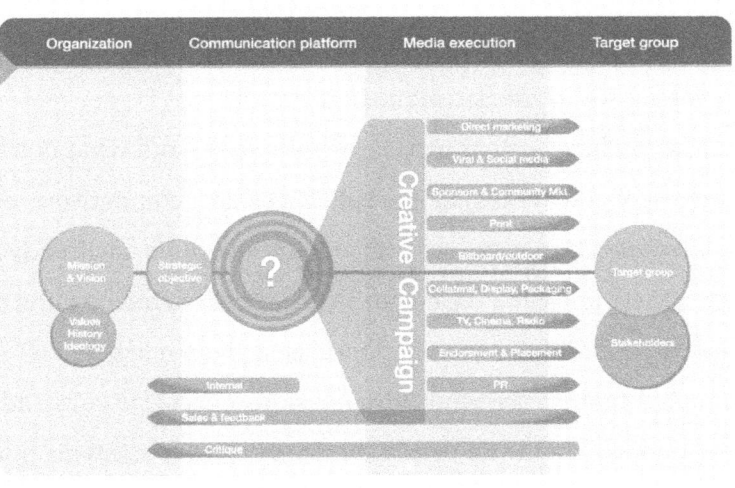

Figure 9.

But before we develop our internal and external communication and branding we need to define our objective. And that objective is based on strategic planning.

Strategic planning consists of two parts: Strategy, or strategic objective, and how to take action, the "planning" process. The analysis is based on the "strategy tripod". It encompasses elements from the positioning school, or what is known as the industry based view, focusing on generic models and industry data. The resource based view, focusing on resources, as a potential competitive advantage. And the institution based view introduced by Mike Peng, focusing on the institutional environment, forces, rules and regulations.[23]

The number of tools or steps in your strategic planning process depends on your defined scope or preferred approach. There are no absolutes. However the following steps serve as a helpful basis.

Step 1. Set-up for strategic planning.
Sometimes you have a clear picture of your scope and what needs to be done, such as if you are losing market shares on a competitive market, setting new sales targets or creating an argument for an already given strategy. Other times you base your initial research on a feeling or ideology, or try to think ahead and foresee a given market development. In this case your initial desk research, surveys and collected data will help you define the scope of your strategic planning process. Make sure to define the people involved in the process and their expectations.

---

[23] Peng, Mike W., Li Sun, Sunny, Pinkham, Brian, and Chen, Hao (2009). The Institution-Based View as a Third Leg for a Strategy Tripod.

Step 2. Mission, vision, values, history and philosophy.

Understand your organisational DNA, your purpose and where you are coming from.

Step 3. Target group.

Define your primary and secondary target group.

Step 4. Stakeholders.

Define your other stakeholders. Who will be affected by, or respond to your strategy?

Step 5. Position.

Use a positioning map to define your position in terms of price, quality etc.

Step 6. Benchmark.

Compare your current situation with your competitors, your past strategies and campaigns, and market development.

Step 7. SWOT.

Conduct a SWOT analysis, including internal strengths and weaknesses, and external opportunities and threats. The SWOT analysis belongs to what Mintzberg would categorise as the design school, as it includes internal and external factors.[24]

---

[24] Mintzberg, Henry, Ahlstrand, Bruce Lampel, Joseph B. (2008) Strategy Safari: Complete Guide Through the Wilds of Strategic Management, 2nd ed. 2nd Edition. Pearson Education Limited.

A few aspects to keep in mind that are covered in the strategy tripod are:

- Your current organisational objective.
- Environmental scan.
- Business model and finances.
- Leadership.
- Organizational capacity.

It might be inspirational to include more specific tools such as Porters value chain or five forces.

Step 8. Product portfolio.

Get an overview of your product portfolio including sales, spending, product attributes, and market share and growth development. The Boston Consulting Group growth-share Matrix serves as a great tool to get an overview.

Remember to subtract points or draw conclusions from each step. Analytic tools offer a great overview, but the key to strategic planning is to link and build on your findings and create a strategic objective and plan.

Step 9. Conduct your strategic plan.

Define your objective and strategy, and conduct an action plan including steps.

The listed tools and steps serve as a great base. Other analytic tools that might be relevant are: Ansoff's Product Market Growth Matrix, Maslow's hierarchy of needs, The Product life cycle model, Push Pull strategy aspects, and many more.

Most strategic plans involve internal or external communication, whether the objective is to build transparency, create awareness or re-brand the organization.

A creative communication campaign is often based on a one-page creative brief, given by the strategic planners to the creative department. The creative brief includes the most important findings from the strategic planning process.

Interviewees.

Dennis Balslev, CEO IKEA Germany. Fmr. CEO IKEA Denmark.
"I think strategic planning today is very interesting because you see more strategic planning but you see very often, stay with the planning. I think very important for the way of thinking if the vision and the mission. Why are we here? What do we want to achieve and what strategic planning will secure we go where we want to be so you always have this clear goal in front of you. I think that's very important and then have short-term and long-term plans in your planning.

The word strategy is very modern today but also be careful with the word strategy because what it's all about is to reach something together and where do we want to be. For us, it's really about putting up the clear goal. We talk about goal which is much more common. Where do we want to be and then we talk about how we get there. Involving the whole organization in the strategy to reach the goal. I spend a lot of time together with my colleagues to get everybody to know where do we want to be as a company and I am quite proud we have reached 86 percent of everybody, of 2,300 people, say we know exactly where the company want to go and that's very high in the retail where we have maybe 50 percent part-timers. If you don't know where you want to go, how fun is to start to walk together with the company. The whole strategy is fine but you really have to get it down to people understand what does it mean for me, how can I engage, how can I be part of reaching the goal, maybe some part goals where I can deliver in my position. We look very much into how can everybody be part of where we want to be as a company."

Birgitte Mabeck, Head of fundraising and marketing Red Cross.
"For me strategic planning, it kind of sounds a little bit old-fashioned, but for me it's very important that it links into a strategic plan, a tactical plan and an operational plan. Those three have to go hand-in-hand. There's no way I would ever just do an operational plan where I would not know what is my tactics, and I wouldn't know what aim am I trying to reach within my strategic plan. I would really use the completely old-fashioned model, and I am using the old-fashioned model saying, "What's our strategy? How does our strategy within my department fit into the overall strategy of the house and for the Red Cross?

116

What are the aims that my department has to be part of them accomplishing? What's the tactics that we should do in terms of reaching these goals, and what are the operational set up we need to have in place to do that?" When you have that, then you also know your resource management. You can start building all of your plans for your campaigns and all the fun. If you start just with the fun what quite often happens, and you just do like a fun marketing plan without any goal-setting, then you might risk not having met the overall objectives of the organization that you are in. It might end up with a very short fun happening."

Lars Seier Christensen, Founder and owner Seier Capital, Co-founder and fmr. CEO Saxo Bank.

"Of course you should have plans because at the end of the day, it makes it more likely that you're going to reach the goal that you define. I think you don't want to do it too detailed again. There's a reason why the five year plans in Soviet Union didn't really work out normally, and that's because if your plan is too explicit and too detailed, you take away again the responsibility for people doing their own thinking and improving with their own ideas and the feedback that they get from reality, from their customers, from the world around them. I would say of course you should have a goal setting, I would say, but I'd be very, very careful to make too detailed plans for... Again, I'm not a big fan of most management theories and huge planning processes, because it actually works quite well if you just let people do what they think is right and test it up against reality, and remember to discard things that don't work and focus on the stuff that does work. At least for what we're doing, it might be different if you have a very complicated, large logistic production or something like that. For us, when there's a lot of personal interaction

with our clients, I think you... I'm a great believer really in just saying this is where we want to go, guys, here's the resources that you're going to get together, and now you come back in a few weeks and tell me what is your plan. Of course, if I think the plan is idiotic, I will tell them, but mostly, it's not because they actually sit down and think about, and I'll say okay, go ahead and show them the money."

Malene Torp. Executive Director, DIS – Study Abroad in Scandinavia.

"When I think of strategic planning I always think of Churchill and he said that, "Planning is everything and a plan is nothing." I don't know if I completely agree, but I certainly agree that the process of a strategic plan is incredibly important and my advice would be to involve your stakeholders in the strategic planning. You can make the most beautiful strategic plan but if you haven't involved people in the making of the strategic plan I don't think you're going to be very successful when it comes to implementing it."

Anders Kryger, Senior Business Strategist, Industrial PhD Fellow at MAN Diesel & Turbo.

"In my research, I'm looking into how employee's stories can drive strategic planning. It might seem a bit crazy to have employee's stories drive the big apparatus of strategic planning in a company, but actually what I'm looking into is having the employee's values, which you can find through storytelling, be the driving force in the strategic planning work that has been done by the finance department. Or by the business development department or the management circle or whatever. I think if you facilitate strategy with storytelling, you will very easily find

through stories, in stories, some of the components of mission and vision, and will very naturally lead you to an action plan."

Peter Holten Mühlmann, Founder and CEO, Trustpilot.

"I think strategic planning is very important for a number of reasons. I think the 2 most important reasons is 1, to ensure that everybody's on the same page; 2, to give everybody a feeling that they're on the same page. If people have a feeling that they don't really know what's going on. They don't really... They're not really sure what everybody else is working on; that, even though you know you're working on just the right things and that thing is going in the very right direction, then they're going to spend a lot of time just thinking about it. That's enormously unproductive. Because they shouldn't.

With strategic planning, 1st of all, my advice is to state your vision. What is it that you'd like to achieve in this life. Then outline, what are your long term... That could be 3 to 5 year strategic goals, where you need to take the business in order to make the world like that. Then, zoom in and say, "Well, Okay. That's our 3 to 5 year goals. What's the 1st step in that direction? That's this year. What are the themes that we are focusing on this year. Then break those themes down to quarterly, or could even be monthly goals depending on how big your business is. Get every team to articulate what their objectives is towards that goal and what key results would be, and to make that in a publicly available format so that everybody in the business can look at what are the other teams goals. That way you can also surf those discussions, like, "Hey. Wait a minute. If I'm working in this direction, why are they working that direction?"

From this way, you go from the top to the bottom and back up from the bottom to the top."

Malene Torp. Executive Director, DIS – Study Abroad in Scandinavia.

"I think we have a very clear mission at DIS and we have a very clear vision as well and I think that is instrumental when you try to have an open strategy process, because if it's not defined what are the goals of the organization and where is it that you would like to go then I think a strategic planning process could go in so many different directions so I think that is absolutely instrumental if you want to be very inclusive and really have your stakeholders' input to a strategy."

Part III. Communication campaign development.

Agency positions and the creative brief.

Agency positions.

Not all advertising agencies are structured in the same way. Titles, positions and workflow vary from organization to organization. Traditional departments and positions include: [25]

Director of account services / Account Management.
The responsibility of the director or account manager is to be the client's representative at the agency, and the agency's representative at the client's organization. It's the obligation to develop knowledge of the client's business, the consumer, the marketplace and all aspects of advertising. Activities are assisted by a secretary or project manager making sure procedures are followed and deadlines kept.

Strategic planning.
Director, Account planner, Strategic Planner or simply Consultant. The account planner's primary tools are research and strategy: consumer psychology and behavior, brand-sales history, competitive sales and

---

[25] Suggett, Paul (2018), The Structure of an Advertising Agency. Get to Know the Typical Make-Up of an Ad Agency.

customer information, consumer demographics, and much more. They use this information to determine how the agency can leverage a brand's strengths.

Creative.

The creative department is responsible for developing the ideas, images, and words that make up commercials and ads.

Creative director: Responsibility for the overall creative development.
Art director: Responsible for the visual creation of general advertising campaigns.
Copywriter: Responsible for generating ideas and concepts.
Illustrator: Prepares a variety of illustrations including design, layout materials, and interpretive drawings.

Media.

Some agencies have an in-house media department while others rely on external media partners. The media department is responsible for placing advertising in the media at the right time and place in order to reach the target group.

Interactive Marketing.

Some agencies may have an independent interactive marketing department while other integrate it in other areas of the organization.

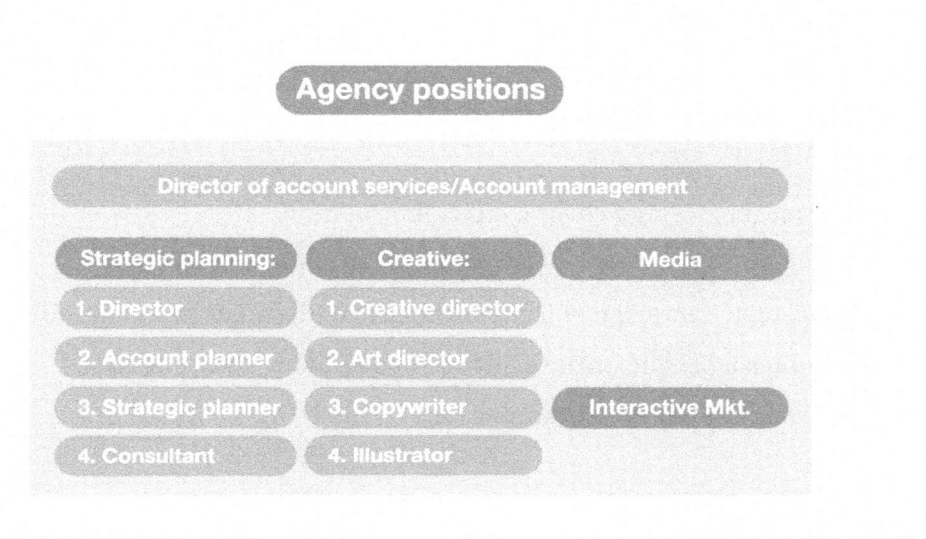

Figure 10.

It's helpful to understand these basic organizational structures and workflows. Some agencies stick to the traditional positions and departments while others form client teams involving both strategic and creative people.

The Creative brief.

A creative brief is a short, written document, usually about one page in length that ensures creative deliverables align with the strategic campaign objective. The creative brief is usually drafted after the communication platform words have been defined, and given to the create people as a guideline. There are no strict rules in terms of what to include in creative brief.[26]

Some aspects to keep in mind:

1. Project name and client contact information.

2. Strategic campaign objective. The goal of the ad or campaign such as, to launch a product, raise sales, change brand perception, raise awareness, employee branding etc.

3. Mission & Vision.

4. History, philosophy and values.

5. Primary and secondary target group, including preferences, habits and values.

6. Potential stakeholders that can either help or harm your campaign.

7. The product or service position. An overview of the competitive landscape, trends and market conditions, traditionally defined as the relation between price and quality.

---

[26] http://www.adcracker.com/brief/Sample_Creative_Brief.htm
http://www.thehealthcompass.org/how-to-guides/how-write-creative-brief
https://www.upwork.com/hiring/design/how-to-create-an-effective-creative-brief/

8. Benchmark. An overview of main competitor campaigns, as a point of comparison or differentiation.

9. Past, current and future campaigns. Considerations in regards to previous campaigns.

10. The campaign and products relation to the product portfolio and markets. Potential ways the campaign may help or harm the overall product portfolio.

11. Considerations in regards to the "Call to Action". The desired action such as, visit a website or store, or sign a petition.

12. SWOT analysis (strength, weaknesses, opportunities, threats). An evaluation of findings leading to a strategy or unique selling points (USPs).

13. Communication platform words. The result of the strategic work presented as 3-5 words or messages the creative campaign should communicate in order to reach the objective.

14. Schedule and outline of the desired deliverables. A timeline and list of work expected to be delivered by the creative department such as: Above The Line advertising material (ATL) for television, radio, print and internet. Below the line advertising material (BTL) such as pamphlets, handbills, stickers, promotions, brochures placed at point of sale, banners and placards. Or Through the line advertising (TTL). A combination of the two.

15. Budget or resources. The campaign budget.

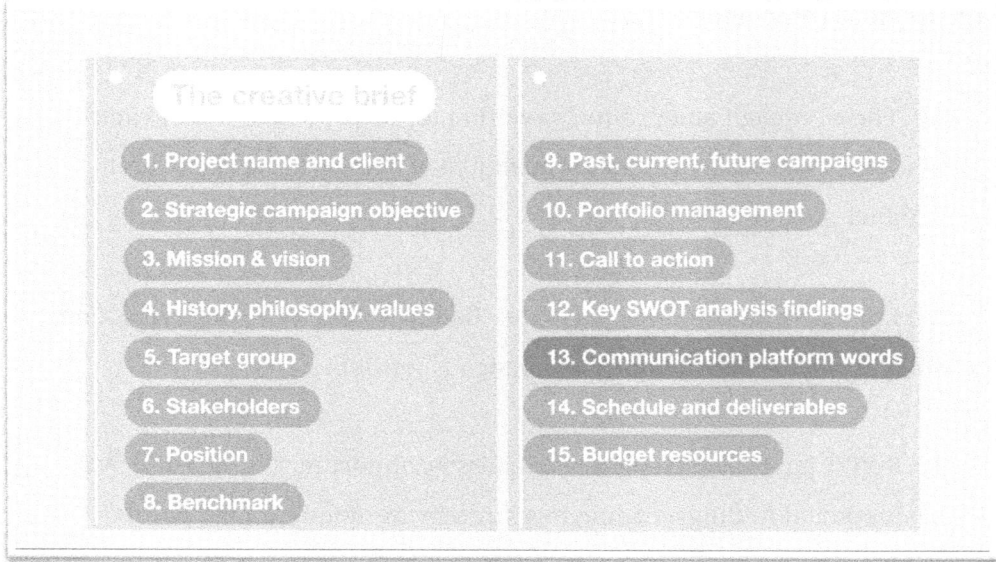

Figure 11.

An example of a company that has aligned its mission, vision, history, values and advertising campaigns is Absolut vodka. In 1986 Andy Warhol became the first artist commissioned to create a portrait of the Absolut Vodka bottle. Following the iconic ad campaign, Absolut Vodka established itself as a way of life: *"One intimately connected with art, design, fashion and creativity."*

The words are taken from Absolut Vodka's corporate web-site and also stated in their mission and vision:

Mission:

"We provide a wide range of premium vodkas in order to create the highest quality drinking experience for our consumers worldwide."

Vision:

"We want to be a role model in our industry and beyond, through innovation, creativity, and progress in every sphere of our production process. Our goal is to be the producer of a vodka that people are proud to drink."

To date, the more than hundred years old Swedish vodka producer has had at least 300 different bottle designs by internationally renowned artists, fashion designers, and glass artisans around the world including a limited-edition bottle called "Absolut 72 Transformations" designed by Chinese Pop artist Gao Yu.

Interviewees.

David Angelo, Founder & Chairman, David & Goliath advertising agency.

"...no matter who touches the brand, it's that person or that entity's responsibility to serve the brand at all costs. A smart marketer and a smart agency owner, or person, understands the true value of collaboration, and that it's so important to make sure that you surround yourself with powerful thinkers.

It's equally important that you stay open to wherever that idea comes from. In many cases a great idea, a great marketing idea, a great advertising idea, can come from the client. In many cases a great business-building idea can come from the agency. It behooves everyone to sort of share this belief of collaboration. If it means writing the brief together, then so be it. Or if it means coming up with the name of the next great burger, then so be it.

Fortunately we work with brands that really believe in that concept, that we're all a team, looking out for the best interest of the brand."

Dr. Kate Stone, Director Novalia.

"We created an invite for Ikea and we thought about the design of how the thing looked and it was for a store opening in Memphis. So, we thought about the people in Memphis, the music in Memphis and what the store means and what it means there. Just trying to take little bits of all of that to create something that's deeper in a way. Cause if you think about things in a more holistic way, then what you end up with is a much deeper connection with deeper roots and anything with deeper roots knows longevity."

Johan Boserup, Global CEO of Trading at WPP's GroupM.

"A good creative brief is difficult to define because it very much ... You can talk about a good creative brief in the context of a good strategic brief and a strategic brief needs to reflect what the client, what the advertiser, the brand, the company sets out to do. What is it they are trying to achieve? If you ask someone like Coca Cola, for example, they will not say... they are not in this world, their strategy is not to sell more Coke, it's

to build the brand because then they will sell more Coke. The same thing goes for Unilever. Unilever don't sell products, they build brands. That's how they will identify themselves.

The strategic brief needs to reflect that. The creative brief needs to reflect that and the nature of the brand. So, "how do we best build this brand?" And I think it's naïve for advertisers to think that they can leave that entirely to a creative agency. Because, I don't think that the creative agency can live and breath a brand the way that the brand themselves can and the company themselves can.

However, they can add a lot of other things to it. So, I think, honestly, that clients and advertisers who leave it entirely up to the creative agency to come up with or to answer a brand brief, I think they're making a mistake. I think it needs to be a symbiosis.

I think they need to work on it together and have the business side of it as well as the creative side of it. So, yeah, the creative side is a very, very important part and the right creative can build the brand."

Steffen Hjaltelin, Founder & Partner at Hjaltelin Stahl.

"In a world where we can divide the marketing challenge in three layers: the platform, the presence, and the peaks ... very different demands to the creative brief. When it comes to a creative brief in Always-on ... How do we become relevant for our clients 24/7 in a thousand different connection points, contact points, touch points over a year? That is one creative brief. It's one brief, semi-creative in that regard. You have to control your structure before you put on the creative part, which is a lot

of design creativity, it's a lot of content creativity, less weird idea creativity. If there's one thing you don't want in a relevant customer journey, it's to be met with some weirdo creativity that takes you out of the process you're in.

It's very different when it comes to the peaks ... we call them ignitions ... where we make the basic, basic creativity that attracts people's attention and from where we can put them down into the marketing system.

The thing that comprehends all creative briefs ... and what clients should focus more on ... is pointing at the problem. What is the actual problem that you want solved? Spend all your time on defining the problem. That is what we see lacking in a lot of creative briefs ... actually defining the problem that you want solved. Typically, in a lot of briefs, people will focus to some degree on the problem, but then they skip over that and come up with ten different ... "It could be solved from this way, that way, that way." But when you look into that, very often that actually implies that it turns out they haven't got a real, real narrow, meaningful understanding of the problem itself ... and trying to be the agency itself.

That doesn't seem to help much. Very, very, tight focusing on the tight, tight problem, and then let creative minds come up with different ways of solving the problem. Also, when you do it like that, it's extremely important that we don't have this closed-box agency thinking where you come up with the problem, and then one month later you hear some different solutions. It is a very, very close working together ... workshops, then you have break-outs, and a few days when the agency works by itself and comes back. But it's close, close interaction in this regard."

Tue Walin Storm, Director, Screenwriter, Founder Storm/Hansen (Nielson, Ford, Pirelli, The Raveonettes).

"Well, as a director, you usually get involved in the stage where the agency have sold the concept into the client and they're now ready to make the film. The creative producer, or the producer from the agency, will then approach various production companies to sort of see who's available to make this type of production. They have specific ideas of what type of director they want. There are sales reps within the production companies that then get in touch with these producers. Based on that relationship or collaboration between those two entities, the producer will then present to the creatives of the agency, a list of various directors. Based on that list, they will look at all the various reels. Based on those reels, they will select three, maybe four, different directors that they would then like to elaborate on with a treatment. So, they will give the directors the creative brief. Then based on that brief is when the director then gets involved to write their treatment. Usually, as a director, when you're shortlisted, you are competing against two to three other directors for the same job."

Molly DeWolf Swenson Founding member / CMO of RYOT.

"...the more specific the brief the better, in particular with regards to budget. When you're doing video production, budgets can range from ten thousand dollars to ten million dollars. So, if there's no budget on the brief, it's very annoying for us creatives. Because, the ideas can be scaled to whatever the budget is truly. So, budget tiers or budget ranges are great. And then when there's sort of a blue sky option where you're just

giving something that's a crazy great idea, we like that too... the "moon-shots"."

Holk's Communication Platform model CPM.

The communication platform model is a concept developed by Benjamin Holk Henriksen. It constitutes the basis for marketing and communication strategies.

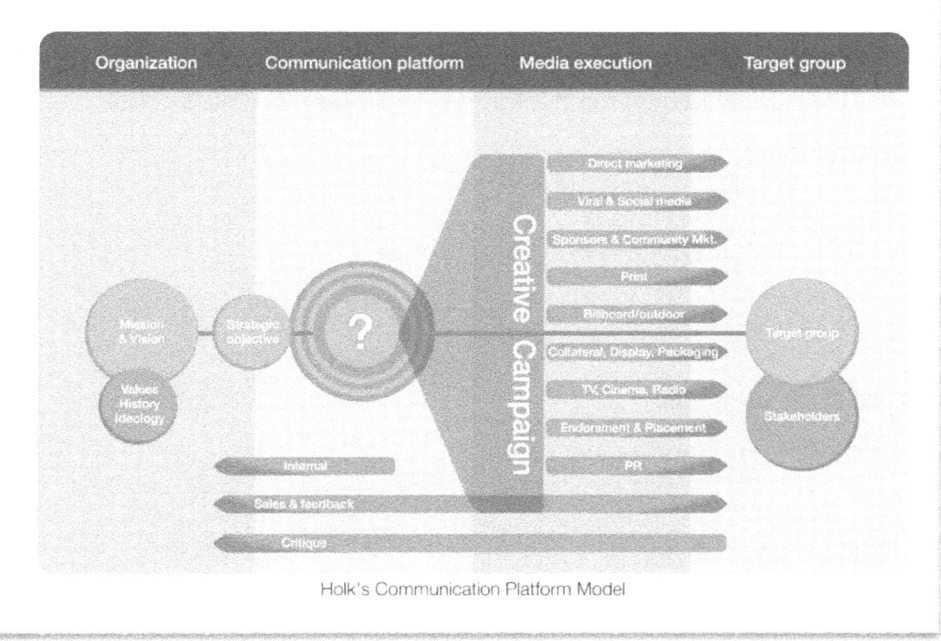

Holk's Communication Platform Model

Figure 12.

The model consist of: The organization or corporation, the communication platform, media execution/activation and target group.

The communication platform defines what a company, organization or specific product wants to stand for or be perceived as, internally in the organization, the corporation, and externally in the market. It's also the

133

foundation when responding to internal and external events and critique.

While the organisation's mission & vision are more or less timeless, the communication platform adapts to the ever-changing environment and strategic objective. Who are we or who do we want to be? What value words or brand comms constitute our communication platform and campaign? For example: serious, playful, friendly, conservative, healthy, luxury, original, responsible, freedom, etc. It's the basis for the creative campaign development and thus an essential part of the creative brief.

Whether the campaign is executed through:

Direct marketing.
Viral & Social media.
Sponsors & Community marketing.
Print.
Billboard or outdoor.
Collateral, Display and packaging.
TV, Cinema and radio.
Endorsement and Placement.
PR.

The organisation's mission and vision, values, history, ideology and strategic objective, and consumer perceptions define the platform. Thus it's important to listen to your organisation, and the market, target group and stakeholders, so that there is a balance between internal and external aspects. The communication platform builds on what is generally considered as corporate identity , the core of the organisation. But it includes strategic concerns and objectives such as selling points, strategic analysis, product portfolio, brand differentiation etc.

An example of a corporation that has aligned its communication platform with its mission for more than 100 years is Coca Cola. Part of their mission is "to refresh the world" and "inspire moments of optimism and happiness...". A brand message that is easily recognised in their slogan's "delicious and refreshing" from 1904, "have a Coke and a smile" from 1979, or "open happiness" from 2012.

A fun and rewarding marketing and advertising exercise is to analyse a commercial. What keywords do you think define the communication platform and why? What can you say about the organisation's mission, vision, values, target group and stakeholders?

Interviewees.

Ole Henriksen, Founder and Creative Director, Ole Henriksen Skin Care Brand.
"The values in my company are definitely an extension of my life philosophy, that of being celebratory of life, having fun. One of my famous sayings is, "A happy face is a beautiful face". And since I'm in the business of skin care, and beauty, that's what it's all about: feeling good about yourself. So that's what I want to bring out in my clients, in my

135

fans around the world, the ones that buy into the Ole Henriksen product line.

So as a platform for the brand, I definitely emphasize the wellness model, because without encompassing all aspects of general health and well-being, you cannot look your best. I'm only happy when, as an extension of that, that people also opt to buy Ole's products. But I must admit, when I'm out meeting clients, travelling the world, speaking on behalf of my brand, that I'm just as happy if I have inspired something positive in them, helped build their self-esteem. If they have come to me and given the impression that they may feel insecure, less worthy, or less attractive, if I can make them feel good, we have laid a great foundation, and then whatever follows is fantastic."

David Angelo, Founder & Chairman, David & Goliath advertising agency.

"One of the big challenges today is that it's been so splintered. There are so many different partners involved in a brand experience, whether it's an agency that has very little digital capabilities. Then you have a digital agency with very little brand capabilities, then you have other different sort of entities, all working on the same brand. I'd say the big challenge there is making sure that everyone is on the same page, because no one is going to be responsible for making it successful. It's going to be the collective whole that helps make it successful. Does that make sense? So it could be social marketing, with the combination of traditional broadcast TV, or point of sale, or PR. Whatever it may be, all of those touch points all need to be aligned with one common truth."

Christina Bilde, Spokes person Roskilde Festival.

"Actually we've created a baseline story you could say or a brand story, which is the story of Roskilde Festival as a city, that will challenge you with music, with art and with culture. That brand story is being used in everything we do. Whether it's design, visuals or the way we speak about the festival, especially in commercials branding and advertising."

Peter Ålbæk Jensen, Producer, Founder & fmr. CEO, Zentropa.

"Opposition is a good word because that's how we started and that's how we still feel our self understanding is, that we are in opposition. The next word would probably be humor, because our partnership me and Lars Von Trier, everybody employed out here, that is with a big sense of humor and a big emphasis on having fun is very vital. The third word would probably be industrialization because we are very much in favor that, even though we are doing art house movies, little strange movies from a peculiar country, we would like to industrialize things. We like that it is, that we think about the process that we try to make it cheaper, more sellable and as much as possible."

Malin Gardeström, International Marketing Manager, Carlsberg & Tuborg.

"When you enter the building, the office building here, it says "semper ardence" above the door which is Latin for "always burning." This used the be the office of Carl Jacobsen, which is the son of our founder which Carlsberg is named after, and always burning is very important and it's part of the culture in Carlsberg. This is always "burning" to us that means doing things better and to always improve yourself. That is very much in line what we do, be it quality, be it marketing, be it everything and the

marketing mix as well. We have a great heritage to build up on. For us, it's about aligning, and what it means nowadays with where we come from."

Benjamin Holk Henriksen, Strategic planning & branding. Lecturer DIS and Copenhagen Business School, Author, Filmmaker "The Mind of a Leader", "Holk Master-class".

"The communication platform is an essential part of the creative brief, like target group, strategic objective and so on. It has to be part of the creative brief. I am a strong believer in building this platform so that creative ideas are not just taken out of the blue, without any context, but based on strategic planning. Furthermore the platform fosters brand consistency... a uniform message through all communication channels. Know your mission and vision. Conduct research and surveys to define values, history, ideology. If you look at organizations like at Ikea, Walmart, Virgin, The Body shop etc. you will see that a big part of their DNA originates from the founders. Define your distribution system, target group and stakeholders incl. preferences, habits, needs etc. Planning should really be from the customers to the organization and not just from the organization to the customers, as my friend and marketing guru Philip Kotler used to say.

Conduct your strategic planning, including market research, surveys, positioning, SWOT, benchmark etc. to define your strategy and objective. Then use the information, your strength, unique selling points, objective etc. as a framework for developing 5-6 mood-boards with words or brand coms that could constitute the communication platform for your creative campaign."

Molly DeWolf Swenson Founding member / CMO of RYOT.

"I think it's a really great exercise for any company to go through... whether you're a small start up or whether you're a giant company. If you were a person, what would that person be like? What would that person look like? And what would they do? Because, it enables... it enables everyone to figure out what brand they should be representing. It also allows for talent acquisition in a more targeted way. It allows for agencies that you're working with, or production companies that you're working with to understand really quickly what type of work you want from them. If you don't have that, you're just going to get a lot of stuff that you don't want."

Matthew Bagwell, Managing Director Naked Communications Europe.

"We would start with researching the client's current position, their competitive environment, how they can create differentiation. We have long conversations with clients about what business they're actually in. Are they staying in the same business or are they exploiting adjacent possible opportunities? We try to understand what that might mean to their customers and their partners, and begin to think about how we then articulate that with things like brand strategy, purpose documents, these types of artifacts. Then how would that be experienced in any given channel, any touch point? Whether it's digital or physical, how would that manifest itself in advertising? Frankly, the brand strategy work is either done, or we need to do it, before we then look at a brand campaign and say, "Well, how do we bring this to life?""

Malin Gardeström, International Marketing Manager, Carlsberg & Tuborg.

"It's of cause important that we are true to ourselves as a company, but also be true to our consumers because they know our brand sometimes better than we do ourselves because the brands are very much in line with the Danish personality of the Danish heritage as such. Although we have this long heritage, we always also need to be very contemporary and not to be modern, but to be in line with the timing. When we're making a marketing platform or a strategy, we need to consider all these things because if we don't, the consumers are going to see right through it."

Benjamin Holk Henriksen, Strategic planning & branding. Lecturer DIS and Copenhagen Business School, Author, Filmmaker "The Mind of a Leader", "Holk Master-class".

"Use the mood-boards to conduct surveys and foster discussions internally in the organization and externally among your target group and other stakeholders. The boards, the mood-boards with the little small piece of text that says for instance three lines that says what the word would be and then you can use some clip photos whatever, drawings to make sure that the internal and external people that you are surveying knows what the boards stand for. And if you do that the boards will ensure that everyone's on the same page, and that the campaign message is supported by the management group.

Once it is in place, the creative agency or art director will come up with an original creative campaign idea and logline, that builds on the communication platform."

140

Peter Giacomello, Sponsorship and Reputation Director, Marketing Carlsberg.

"Roskilde, as a big cultural music festival, it's a perfect match because our communication platform is music. We actually have 2 on Tuborg, we have humor and we have music, so it fits the music platform perfectly. We use it in campaign, in store, outdoor, above the line marketing. The whole 360, so it's a perfect match."

Lars Liebst, CEO Tivoli.

"Since our history goes all the way back to 1843, we have a long history, but we also have a new history, where we try to be on different digital platforms, where we try to see if it's possible to enhance new guests. That is what we call them, we don't call them customers or client, we call them guests. Of course, we pay a lot of attention. We pay attention, depending on what kind of platform we are, but there has to a be a red line that goes through all of it. Tivoli, as it never has been before, could be one of those slogans that we try to enhance and we do a lot. As probably everybody knows, this is probably just the beginning, because what will tomorrow bring? It is difficult to tell."

Aristotle's Modes of persuasion.

"Persuasion is clearly a sort of demonstration, since we are most fully persuaded when we consider a thing to have been demonstrated. Of the modes of persuasion furnished by the spoken word there are three kinds. [...] Persuasion is achieved by the speaker's personal character when the speech is so spoken as to make us think him credible. [...] Secondly, persuasion may come through the hearers, when the speech stirs their emotions. [...] Thirdly, persuasion is effected through the speech itself when we have proved a truth or an apparent truth by means of the persuasive arguments suitable to the case in question." [27]

In marketing and communications we refer to these three means as: Ethos, Pathos and logos.

Ethos.

Ethos is an appeal to the authority or credibility of the presenter. The ability to convince the audience that he or she is qualified to speak on the particular subject. The speaker or endorser of a product or service could be a professor, top athlete, business executive or any other expert related to the subject in question. By using impressive logos the speaker demonstrates that he or she is knowledgeable on the topic.

Pathos.

---

[27] Aristotle, "Rhetoric", 350 BCE.

Pathos is an appeal to the audience's emotions. It can be in the form of storytelling, a metaphor, simile or a passionate delivery. It may appeal to emotions such as fear, hope etc.

Pathos can be particularly powerful if used well, but most communication campaigns do not solely rely on pathos. Pathos is most effective when the message demonstrates agreement with an underlying value of the audience.

Logos.

Logos is logical appeal. It is normally used to describe facts and figures that support the communication campaigns or speaker's claims.

Ethos, Pathos and Logos are oftentimes used in conjunction as Ethos and Logos support each other while Pathos adds an emotional value.

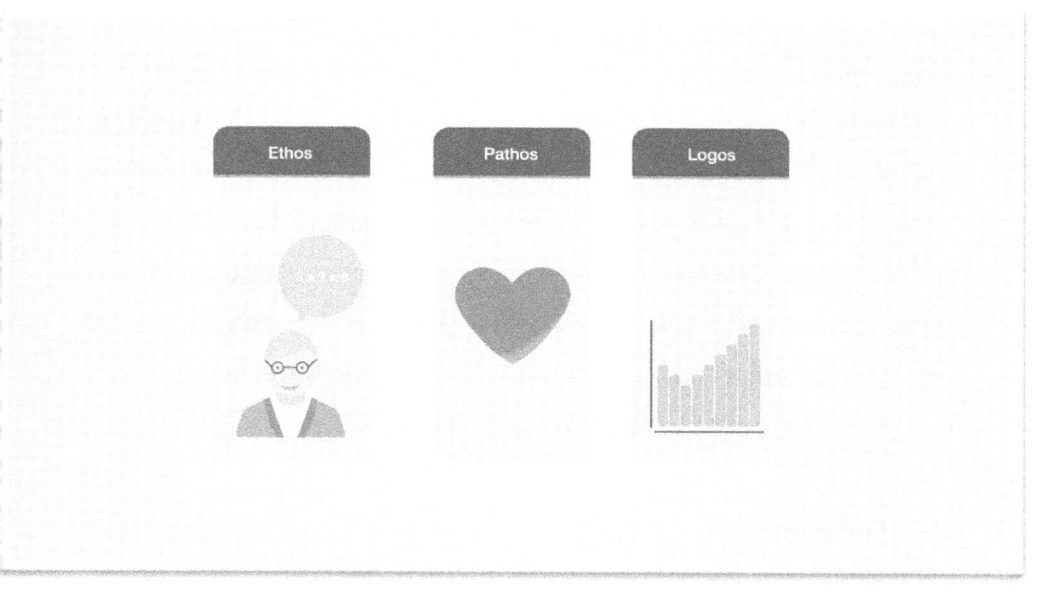

Figure 13.

Interviewees.

Ole Henriksen, Founder and Creative Director, Ole Henriksen Skin Care Brand.

"I think, when I appeal to people, get my message out there, it's definitely based on the product, first and foremost. Because that's the foundation for it. Without a good product, you're nowhere. That product has to repeat sell. You don't just want a one-time sale. So it's the integrity of the formula: what it does, how it performs, how it feels. And what's fun about is, it allows you to educate your clients in skin care. And my aim is always to make everyone their own best skin care expert, to empower these women and men to really know what's best for them. And then of course, there's all the other aspects that come into the equation. Because that's where the wellness model, again, is a key partner in this messaging.

And then the celebrities ... Oh gosh, I grateful for the many celebrities that I have laid hands on, treated their skin if you will, for decades, and that my staff at the spa treat. Because celebrities today, they sort of rule the world, in the sense that they are icons. You put Charlize Theron on the cover of In-style magazine or Vogue, she happens to be a client- and the world will say, "Wow, that woman is hot". And she is, she's beautiful. And if it's an image that encompasses, again, that natural healthy lifestyle that I'm a fan of, well then it's a win-win.

But at the same time, I do believe that a brand, for it's longevity, needs to stand on its own feet with its own identity, and based, in essence, on the quality and the integrity of these formulations that they elevate skin to the best it can be, that they really are transformational. And I can say that, in the world of Sephora, being my biggest retail partner in the world, on the number 1 repeated business. That is, people come back continuously to replenish more for the Ole Henriksen product than any other brand in the world of Sephora. So that's of course a plus, and something I'm very proud of."

Asger Leth, Director & Screenwriter, DGA award winner. (Ghosts of Cité Soleil, Man on a Ledge, Five Obstructions, Move on (Telekom)).

"What do I consider the most effective? Look, I actually think there's a marriage between things. If I had to choose, it's like the, you can bring one thing to the island. Which one are you going to bring? I would bring emotion, because that's ultimately where we want to end up. Now, I actually think that emotion is better served and landed with an audience if you use storytelling. Storytelling often has to do with structure. That also means facts and logic. That means that although I want to get to the emotion, I don't think that it works if the facts fall apart. Oftentimes, you have stories where the story structure or the factual logic of the story falls apart because of some crack in the writing of it or the conceptualization of it. When that falls apart, the storytelling doesn't land with us as human beings. Then we don't really get to the emotion. Those two, logic and emotions, are married, in my mind. There's no doubt I want to reach the emotion. That's the whole point. You're not selling anything. The story, a product, or anything, a brand, if you don't reach some sort of emotion."

David Angelo, Founder & Chairman, David & Goliath advertising agency.

"...Brands can basically take 2 paths. One is to scream and yell at a consumer and tell them who they are and what they're made off, and all that. Or treat them like a friend and speak to them in a way that respects their intelligence. I believe that the brands that do the latter, the ones that get to know the consumers better, and really understand what makes them tick, what makes them laugh, what makes them cry, what makes them feel, are the brands that transcend the business from being just a product that's on a shelf, to a friend that fits in their life.

Emotion is the one thing that people remember. They remember how you made them feel, so I believe that emotion is an amazing, amazing aspect of what we do. If we connect with people on an emotional level, and we get them to feel something about us that they never did before. When you get that, when you get that sort of connection between the brand and the consumer, and it's an emotional connection, they no longer see you as a product anymore, they see you as this amazing partner that's going to be around their lives for many years to come.

That's the way I see it, and I believe that today's consumer is so much more savvy than ever before, because they have such a bigger soap-box, you know that they could stand on and either create or destroy brands. It behooves you to form that authentic connection with them. The only way that you can do that, I believe, is through emotion."

Malin Gardeström, International Marketing Manager, Carlsberg & Tuborg.

"When we are planning to make a marketing campaign, historically, and if I take Tuborg to begin with, it has always been a lot about humor.

Humor is the number one ingredient, and of course humor is very close to an emotional response. For Tuborg we use a lot of humor, a lot of being present. We do use celebrities sometimes, but that is not to be more persuasive, it's more to get that immediate attention because you get that much faster with a celebrity than you do without. It's not to have a specialist as such, we're not a toothpaste, so we're not want to tell people what they can and cannot do.

But I have to say, as times are changing, the whole specialty beer also entering the market, it's much more talking about quality and talking about facts and these kinds of things. For the Carlsberg brand, yeah, we are doing a little bit more than we used to before, to tell the stories as people are also getting more into beer and into what's behind a perfect brew. It's becoming a little more educational than it used to."

Peter Ålbæk Jensen, Producer, Founder & fmr. CEO, Zentropa.
"Always emotions. Nothing but emotions because our product is emotions. That's strange that the emotion, the enthusiasm of the seller spreads to the buyer, to the release, to whatever you know. So, emotions, emotions, emotions."

Matthew Bagwell, Managing Director Naked Communications Europe.
"In almost all of our communications planning, it's a balance between those three actually. As opposed to simply using one and not considering the other two. We may know that we will get a particular reaction from over-indexing on emotional appeal, we may know that if we go too far into emotion, it may mean that people can't understand the practical

product benefits, for example. Therefore you're trying to balance the rational with the emotional.

Very often we and our clients are interested in whether a third party expert, or the opinions of others, and the whole idea of influences, can be used to either deliver the emotional or the rational message on behalf of the client in their communications. I think where we start is, what are we trying to achieve? What behavior are we trying to change? Do we have enough evidence to suggest that you need to over-index on any one of the three, or blend the three simultaneously?

If we're doing a sort of a brand campaign, particularly for example, we may be over-indexing on emotion. If we're doing a price-led campaign, and to compete on a very practical level against the competitor, we may be in the very rational territory. It's often the case that a third party will be as convincing as anything that the brand actually can create or communicate. It's a blend of the three, no simple answer."

Asger Leth, Director & Screenwriter, DGA award winner. (Ghosts of Cité Soleil, Man on a Ledge, Five Obstructions, Move on (Telekom)).

"I would say that using endorsers or people or presenters, authentic characters, for me, it's about character-building more than endorsers or whatever. I think that whoever you're using in your storytelling, in your spot, has to be believable and trustworthy. That's it. It's really a danger zone for me. If you use people that you don't trust, that's a big problem. Audiences sniff that out in split seconds. That's why it's a constant battle and fight when you do commercials to fight over casting decisions,

because a lot of times, there's a little bit of a direction for the client and so on to cast that beautiful girl or this. I don't mind beautiful people, but they have to have character, because without character, they're not believable. That's a fight you have to find. I absolutely find that just casting surface looks over substance will kill whatever you're trying to tell."

Lars Seier Christensen, Founder and owner Seier Capital, Co-founder and fmr. CEO Saxo Bank.

"Aristotle is an interesting philosopher. I'm a big fan of Ayn Rand, that is a Russian-American philosopher that built a lot of her thinking on Aristotle. A is A, which is very evident, but still very important to remember, simply because what he's really saying is that reality is reality, and reality, you need to deal with, emotions are not really going to help you if the reality is different to what you would like it to be.

If a competitor has a better product than you, you better face up to it, rather than being emotional about it and say ours is really better and trying to convince your clients that it's better. You should fix it and make sure that your thing is better than the competitors.

Facing up to reality, I think, is the main message of Aristotle, actually, and is also a very good message to wannabe entrepreneurs, because it's very easy to dream up something and you see it very often, that people have great dreams. It's great to dream, but if those dreams are unrelated or it's not subsequently verified by what happens if you don't get the customers that you expected to get, because you release a nice widget, you need to look at that widget again. It's not the customers that are wrong, it's you that's wrong."

Creative development, Tagline, Logline and structure.

There are many ways of developing or structuring creative ideas. The process usually starts with an idea or the framework for an idea such as a creative brief.

Tagline, logline and mood-boards may serve as important tools in terms of the creative development process and output.

1. Tagline.

A tagline or slogan is a small amount of text used in marketing materials to clarify a thought.

2. Logline.

A logline is a one or two sentence storyline. It serves to pitch a concept or to stay focused as you write or work on a treatment or creative idea. An example of a logline is for the movie Alien:

"The crew of an interstellar cargo ship battles a dangerous creature they find in a wreck of an alien spacecraft".

According to industry rumors the high concept project was sold in as "Jaws in space".

In advertising a good logline includes the relation to the product. A made example could be:

"Hungry man in locker-room is visually presented as grumpy diva, but calms down and become himself after eating a bite of a Sneakers".

3. Mood-boards.

Mood-boards with photos, images and text serve to demonstrate the visual style of a concept.

4. Advertising forms.

Basic advertising forms include: [28]

1. "Announcement", based solely on facts.
2. "Association transfer", such as life-style, metaphors, metonymy and celebrity transfer.
3. "Lesson", using a presenter, endorsement or testimonial, a demonstration, comparison or how-do use lesson.
4. "Drama", such as a slice-of-life story, problem solution or vignette.
5. "Entertainment".
6. "Imagination".
7. "Special effects".

---

[28] De Mooij, M. (2014). Global Marketing and Advertising. Fourth edition. Sage publications.

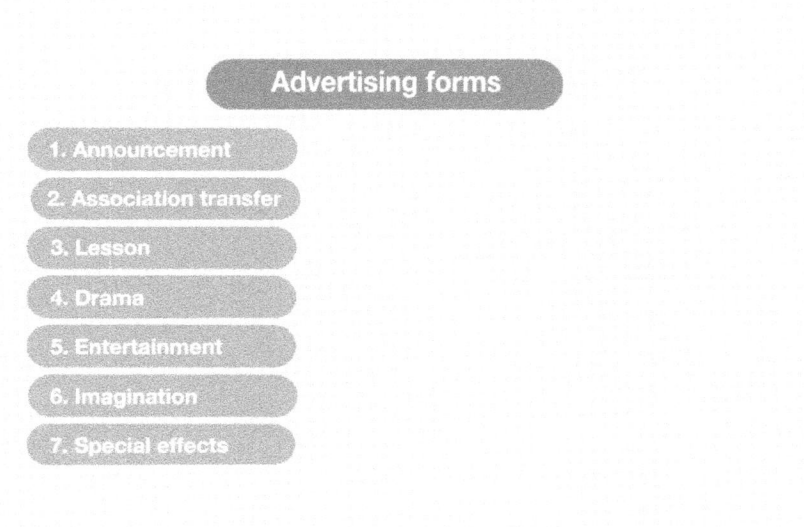

Figure 14.

5. Three-act structure.

Most stories are based on a three-act structure: 1. Setup. 2. Confrontation. 3. Resolution. They usually contain a motivational objective, and some kind of obstacle or conflict, such as "Man vs. Nature", "Man vs. Man" and "Man vs. Self".[29]

---

[29] Katz, S.D. (1991). Film directing "Shot by Shot" visualizing from concept to screen. Mackendrick, A. (2005). On Film-making 'an introduction to the craft of the director', Rosenberg, J. (2010). The Healthy Edit. Focal Press.

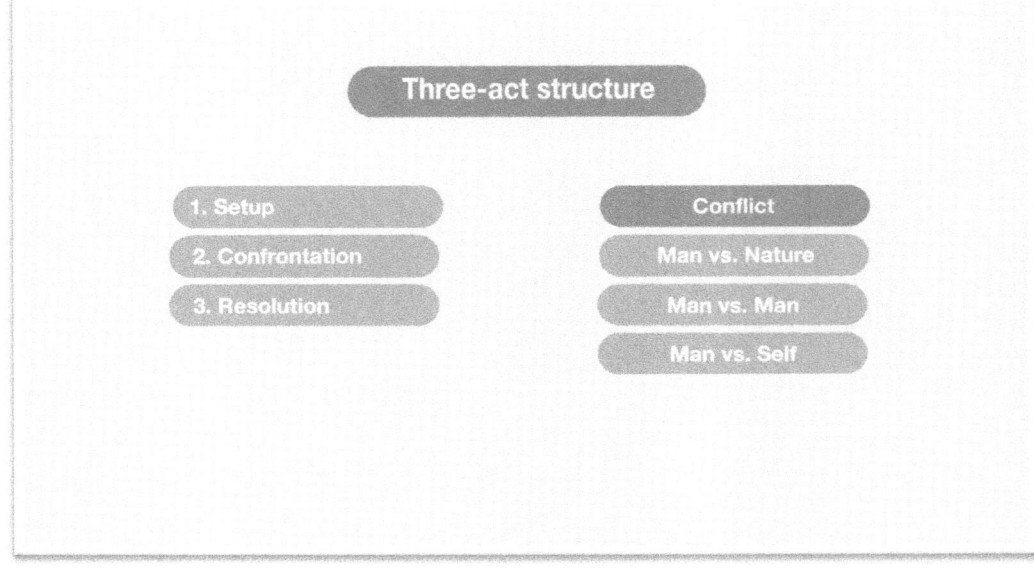

Figure 15.

Suspense can be added in the form of a "ticking bomb", meaning a deadline to resolve the conflict. Many great storytellers will tell you to learn the rules only to break them.

Interviewees.

Asger Leth, Director & Screenwriter, DGA award winner. (Ghosts of Cité Soleil, Man on a Ledge, Five Obstructions, Move on (Telekom)).

"Do I use storytelling in my commercials? You bet I do. The more of an experienced filmmaker I am, the more do I love the original concept of what storytelling is. Going back to the origins of drama and dramatic structure and so on, when I was younger, as in any other young

154

filmmaker on anything, different arts where you want to break all the rules and tear everything down and you always think you're going to reinvent the plate. I did that, too, when I was very young. The older I get, the more I just love the bare bones of what it is. The more I realize that I need to use storytelling with all of its tools for the betterment of everything. When I have those tools in place, then I can feel comfortable experimenting with breaking some of the usual ideas, some of the, what do you call it? The consensus of what storytelling is. If I feel comfortable that I have all the bare bones and the structure in place of what storytelling is, of how to tell a story, then I start feeling comfortable in breaking the rules on purpose here and there, because I know I will get back to it."

Tue Walin Storm, Director, Screenwriter, Founder Storm/Hansen (Nielson, Ford, Pirelli, The Raveonettes).

"Well, I'll have to say, that based on my own personal experience, the logline is not so prevalent. I feel like what really sums up the idea of the film is the title. The title kind of becomes the logline. I'm just thinking back in the previous projects that I've done, I don't remember seeing a specific logline that defines the core concept or the idea. I think, again, when you write the treatment, I think it's your job as a director to somehow rephrase that logline and you sort of write the opening sentence oftentimes is to sum up the essence of what the times are about, how the product relates to current times, and so on and so forth. I feel like the title is the one that defines the essence of what the film and the project is.

For instance, the most recent commercials that I'm currently working on is one for Pirelli Tires and it's called "The Alert", which sums up the idea of what the whole thing is about. It's a tire that has a smart chip, you hit it, and there's a phone that responds to it and there's alert on it. That's the whole spot. The previous spot was one for Ford, which is called "The Bravest". The Bravest is more or less the idea that it sums up the people that is the target group for the film, which are the hard-working people of America. They are the ones who are the bravest. Of course, there's many more aspects to it, but The Bravest somehow sums that up in its essence."

Molly DeWolf Swenson Founding member / CMO of RYOT.

"Yeah. All the time. Especially in our television pitches and documentary film pitches. There are two that come to mind for me. One is we were developing this MTV documentary series where there, it was going to be host driven and it was going to be someone young, out in the world, doing investigative, sort of, reporting but the audience was younger and the log line for that was, "Front line documentaries for a Snapchat generation." And we can sit there and for ten minutes describe what this concept was, but that log line summed it up perfectly.

In another, I was sitting at lunch with a friend who is developing with Ben Stiller, this show about the Iran contra crisis. The story within it being, you know, this series of mishaps and human idiocies leading to all of this crazy sort of stuff happening in international politics. My first reaction to it was, "Oh, so it's Argo meets Fargo" and he said, "Yeah, exactly." Only because I had just seen both of those movies did that come to mind. It wouldn't have other wise. But, to me a film that's "Argo meets

Fargo" seems great and I would love to watch it, especially if it's a true story."

Tue Walin Storm, Director, Screenwriter, Founder Storm/Hansen (Nielson, Ford, Pirelli, The Raveonettes).

"In feature films, there definitely is a logline. The logline is the essence of what a film should be about. Loglines are tremendously difficult to write, or it can be very easy. As a screenwriter working together with my writing partner, we definitely sort of try to... Maybe in a much later stage and what you're supposed to do, film school books and writing books always say that write the logline first. The logline is sort of the ... That's your fallback. That's the line that whenever you're in doubt, you look at the logline and then whatever you do sort of stems from that. Oftentimes, I don't think the way that I work with my writing partner, it's not like that.

You write what you think is interesting. You have a core idea and you've sort of see where the story develops. Then afterwards, in retrospect, you can look and say, "Okay. This is what the logline is." You discover what the logline is. You discover the essence of what the project is as you do it. For commercials, it's different. I mean, again, you have an agency that's developed this ... I'm sure they have internal loglines and they sell that to their client. It might be communicated to us directing it, but usually not. I feel like a good creative brief and a good pitch will have somewhat of a logline within it, but not always so."

David Angelo, Founder & Chairman, David & Goliath advertising agency.

157

"There's an old saying that tell the truth, it's the easiest thing to remember.

If you tell the truth of your brand, then you don't ever have to worry about whether or not someone is going to call bullshit on you, because all you're doing is you're speaking from your core. If you can connect with people from your core of who you are, and tell them a story in a way that is engaging, and a way that's sort of could make them cry, could make them laugh, could make them whatever, cheer for you, then I really believe that you will connect with more people than you ever imagined. That's what the great storytellers do, right? Have you ever sat in a room with somebody who couldn't tell a story? Have you ever sat by a campfire next to somebody who couldn't tell a story? All the great sort of storytellers out there all started from this concept of speaking from the core. Because when you speak from the core it's just fluid, it's more believable, it's more authentic. You end up connecting with people on a completely different level."

Tue Walin Storm, Director, Screenwriter, Founder Storm/Hansen (Nielson, Ford, Pirelli, The Raveonettes).

"I don't think we've ever done anything with announcements or celebrity or anything like that.

I think that what we find interesting in terms of working with are films that are miniature stories. Little films that last 30 seconds to a minute. Usually the minute is much more interesting than the 30 seconds because you have enough time to develop some real emotion and some characters. You have time to build a set-up and a payoff. You have time to make establishing shots and introduce characters and return to them.

It's like creating little movies. It's what we find really interesting. I think that's the type of work that we'll end up doing. There are other directors who are very strong visual that create moods and atmospheres, and then it's much more poetic and ethereal.

We've done some of that work. I think maybe we'll continue to do so. For us, as storytellers, we always come back to the idea of communicating story and communicating emotion through story. You can take some of those abstract and poetic ideas and then infuse that into your storytelling to sort of create, again, a subjective mood and understanding. The type of work that I do, and with my directing partner, has always been stories. Little stories. I think that's the type of work that we'll continue to be doing. Vignette films, they often call these things as well. We sort of have multiple little mini stories that take place, that can be told in one or two shots combined to tell a much bigger story.

With the previous one, again, I was just finishing a spot right now for Pirelli, which is a little Pixar animation. It's literally just three characters: a working robot and a surveillance drone that are distracted by a live bird. Within that relationship of these three, you get to tell a little human story."

David Angelo, Founder & Chairman, David & Goliath advertising agency.

"Harry Potter, right? Harry Potter has many volumes, right? It's created a mass following, probably one of the greatest brands in the world, through the art of storytelling, to the point where people are getting tattoos of Harry Potter all over them.

159

What is that, the art of storytelling? The art of storytelling is the ability to sort of speak from your core and to be able to connect with people on an emotional level, in a way that has them waiting with bated breath, for your next word. That's what great storytelling is all about."

Tue Walin Storm, Director, Screenwriter, Founder Storm/Hansen (Nielson, Ford, Pirelli, The Raveonettes).

"I mean, I think writing a script and a treatment are two very separate things. I think what combines them is storytelling. I think a good storytelling and, again, the type of commercials that I like to be involved in have stories. Within that storytelling, you need a setup, a payoff. You have establishing setup and payoff. You have these different elements. In the telling of story, that automatically comes to you. I'm sure you can learn this in school and you sort of learn that when you start analyzing good storytelling. You figure out like, "When was there a setup and what's the payoff?" You can trick the audience, or you can guide the audience, or you can define how you want to tell the story.

Obviously, in a commercial, in a feature film, there's some sort of resolution. The resolution ... The bigger the drama or the bigger the tension, the bigger the resolution is. So, depending what type of story it is that you're telling, you can use various mechanisms to achieve this. Obviously when you start writing your treatment, you think about this. This is part of the brainstorm and part of how you want to tell the story. I don't think there's much of a conscious thought about it. I think it just comes automatically. Once you start telling stories and you do it for a while, that's the way you think. On the other hand, writing scripts, I'm

160

much more aware of using the three-act structure, because there is a formula for a script that is quite consistent, or at least that's a proven formula that works.

When I'm writing a screenplay, that formula is much more present consciously as I'm writing. That's just for me. I have a writing partner and he doesn't think like that at all. It's much more about intuition and flow than get structured. Commercials don't have the same structure as a feature film. Commercials can have anything. It can be a single shot with a person talking that can have great tension and a great setup. It can have a beautiful establishing shot, and then you introduce a character. That then introduce another character and within those presentations, you create tension that then has a resolution, or it's something completely different. A carton of milk that's being poured in a beautiful way to sell milk. Not the type of commercials that I like to do, but it happens. Of course, there's not much drama within that."

Storytelling.

Stories or narratives have been shared in every culture as a means of entertainment, education, cultural preservation, and instilling moral values.

Storytelling is a method of explaining a series of events through narrative. The events can be real, fictional or some combination of the two.

Marketers use storytelling as a tool for illustrating an otherwise difficult concept, to drive home a point or to encourage consumer loyalty through entertainment or emotional connection.

As a marketing tactic, storytelling is based on the premise that people remember information better when it's told as a story rather than presented as a list of facts. This is largely because stories are more relatable and inspire an emotional reaction in an audience.

Storytelling also helps to foster a brand's voice and personality. It involves the audience in the process by engaging their brains at multiple levels and, often requiring them to take a stance. Storytelling also speaks to an audience that may not otherwise show interest in a product.[30]

---

[30] Katz, S.D. (1991). Film directing "Shot by Shot" visualizing from concept to screen. Mackendrick, A. (2005). On Film-making 'an introduction to the craft of the director', Rosenberg, J. (2010). The Healthy Edit. Focal Press.

Interviewees.

David Angelo, Founder & Chairman, David & Goliath advertising agency.

"Storytelling is the foundation of communication. If you're good at it, then you will have the ability to sort of capture an audience and hold them right on the edge of their seats for a very long time. I always compare storytelling to life. It's this whole notion of if your life were a movie, would you watch it, right?

Making sure that A) you have a good story to tell, is very important for any brand. Very important for any person too, right? Telling a story in a way that engages people, that sucks them in, that makes them feel like they're living it, that they're experiencing it, that they're right there with it, is not an easy thing to do. It does start with one thing and that is the truth. If you take the truth of who you are, like what I've just been talking about, where I'm from, then it's an easier story to tell."

Lars Liebst, CEO Tivoli.

"I think with the age that Tivoli has, it's obvious that we use storytelling, but there is also the flip side of the coin is that we shouldn't use it all the time, because then everybody knows well this is this story and this is that story. We would definitely like to be sometimes, a little bit on the edge and try out the market. Yes, we use our storytelling, but definitely not all the time, because we have to look into the future, more than looking into the past. We shouldn't forget the past. We should bring the past up to today but we have to look into the future. Right up there, there is the

founder of Tivoli and he said, all the way back in 1845, Tivoli will never be finished. That is actually my inspiration, that is where I pick up the inspiration for working in Tivoli, knowing that the founder of Tivoli said those few words."

Malene Torp. Executive Director, DIS – Study Abroad in Scandinavia.

"I think first of all storytelling is interesting to me because it's when you're delivering a message over and over again, if it's not interesting to you, it's not interesting to your audience either, and storytelling is a way for me to keep it interesting and fresh. Being able reflect on what is the message that I want to convey and then finding examples, cases, personal anecdotes that can support that is something that keeps it fresh, I believe, hopefully also for the audience. I also think that storytelling has an advantage to underplay the business side of things. Sure, I'm selling a product but if you're in a business where you sell experiences and in my case education then it's about the human relations. You're not selling a product per se, but you are selling an impact on people."

Anders Kryger, Senior Business Strategist, Industrial PhD Fellow at MAN Diesel & Turbo.

"Storytelling, I think is very important or has the possibility of being very important for strategy. At MAN, and what I'm researching, is to apply storytelling techniques in strategy facilitation. Imagine an organization where strategy is made in a small, dark room at the very top floor of the largest, tallest building with glass on all sides by some people in dark suits. That sort of vision is usually infested with words that are difficult to understand for many of the employees, the man on the floor.

164

Then imagine another type of organization where strategy is a collective patchwork of stories that are gathered from all parts of the organization. Those stories are somehow aggregated and are co-created by the employees and management or strategy facilitation team to be the company's strategy. I think that sort of strategy where you involve the employees, what I would call bottom up strategy, is much more easy to have affinity with. It's easier for the employees to understand because it's based on their own stories."

Benjamin Holk Henriksen, Strategic planning & branding. Lecturer DIS and Copenhagen Business School, Author, Filmmaker "The Mind of a Leader", "Holk Master-class".

"I believe storytelling isn't just a matter of creating an advert with a narrative. It's about telling the story over multiple platforms, multiple times using different tools. Honesty and transparency are key factors otherwise you will risk creating some kind of a communication gap. Also it might be beneficial to implement characters and personalities in the story and to have thought of a beginning middle and an end.

An example is the Scarecrow, a small animated story created by Chipotle and by the Los Angeles based marketing team CAA. They wanted to raise awareness to two concerns. First their ethical raised livestock but also the fact that they were no longer associated with McDonalds. The story features a small little guy that eventually becomes a farmer. He lives in this industrial mean world, dystopia, and starts his own little burrito shop where it's all about happiness and ethical raised livestock. Great little story you should check it out."

Malin Gardeström, International Marketing Manager, Carlsberg & Tuborg.

"I have to say I am a fan of storytelling. I love it. I remember also from school stating "we are storytelling animals", isn't that the claim? And I think Danes are leaders in terms of telling metaphors, just selling in a concept, they use a lot of metaphors. I found it very amusing and very effective. Yes, we do that of course also in selling in new products to our sales force or to consumers, or in all touch points. Storytelling is very effective. We do it with Tuborg, in our last commercial with the two gentleman, our drivers taking around our beer. Them showing very much about themselves. Letting consumers see kind of inside Tuborg to feel what it's all about, the informal atmosphere that these guys are having, and how they're playing with each other. Everything is very much in line with how Tuborg is as a brand. That is really supporting what we want to communicate."

Asger Leth, Director & Screenwriter, DGA award winner. (Ghosts of Cité Soleil, Man on a Ledge, Five Obstructions, Move on (Telekom)).

"I think storytelling is a way to tell stories or to tell, to tie events down, human condition, human emotions. In all sense of stories, in all aspects of storytelling, there's always something universal that I always find are the most interesting and inspiring traits of any story. In those universal themes is an engine for how to tell that story. Then you use the tools of storytelling, what you've learned of dramatic structure and three-act structures and protagonism, antagonism, and all that stuff, to bind it together as a textualized piece that will drive logic, but then use emotion.

To get the story told or to tell a universal theme, you need storytelling to take you from A to B and deliver you in the right place… So I think storytelling, using storytelling or using storytelling tools are universal for all kinds of storytelling, long-format films, documentary films, feature films, but also documentaries. I would actually go so far as to say that the more short-format you go, the more you're working in the commercial length, 30 seconds, 40 seconds, 45 seconds, 60 seconds, the more important it is that you know your rules, that you know how to build a story. You need to condense time, place, emotions, action, suspense, all kinds of storytelling tools into the shortest possible time. I don't think you could do that without having your toolbox sharpened."

Matthew Bagwell, Managing Director Naked Communications Europe.

"Vodafone Firsts was the global campaign that myself and a couple of colleagues from other agencies conceived with Vodafone, which was from the central marketing team, and then distributed into the ten markets internationally. It was the story of people achieving things for the first time. The reason why Vodafone wanted to own this territory was because many people achieve things for the first time because of the empowerment of connectivity. Whether it's our first experience of a new country, finding a piece of information on Google, the mobile phone is often the first part of something that we want to achieve. Then we use it to achieve something for the first time.

We all know how positive that is, when we accomplish something, whether it's the first time we skydive, or the first time we try sushi, or the first time we accomplish something that we've always wanted to do.

167

Vodafone told multiple stories across many different channels, about people achieving something for the first time. Some of that was long-form storytelling, so we did, I think it was something like 32 stories across 18 months. Some of them had physical, experiential components within them, and then we filmed and then amplified those films through digital channels. Some of them were purely digital sort of stories, some of them lasted moments, some of them became episodic across the course of an 18 month period."

Asger Leth, Director & Screenwriter, DGA award winner. (Ghosts of Cité Soleil, Man on a Ledge, Five Obstructions, Move on (Telekom)).

"I think basically, you can have commercials that are just pure emotion. You can also have commercials that are pure visual overdrive. Those serve a purpose, too, and if they're well executed, will hit a spot somewhere. I think storytelling hits a universal human gene. We all are much more used to storytelling and stories than we are really aware of. Basically, we all know the general structure of storytelling, without knowing how to put words on what those elements are. It's just as much a part of your language as your spoken language. In a way, if you take, it can be in real storytelling of movies, themes, human universal stories, or it could be products or concepts or brands that try and attach a story to them. The moment they try and tell their brand or their product in a storyline, attach characters to them, a protagonist, antagonist, overcoming, succeeding, victory.

Those kinds of stories just resonate with us, so apart from being just an emotion, we can connect a story to it which makes it easier to retell to yourself, makes it easier to remember. It also makes it easier to tell to your friends. It's much more difficult to go down after seeing a spot or an advertisement for anything and just say, "This was about that feeling." No, that's difficult to tell. No, you tell the story. With the story, you tell emotions. This is how we've done it since before we could read and write, when we were sitting around a bonfire or even before fire, and we would almost grunt stories to our monkey ancestors. Human interaction is about storytelling, and that's how we portray emotions. Ultimately, that's how you connect brands, products, and anything with filmmaking."

David Angelo, Founder & Chairman, David & Goliath advertising agency.

"Every brand is a story. You have, the title of the story needs to be what the brand is. That's what's on the cover of the book. You open up the first chapter and that's the beginning of the story. That is basically the brand telling you what it's going to do. Then chapter number one is the first experience of that story, what did it do? It created this amazing campaign that attracted millions of people. Could be a stunt, could be experiential, could be a TV campaign, whatever it is. Then the second chapter still needs to be connected to the first chapter, but it has to be even better. That as you build that story throughout, each chapter gets more and more exciting, to the point where you just can't put the book down."

Part IV. Media activation.

Push Pull strategy.

Two well-known sales & marketing strategies a company can use to reach its target group are the Push and Pull strategies.

A push promotional strategy involves taking the product directly to the customer to ensure the customer is aware of your brand at the point of purchase. Trade show promotions, showrooms, positive negotiation with retailers, an efficient supply chain, your packaging design or point of sale displays, are good examples.

A pull strategy on the contrary involves motivating customers to seek out your brand in an active process. You depend on advertising and mass media promotion, word of mouth referrals, customer relationship management or sales promotions and discounts.

In conclusion a PUSH strategy is typically relying on a sales force to PUSH the product through the distribution system, whereas the PULL strategy relies on bait such as commercials to pull the consumers closer to you and the product.[31]

---

[31] Robertson, T. (2018). Difference Between Push & Pull Marketing, smallbusiness.chron January 31.
Debasis Pradhan. (2011). To push or to pull: Dynamics of promotional strategies: Tale of three rural industries.
Hopp, Wallace J.; Spearman, Mark L. (2014). "To pull or not to pull: what is the question?". Manuf Serv Oper Manage. Retrieved 13 June.

Interviewees.

Ole Henriksen, Founder and Creative Director, Ole Henriksen Skin Care Brand.

"For me, a sales force has always been number one as far as getting that message out there. Sharing in the new product, or in the philosophy of Ole Henriksen in general. So I have sales forces all over the world. And these are of course women and men that are out there, being, if you will, an extension of Ole Henriksen himself... Because I work with these people. We meet, of course. We have our events together and inspire the best in each other, and the reason it's so impactful is, you get to touch the sales staff in the stores, and then in turn you empower them to do an even better job.

And the fact that they have met with someone from the Ole Henriksen company that cares so much, and then the fact that Ole Henriksen... I'm one of the few founders in this business that actually travel the world. And we'll go into a small community as well as the big stores in London. I'll be anywhere at any time. And that has paid off big dividends, because it's the caring touch. And I'm just as enriched when I leave, and as inspired as hopefully they are. So it's a win-win."

Dennis Balslev, CEO IKEA DK.

"With the background, I have worked with the concept which was quite specific in how do we want to approach our customers and also now as a retailer. I think again, listen to our customers and then when you decide how to do it. It's very interesting to be in retail because you can have the

same product but you can show it in different ways and you see the sales go up or go down. That's really amazing to be in retail. You can steer a lot in the way you are working with your store, with your layout, with your communication around the products. It's a lot up to us how we do it, but always of course with the customer in mind, so how the customer should meet the different products. I think there's a lot of opportunities in retail, how retailers can be much more aware of what's going on.

Manu retailers they have a quite... they do what they always have done and I think that's the big challenge for the future. You can to renew yourself or you will disappear from the market. It's going so fast today. Some big players coming in from e-commerce, what it's called, Alibaba and Amazon and so on. They're really pushing the retail in many different countries so we have to look into how we work in the stores. I think the focus we have in the stores and how we merchandise the products, how we meet the customers, how we change, and spend a lot of money in changing all the time. That will make the big difference for us. Inspiration, vitality, a reason or me to go there means a lot for many retailers and I think even just changing a small window in a shop can make a big difference for a consumer to understand why should I go there next time.

For us again, it's not about one or the other. It's about the totality. It's a small circus sometime if you want to call it like that. You have to give an interest for people to come to you. We have to add, like the restaurants we add into it. It's not only to come here and spend an hour. You get hungry, how do we secure you can stay another hour in our company? That's really something we focus on to make it a fun day out for the family. That's very important for the way we work, which means we have to play on all different instruments."

Birgitte Mabeck, Head of fundraising and marketing Red Cross.
"At the Red Cross we are using both the pull and push strategy. Really you could say, if you look at push and pull strategy, the sort of original concept, you would also have to have a middle part. You would have to have somewhere that you are selling a product to if you are looking really at a push strategy. We don't really have a product per say and we don't have anyone, a middleman handling our products out to the customer, the donor. In this sense we are acting as both the middle channel or the middleman and the owner of the product. That's important for us to push our message all the way through to the donor. What is it that the Red Cross is standing for? It's important for us to keep having that message out there. This is who we are, this is where you can get support and this is also where we are supporting, so that we are the carrier of our message and not someone else is the carrier of our message.

If we then look at the other side, we would also like, when there is an emergency situation, we would like to be the organization that people, they would seek up. That they automatically would go back to and say, "The Red Cross is a place to go to now we've heard that there is a disaster in Nepal, or the Philippines, or wherever. The first place I will go to is the Red Cross. I know I have to donate through the Red Cross because now I know that they are definitely out there." We would like to build that pull/push by using pull, push strategy. We would like to build that awareness in the donor segment."

Mikkel Borg Bjergsø Founder and CEO Mikkeller brewery, bars and restaurants.

"...we focus on people's desire to chase our products. We do have a sales department, we have sales people, but they're main job is to take in orders. Until now, and I'm saying this because I don't know if that's going to change some day, but until now, the way we sell our beer is that we send out a price list, and then we take in orders. We don't have people in the fields pushing customers to buy our beer or showing up with samples and stuff like that.

It's like when we talked about the marketing. I don't want people to buy my product because somebody tells them to buy it. I want them to buy it because they think it's the best beer, and because they think it's interesting and they want to be a part of our world, and they want to showcase our art, and stuff like that. We don't do a lot of active sales."

Malin Gardeström, International Marketing Manager, Carlsberg & Tuborg.

"In terms of pull and push, of course both are important. We work very much with both the BTL and BTB marketing. We have at the Danish market, a very big sales force. Making sure that our product, as it is fast-moving consumer goods, we always need to be out there and make sure they look good. Of course as competition is increasing, our customers are having a hard time getting our consumers to their shop and not everybody else, so we do need to help them out as well to drive traffic. Therefore of course, we need to focus on both, so heavy market advertising, but also to be physically available."

Leif Rasmussen. Strategic Branding. Lecturer, DIS – Study Abroad in Scandinavia.

"Yes, that's a very good question because many, many companies struggle with that. It is depending. As most questions can be answered, is it depends. I would say this mainly depends on the position of your brand in the marketplace. If you're having a very strong brand which is pretty well known you tend to, which is wise as well, to spend most money on a pull strategy because your consumers or your target group will react because they know of your product. The idea behind the pull strategy is that they then will go to the retailers, if it's a product for consumers or brand for consumers and ask for it and when they ask for it they need to buy from the producer or the market share or the brand owner, which in this case is me."

Christina Bilde, Spokes person Roskilde Festival.

"It's a combination because in Denmark it's not really necessary for us to... Actually it's not that necessary for us to advertise because we're so well known and of course we also advertise. Outside of Denmark, we have a huge audience in Norway and Sweden and Germany, also in England there's actually, and people coming from thirty-eight different countries this year. We would like to have more and that's a matter of combining both things. So it's a matter of advertising but it's also very much a matter of putting forward the new offer and new ways of getting to the festival, for instance. So it's a combination of both."

Leif Rasmussen. Strategic Branding. Lecturer, DIS – Study Abroad in Scandinavia.

"Yes. It is necessary if you're having a brand, a product, which is not very well known, you need to create distribution before you can actually start using the pull strategy which I just mentioned. In that case I would absolutely prefer to use the push strategy because you push your products, your brands, out into the retail and you enable your customers or potential customers to come around and actually buy it. In general, as a conclusion, you can say that it depends completely on what is the position of your brand if you should choose push or pull or a combination. So, basically you can say first you use push in order to create distribution. When you have a distribution, you start using pull because your product's out there and you can start convincing the consumers to go and ask for them. If they do so, you will generate better and better distribution and sales."

Ole Henriksen, Founder and Creative Director, Ole Henriksen Skin Care Brand.

"Today, advertisement as such, of course, has taken on a whole new profile, because the printed media is not as important as it used to be. So social media now is where it's all at. And then when you juggle the two, the social media with, again, the personal touch, great sales force, you have a win-win situation. That doesn't mean the printed media is not important, but actual, traditional advertisement, I've never done. I've done a little of it. It's never been important for me and I've seen other brands grow and be successful following a similar model. So that... I love the fact that we can be such a hands-on, approachable brand, via these amazing talents that are out there and spreading the Ole Henriksen philosophy of wellness and health, and just being celebratory of life."

Community Marketing.

A company has a variety of ways to activate a campaign and reach its target group. Media execution channels such as:

Direct marketing.

Viral & Social media.

Sponsors & Community marketing.

Print.

Billboard or outdoor.

Collateral, Display and packaging.

TV, Cinema and radio.

Endorsement and Placement.

PR.

Whereas marketing communication strategies such as PR and sales oftentimes focus on attaining customers, Community Marketing focuses on the needs of existing customers or the relationship with a community.

People often differentiate between two types of Community marketing. Organic marketing that occurs without the assistance of the company, such as word-of-mouth. And sponsored community marketing, promoted by a company through activities like investments in the local community or corporate social responsibility.[32]

---

[32] Fournier, S. & Lee, L. (2009). Getting Brand Communities Right. Harvard Business review, April issue.
Faris, R. (2015). Market to Millennials by Getting Out of the Way. Harvard Business review, December 09.

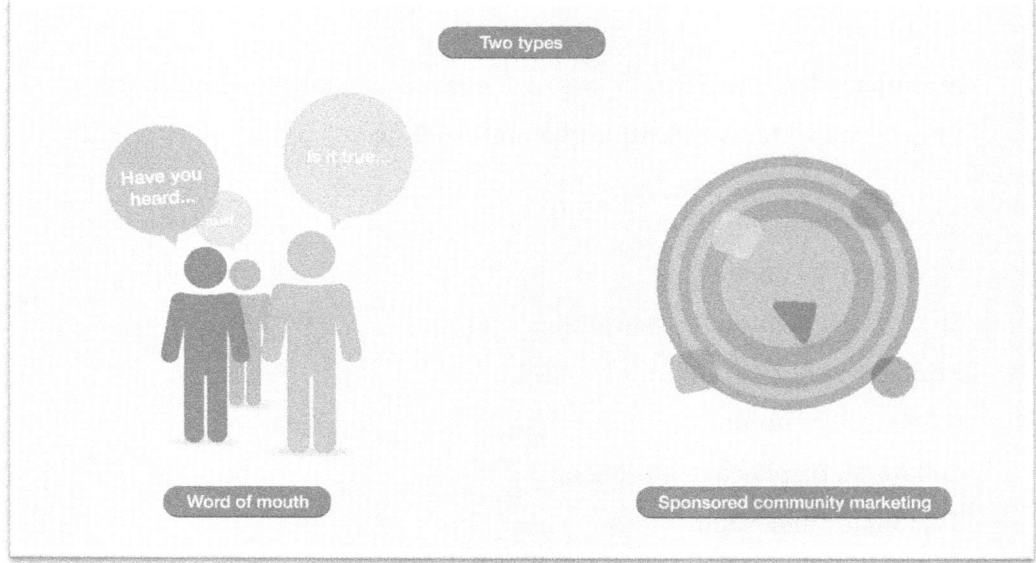

Figure 16.

Walmart is an example of a company that used this strategy after experiencing problems in local communities because their department stores were said to kill the smaller family-owned businesses. In recent years we have seen community marketing evolve into new shapes involving digital media, product endorsement and placement at events.

Interviewees.

David Angelo, Founder & Chairman, David & Goliath advertising agency.

"Interesting. Define community. A community is a group of like-minded people, right? Millennials for instance. There's a lot of talk right now about millennials and everywhere you look there's a person claiming to have the secret to marketing to millennials. They make millennials, the millennial audience, out to be like aliens, like they're some weird sort of foreign object, or whatever. What they don't realize, that millennials it's less of a community, but more of a mindset, a shared mindset.

For instance, if you were to look at technology right now, technology is growing at an exponential rate, faster than we've ever experienced. It continues to sort of pick up speed. The people that are at that sort of, at the same pace, are the millennials, right? They're the ones that are challenging convention, they're the ones that are right there at the same sort of pace as technology. It's not an age group, it is a mindset of people that think differently. There are people that think different of all ages, all races, all creeds."

Peter Ålbæk Jensen, Producer, Founder & fmr. CEO, Zentropa.
"We are addressing all our films to a little community which is females around thirty to sixty years old and they are educated. So you can say, even though how much we feel we embrace the whole world, we have very specific target group for our films. Again, we know that since they are an educated audience, they search information themselves and they are pretty much aware of what's going on on the cultural side. So, for some strange reason, they know whether they want to see a film or not. Maybe even before the marketing or the premier of the film. We are a little bit reluctant to try to be too smart into these activities. We try to have an eye on what type of films we are making in order to getting the

best sales result, but the few times we have tried to be too clever, too much thinking, I think we have failed. Maybe because we are not too clever, and too well thinking here. There's a certain energy in creating the product, and selling and marketing it we have been lucky, successful with. Mainly due to the fact that there was a certain cult around our type of films that are hard to reach, but when you have them, then they are pretty loyal."

Andreas Rasche, Professor at Copenhagen Business School. Department of Management, Society and Communication.

"Community marketing, we have to distinguish a little bit. Some people look at community marketing in the sense that this is word-of-mouth propaganda for the corporation. There's also more deliberate type of community marketing which is often tied towards CSR efforts. For instance, if a corporation invests in a certain community and then of course, it hopes to get authenticity and to get loyalty from it's customer. I think it is a very good tool if the corporation has strong ties towards its community, not all corporations necessarily have that. Corporations who have strong ties towards their local communities who even work with these communities, for them community marketing is a very important and also timely tool."

Matthew Bagwell, Managing Director Naked Communications Europe.

"So in terms of sort of community marketing, if it's genuine, and it's part of your brand, I think it can be incredibly provocative. If it feels as if it's simply being done to divert attention, or because there's a sort of a checklist of things that you need to do for CSR or sustainability agendas,

then I think that it can feel less than authentic, and can actually be quite damaging."

Peter Ålbæk Jensen, Producer, Founder & fmr. CEO, Zentropa.

"The DOGME 95 movement, which now is twenty years old, was fun since it was a rebellion. There was ten commandments that I can remember which was that we filmed in academy, which was a very boring form, very old television like form. It is not so widescreen. We are not making genre movies. The director is not allowed to be credited, which was hard for them due to their big egos. The demand that we give a shit about continuity, which means that in one shot I could smoke a cigarette and in the next, the cigarette was gone, and in shot number three the cigarette was back again. So, this continuity thing that we have spent so much energy on while we're making film, we found out meant nothing to the audience. Music has to be made on the set directly, and not afterwards. No grading, which means no correcting of color and light afterwards on the images. Makeup, wardrobe, whatever had to be the natural makeup and wardrobe of the actors.

Probably today you would have made some kind of environment around the whole operation. We tried to do it. We had an office around here for some years that was responding on questions and mails, no that was even before the emails probably, so letters and fax or whatever it was. So we tried to be communicating around it yes. That's probably the only time we tried to make also a movement in the film industry. We were happy to start and we are also happy to stop it again."

Birgitte Mabeck, Head of fundraising and marketing Red Cross.

"Door to door collection in Denmark has a little bit of a tradition. We have as the Red Cross been doing the door to door collection for many, many years, more than nearly 30 years so it's a long tradition. First of all, of course traditions we don't want to kill off, so traditions we'd rather honor and continue. That's one thing, and one reason that the Red Cross can still do that. Another big reason is we have a huge network of volunteers who would like to show, you could maybe say it's what we do today in social media when we tag ourselves and say, "Hey, I'm a cool guy, I'm doing this." This is sort of the old fashioned way of tagging yourself. You are going out into the community and you are showing the community, "I am supporting the Red Cross and this is my belief and I would like to help them."

That's one of the reasons that the volunteers definitely are doing it and they are doing it year and year as a tradition. Another thing that we believe that it's a good way of collecting the funds is that when you have the face-to-face contact with people, it's really difficult to say no. When someone is knocking on your door and they have taken the time to go out with the drain of sun or whatever and they are standing there knocking on your door, then you give them some money. It's difficult to say no. That's another reason that we will continue this effort and hopefully keep getting the increased donations."

David Angelo, Founder & Chairman, David & Goliath advertising agency.

"Life is very much like casting, right? You cast the right person for a movie, you cast the right director to shoot that movie, you cast the right set of friends, you cast the right spouse, you cast the right agency to work

182

for a client or a brand. If you get the casting right, then your parties are so much better. If you throw a party and you invite people that don't share the same mindset as you, then that's going to reflect the party. If you throw a wedding and you don't invite people that reflect that mindset of the person who's throwing it, then it won't be a great wedding. But if you can really look at the world through this idea of casting, when you cast the right people, then you really don't have to say a lot. You don't have to say a lot, and that becomes a community in itself.

You've created a community through like-minded values, and the sooner we can get to that, the better off everyone else will be. Then you'll have less disruption of the wrong agency with the wrong client. You know what I'm saying? You'll have the right coach on a football team and the right players playing for that coach. You have to start from there, you start from the core truth of what the product is, whatever it may be. It could be a football team, it could be a bar of soap, whatever it is. Then what you need to do is find the people that reflect the same values as that product."

Malin Gardeström, International Marketing Manager, Carlsberg & Tuborg.

"Tuborg and music goes hand in hand. Live music sounds better with a cold Tuborg in your hand. It's part of having fun with your friends about being relaxed, laid back, and just enjoying yourself. So Tuborg music has always been very much linked together. Tuborg has worked with music for over 30 years. We created The Green concert over 30 years ago which is now the biggest music event in Denmark. Of course we have a very big sponsorship. We have a lot of big sponsorships, Roskilde Festival being

the biggest one. Out during the summer with Tuborg, we meet over 50,000 Danish consumers. Of course it's important for us to be part of a good experience with music to give something back which is also very much part of our heritage, to give something back to community. Here we have opportunity to give our consumers also very good experience with of course, brand in hand, so that we are part of something bigger."

Peter Giacomello, Sponsorship and Reputation Director, Marketing Carlsberg.

"Roskilde Festival is a big marketing investment. It's not about the sales on the ground. They are huge, but it's not about it, because we still, netto invest a lot of money in Roskilde. This is all about building a strong Tuborg brand together with Roskilde, and showing that Tuborg is a perfect match for when young people listen to music."

Benjamin Holk Henriksen, Strategic planning & branding. Lecturer DIS and Copenhagen Business School, Author, Filmmaker "The Mind of a Leader", "Holk Master-class".

"It has been argued that community marketing is often time less costly. If you focus on existing customers you do not have to spend big money to attract new, and if you stay close to their communities you do not need to make a lot of market research to tell you what people want. In fact some of the world's strongest brands were initially built through low-cost community-based marketing.

It has also been argued the Community drives Innovation. Take Vans. The brand Vans. They started out making heap deck shoes – but followed the interests of their customers to expand into custom surf shoes, surf competitions, skateboarding shoes and gear, skateboarding parks etc. They were also part of music festivals, touring music festivals etc. And within each of those businesses, they were able to develop new products segments and marketing methods emerged all due to this thought of grassroots approach. So by tapping into the community segment you might be able to learn, develop and form a unique customer bond and loyalty."

Peter Giacomello, Sponsorship and Reputation Director, Marketing Carlsberg.

"There's one very big issue. You have to think of sponsorship as long term. You can't really make anything happen within a couple of years. You have to... I'd say at least 5 years as a partner, before you can benefit from the things you bought."

Print.

Print advertising is an ad in a printed medium such as a magazine, newspaper, trade journal etc. This encompasses media with a broad readership base as well as narrowly targeted media.

One form of print advertising is "classified advertising", which allows private individuals or companies to purchase a small, narrowly targeted ad. Newspaper classifieds are typically short, as they are paid for by the line. Another form is the display ad, which is generally a larger ad with design elements.[33]

Visual patterns.

The visual hierarchy is a concept in the field of advertising dominated by effective communication, visual recognition and motion.[34]

1. The rule of thirds.

The rule of thirds guideline proposes that an image should be imagined as divided into nine equal parts by two equally spaced horizontal lines and two equally spaced vertical lines. Important compositional elements should be placed along these lines or their intersections.

---

[33] https://webdesign.tutsplus.com/articles/understanding-the-f-layout-in-web-design--webdesign-687
http://linchpinseo.com/effective-print-advertising-design
[34] Eldesouky, D. F. B. (2013). Visual Hierarchy and Mind Motion in Advertising Design. The arts Journal.

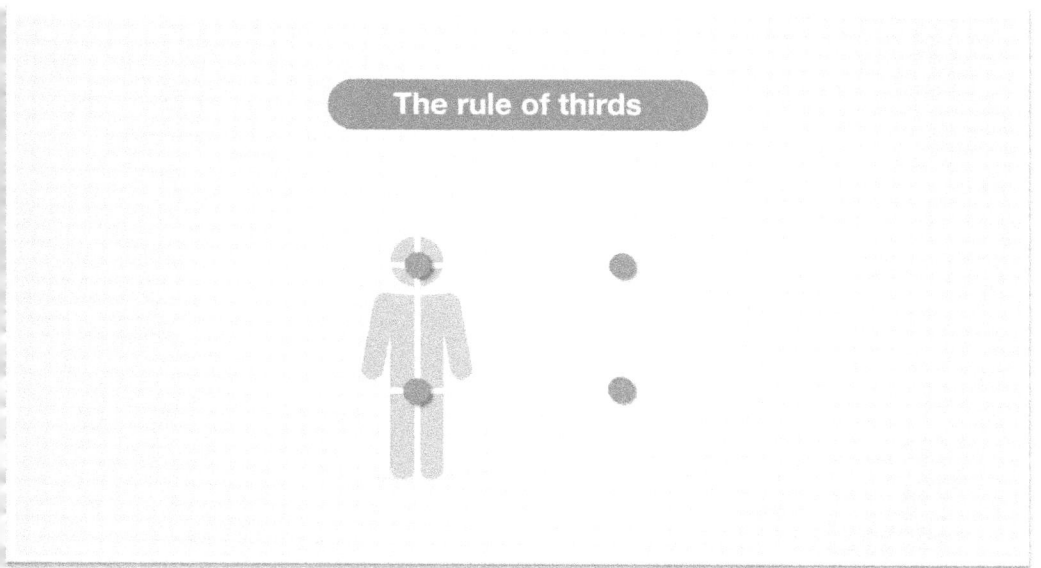

Figure 17.

2. The Gutenberg Diagram.

The Gutenberg diagram describes a general pattern the eyes move through when looking at evenly distributed, homogenous information. This pattern applies best to text-heavy content as its in harmony with natural reading gravity.

The Gutenberg diagram divides the layout into 4 quadrants.
• Primary optical area located in the top left
• Strong fallow area located in the top right
• Weak fallow area located in the bottom left
• Terminal area located in the bottom right

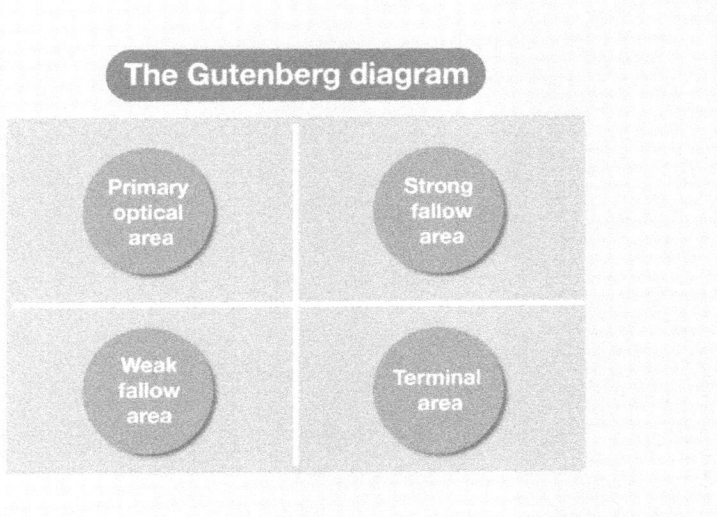

Figure 18.

The pattern suggests that the eye will sweep across and down the page in a series of horizontal movements called axes of orientation. The Gutenberg diagram suggests that the strong and weak fallow areas receive minimal attention unless emphasized visually.

3. Z-Pattern Layout.

The z-pattern layout follows the shape of the letter z. Readers will start in the top left, move horizontally to the top right and then diagonally to the bottom right before finishing with another horizontal movement to the bottom right. The z-pattern is good for simple designs with a few key elements that need to be seen.

188

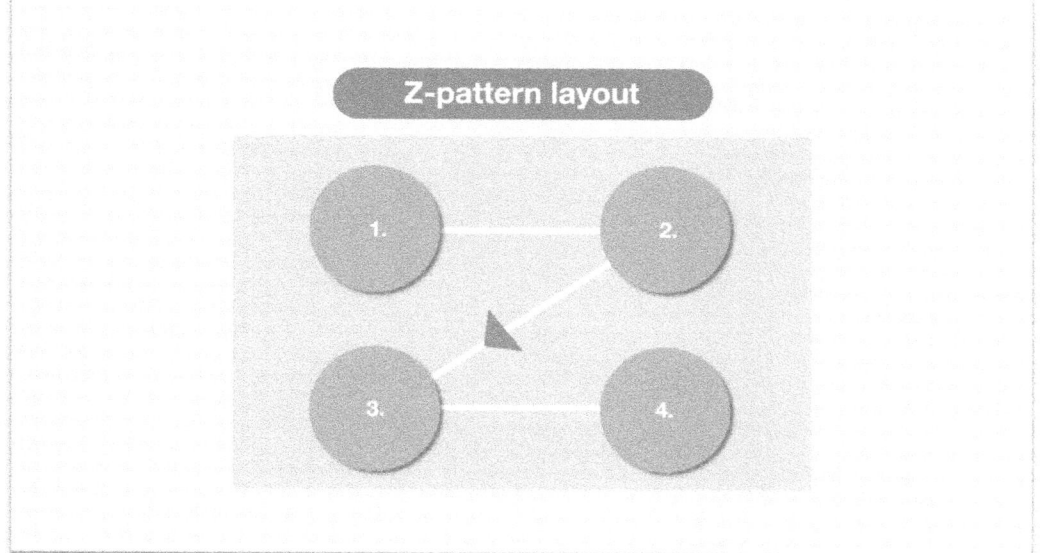

Figure 19.

4. Golden Triangle Pattern.

The z-pattern also leads to what's called a golden triangle pattern. If you take the first horizontal and first diagonal movement and then close the shape you end up with a right triangle whose right angle is the top left corner. This triangular area at the top of the page will be the area most seen, where you most important information needs to be placed.

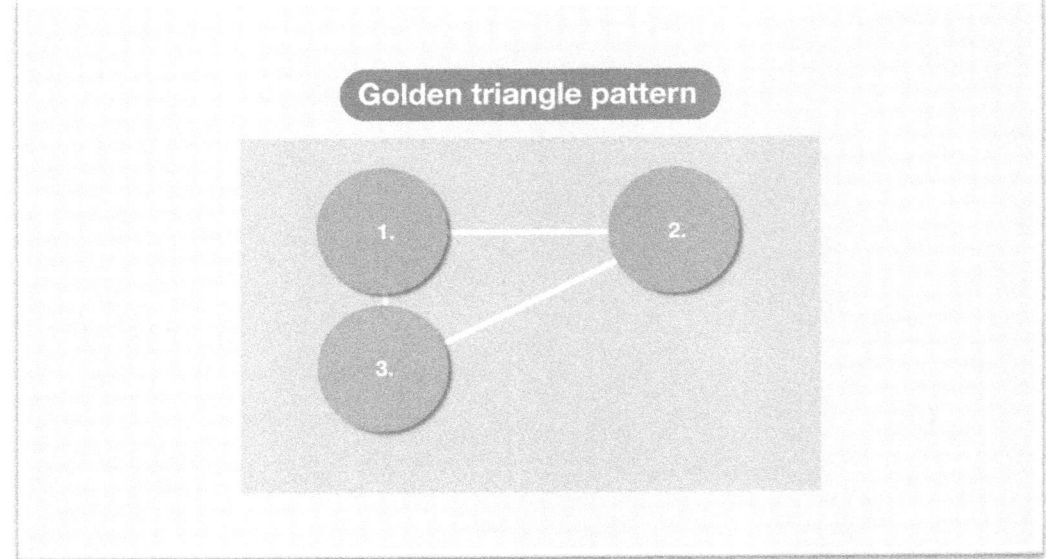

Figure 20.

5. F-Pattern Layout.

The f-pattern follows the shape of the letter F. Eye starts in the top left, moves horizontally to the top right and then comes back to the left edge before making another horizontal sweep to the right. This second sweep won't extend as far as the first sweep. The f-pattern suggests that lesser information should be placed along the left edge of the design often in bullet points where little horizontal eye movement is required to take everything in.

190

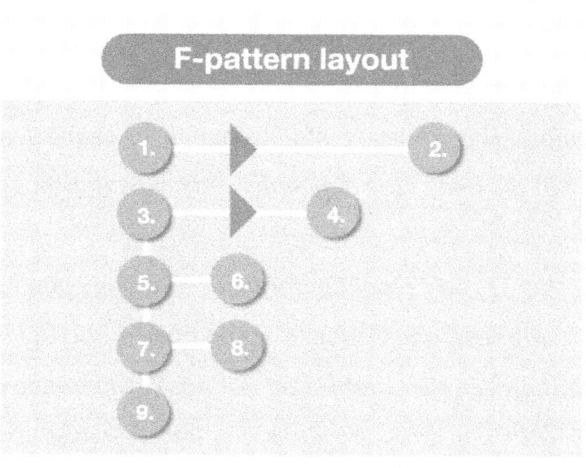

Figure 21.

A few other things to keep in mind when creating a print ad:

Consider the creative brief and objective.

Use an updated Logo.

Select the right color scheme.

Use the right font.

Be aware of using too much text.

Consider the size of the design and visual hierarchy.

Incorporate a call to action, such as a bar code for smartphones, website, phone number, store location etc.

Interviewees.

Steffen Hjaltelin, Founder & Partner at Hjaltelin Stahl.

"Print campaigns... I actually used to be Vice President at Politiken, a newspaper, so I've worked a lot with print campaigns. For most of our communication, print campaigns, when it comes to newspapers, is not relevant anymore. It is, however, still extremely relevant if you are in the tactical mode in the end stage of people's purchasing process.

You can note this: If you're looking for a car, suddenly you see all the cars ads if you actually read a newspaper. If you have a hurting back, you see everything that ... even the smallest ad if it has the message of curing a hurting back. That's how it is. So when it comes to newspaper advertising, I would forget about branding. That is not the right place to do branding. It is relevant if you have... in two ways. One, if you have a very tactical message, and the answer is just put it as big as it is, because you're going to reach people for whom it's meaningful, because they're very close to choosing between this and that... very close to an actual purchase. That is one.

There is actually another. We do a lot of political campaigns. There is another use of print media, if you want to speak to society, because there is one group that definitely still reads newspapers, and that is journalists. That means if you want to get on TV in the evening, they all read the newspaper in the morning. If you want to have a message to society, a CSR message, just a message in general to society, newspapers are extremely relevant.

When it comes to outdoor... outdoor has not decreased in relevance at all. You could actually say that if you look at media in 2017, it's mainly digital. And then there are two other media that are extremely interesting, and that's TV... TV still works... and then there is outdoor. Outdoor has this strange thing of being... it's sort of the only physical thing left. We can see that, for instance, for e-tailers. It is extremely relevant to show a physical presence in the outdoor. There are different rules when it comes to outdoor. The most efficient outdoor... and this becomes very practical, but it still works, big faces with eyes looking out. There's a lot of evidence showing that people cannot help looking at big faces when you're out in the city, the landscape. That's just a whole basic nature thing. That means that you will direct your attention to faces with eyes being live or being in print. And you see that from a lot of outdoor commercials. People are actually taking this into account. You also see some bad ones where's there a lot of copy and some of it... like this and in the bottom, where are the bicycles are parked. Those are useless. But a simple message with faces is very... it sounds like seventh year school grades, but that is actually what works when it comes to that."

Molly DeWolf Swenson Founding member / CMO of RYOT.

"Well, what I've seen recently that's really exciting and that is something that is Riot is starting to work on in very early stages is this intersection of print and digital using augmented reality. Basically, we've developed, with the help of our parent company- Verizon, an augmented reality technology built in Unity, which is a gaming engine, that can be integrated into the back end of an existing app and then you can use anything... any image anywhere as an image trigger to deliver additional content. So, for Elle magazine and Cosmopolitan magazine, for instance, we built this SDK into their apps and when you got your Elle "Women of Hollywood" issue, if you had the Elle Now app, you could hold your phone

over the cover of the magazine and the Women of Hollywood would come to life and it would give you on your phone video content, interview content that you couldn't get anywhere else. So, it was a way for them to drive app downloads by using the magazine because the magazine itself was a delivery mechanism or a vehicle for content using image trigger technology. So, it's basically a fancy QR code but instead of a little square box, it's, you know, Helen Miren or Kristen Stewart of one of the cover women of that issue."

Henrik Fisker, Automotive designer and entrepreneur (BMW Z8, Aston Martin DB9, V8 Vantage, Fisker Karma, Mustang Rocket, VLF Force 1, Destino V8).

"With my companies, I have been involved, with my own company is always involved in any print advertising or whatever we might do. I want to sign it off. I want to see it. Sometimes as a leader, you go in and have to make a decision in something that quite frankly, you may not have that much knowledge about but because you're the CEO or a large high corporate manager or whatever you might be, you have to make that decision. In the case of print advertising, we'll say, yes, I can understand the visual and all that but unusually in this area, I would definitely want to have my experts with me and discuss it. For me, when there is area where I know that I'm not the top-top in knowledge, I would always encourage a discussion before we make a decision. When it comes to print advertising, I would always encourage a discussion. I think it's a very difficult area because certain ads may appeal to me but not actually to the customers or some customers or a large enough customer group.

For me, that's a tricky area to understand and again with the way the print media has changed and really figure out who is actually looking at this print and what are our measures because sometimes the measure is you're trying to sell something. Sometimes you're just building the brand. Those are two different things. Yeah, I've been involved in selecting print media. Not so much in the corporate, when I worked in the corporate world because in the corporate world, you have departments that do that. You don't really involve people who is not in the department."

Dr. Kate Stone, Director Novalia.

"A good print ad... Hm. I think, maybe something that doesn't stand in the way of you trying to read what you actually want to read or look at. In some ways, it complements or has the same feeling as the thing you're looking at and reading. Otherwise, it's going to annoy the person who is going to have to look or see something that is not necessarily relevant and it's distracting from what they're trying to look at. If that's the case, it's also going to annoy the advertiser as well. So I think... thinking of creating a good ad is complementary to also what's there in the content, not just directly trying to hit the person who might be reading it."

Steffen Hjaltelin, Founder & Partner at Hjaltelin Stahl.

"When it comes to outdoor, again, I made all the political campaigns for a leading political party in Denmark "Venstre", all election campaigns since 2004. In that regard, outdoor is extremely relevant. We can just tell from the tracking afterwards that it has a major impact.

When it comes to political campaigns, it's all about the faces. If you make a political campaign with just statements on it, it's extremely difficult. If you make them with the faces and they look trustworthy, it has proven to be very, very relevant and effective, and still is. Not totally... and that's actually perhaps the most interesting... totally unchanged by all the digital. My thinking is actually that since we took away almost all physical marketing, there's always one thing standing back and that is outdoor in the widest sense from the buses to the billboards. And that is completely relevant still."

Product Placement.

Product placement is one of the methods or media channels a company can use to activate a marketing campaign.

It's the paid inclusion of branded products or brand identifiers, through audio or visual means within mass media programming such as movies, music videos, `news programs, videogames etc.

Corporate cameos have been around for decades, at least since Katharine Hepburn dumped Gordon's Dry Gin overboard in "The African Queen," but placement, as a paid strategic marketing tool, first really received attention during the 1980s, following the movie E.T. The decision to feature Reese's Pieces in ET catapulted the product placement craft into the Hollywood mainstream. Reese's Pieces leapt onto kids' mental menus and sales shot up 65%.[35]

Product placement can also enhance brand value at strategic times. When Tom Cruise visits Gene Hackman in the Cayman Islands, in the feature film 'The Firm', Hackman suggests that he "grab a Red Stripe," so Cruise opens the fridge for a bottle of the Jamaican-brewed beer. Within a month of the film's release, Red Stripe sales in the U.S. had

---

[35] Karrh, James A., McKee, Kathy Brittain, Pardun, Carol J., (2003). "Practitioners' Evolving Views on Product Placement Effectiveness". Journal of Advertising Research; Jun, Vol. 43 Issue 2, p138, 12p .

Peebles, M. Ellen. "And now a word from our sponsor". (2003). Harward Business Review, Oct, Vol. 81 Issue 10, p31, 9p, 2c, 4bw.

Russell, Cristel Antonia. (2002). Investigating the Effectiveness of the Product Placement in Television shows: The role of Modality and the Plot Connection Congruence on Brand Memory and Attitude. Journal of Consumer Research, Dec, Vol. 29 Issue 3.

Kogtvedgaard, Mogens. (2002). The law of competition (konkurrenceret).

Govani, Shinan. (1999). Product placement in movies – Is it really so bad? February 10, www.csmweb2.emcweb.com/durable/

increased by more than 50%, and just a few weeks later, company owners sold a majority stake in their brewery for $62 million to Guinness Brewing Worldwide.

Other known examples of product placement are: James Bond's association with Visa card, Avis car rentals, Aston Martin, BMW cars and motorcycles, Smirnoff vodka, Heineken beer, Omega watches, Ericsson cell phones, L'Oreal makeup etc. And AOL's signature smiley-face logo in "You got mail", staring Tom Hanks and Meg Ryan. The placement was reportedly worth between $3 million and $6 million.

The industry involves two primary groups of professionals, placement agents and programme producers. Agents function as middlemen between marketer and producers, typically working on a retainer basis. The major movie studios have their own departments for handling product placement opportunities, and work with placement agencies as well. Advertising agencies and public relations firms may also become involved in negotiations for their clients.

One of the negative aspects of product placement is the lack of control. It's highly unpredictable exactly how much, and when, a director wants to use a specific film sequence, and thus how much the company gains from the investment.[36]

---

[36] Hip Hop: Are we selling the song or product? July 9, 2003 www.pub12.ezboard.com
"Gimme a Bud"! Promotion, www.Advertising.utexas.edu
"Product placement in movies" www.propguys/htdocs/pages/product/
Buss, Dale: "A product placement hall of fame" Date 06/22/98 online original.
www.businessweek.com/1998/25/b3583062.
Gene Emery, Reuters "What's in a name: Product Placement in games"
www.usatoday.com/tech/techreviews/games/2002/1/30/spotlight.htm
"Pepsi adds splash of color" www.hollywoodproductplacement.com

It's been argued that the use of product placement will increase due to the emergence of hard-disc recorders such as TIVO, that enables you to skip commercials, but only time will tell.

Interviewees.

Asger Leth, Director & Screenwriter, DGA award winner. (Ghosts of Cité Soleil, Man on a Ledge, Five Obstructions, Move on (Telekom)).

"Yeah. I did this massive T-Mobile campaign where basically we were doing a road movie of eight episodes in eight different countries. It was a T-Mobile project there were phones thrown in here and there, which would tell the story that this is about telephony somehow, but apart from that, if I didn't have those props in, actually I felt that the stories that we were telling would not have connected with what we were trying to tell. Sometimes, product placement can help you tell the story. Sometimes, there is no story without the product. In that case, it was a perfect example of how to use that."

Peter Ålbæk Jensen, Producer, Founder & fmr. CEO, Zentropa.

"We've done it a lot of times with no success at all. We made a film, a loaded comedy called "Clown", where we had an alcohol based drink that we included which was Jagermeister or... was it Jagermeister ... I can't remember. That was something that was regarded as liquor here in

Product placement with a "twist" Hollywood takes a hit from the internet & moves towards guerilla style "permission Marketing" www.hollywoodproductplacement.com
"Coca-Cola revises its guidelines in school nutrition, commercialism" (Atlanta Business Chronicle) www.atlanta.bizjournals.com/atlanta/stories/2003/11/17/daily3.html

Denmark and that worked quite well. No problems, and then we sold the film to the U.S. where the same fucking drink was not regarded as liquor, which meant that is was put on the shelf in the supermarket together with alternative medicine treatments, herbal tea, whatever. So, suddenly we had a film that was promoting the fluid here as alcoholic, which was what it was. Then suddenly they had the problem that they had to face that the product had to be removed from all the shelves in all the supermarkets in the states. It ended up that we had erase in the movie all of the little marks saying Jagermeister on all bottles, everything. That started happy but ended very unhappy. It's unpredictable what types of problems it can involve. Actually, it was not our fault it was the fault of the company that they never thought that we would sell this product in the states where they have this specific problem. Funny."

Lars Liebst, CEO Tivoli.

"To be very honest, I don't think we have done it. Will we do it in the future? You should never say no, but maybe we are a little bit privileged because quite a lot of movies are actually shot in here because the atmosphere is pretty okay, so that is something. Every morning there is live TV coverage, Good Morning Denmark from Tivoli. In one way another, is that product placement, I don't know."

Tue Walin Storm, Director, Screenwriter, Founder Storm/Hansen (Nielson, Ford, Pirelli, The Raveonettes).

"Obviously, product placement is not that interesting in commercials, because commercial's all about product. Product placement becomes interesting when you try to sell something else. Especially in music, a musical artist for a music video. I've been involved in a music video for a

band called *Gym Class Heroes* where we filmed in Vegas. The budget is a good budget, but it wasn't good enough. In order to enhance the budget, the record label started making deals with various products to have them featured within the music video to be associated with the band and, of course, gain commercial value through that. There was a couple of different things that were introduced within the music video.

The main one was a Jeep that had to be featured. So, the band is arriving down the Las Vegas strip and they're driving this Jeep, obviously. But there are very strict demands from Jeep in terms of what they need to be featured. The Jeep could open its doors all four ways. They needed to see that. They needed specific angles. Suddenly you have the idea of a music video, which, to me, has always been the most true, creative form within all of these things because there is no real brief. The artist might have an opinion, but there is nothing... It's pure art, so to speak. The minute you start infusing products into it, and the product starts having demands about how they want to see the label, how the car should be featured, when to see the grill, when to see the doors opening, see the dashboard. Obviously, you being restricted creatively in order to incorporate this, it becomes much more like a commercial.

The advantage is, of course, that you can get some interesting products that the band would like to be associated with. Grosby clothing. They're wearing specific clothing that they like. Beverages are very common to put into a music video. The U.S. is non-alcoholic because they can't show that on MTV. In this particular case, the Jeep was definitely the biggest item that had to be in and that demanded the biggest change on the creative level, because it suddenly sucked up so much time of the music *video... in order to feature all these elements that Jeep required to be featured. A necessary evil in this type of music videos."*

Peter Giacomello, Sponsorship and Reputation Director, Marketing Carlsberg.

"I'm responsible for all our sponsorships, and you can divide them in 2. For Carlsberg, it's football, soccer, and for Tuborg it's music. That's the strategy, so it's pretty easy to choose which sponsorships to look at. Within the music category, we choose the strongest."

Asger Leth, Director & Screenwriter, DGA award winner. (Ghosts of Cité Soleil, Man on a Ledge, Five Obstructions, Move on (Telekom)).

"Product placement can be a really, really great thing for a director if it adds to his toolbox. If it gives him more money for the budget, to do other stuff that he wants to do, if it gives him sometimes specificity for the scene that he needs, actually, a product, then if you need it already, let's say you need a hammer. Why not go with a hammer that's this and that brand, who actually will put money into the movie by you using that? In that case, I see only advantages. The disadvantages are when producers are not aware of the dangers. That means, some producers are happy to sign a product placement deal that says, "X amount of seconds and X amount of scenes does this product have to in the movie." That's very, very dangerous. I, as a director, would never sign up for that. I think the best producers wouldn't either.

I think you have to have, if you want a minimum, it should be an extreme low minimum, but you should more make a friendship with your brand,

202

with the product that you want to put in. You should shake hands and say, "We'd love to make a product placement deal with you guys. We're going to put it as many places as we can, because we love the product, but we're not going to put it in places where it hurts the story." Ultimately, if it hurts the story, it hurts the product. I think it's in everybody's best interest, the product and the film, that they come to some sort of gentlemen agreement that doesn't have to be ironed down where you tie yourself up in editing or for a director, because those kinds of deals don't work. That's my basic take on that."

Mikkel Borg Bjergsø Founder and CEO Mikkeller brewery, bars and restaurants.

"Not actually. We have been, but it hasn't been our decision actually. Which is then, I guess, is not product placement. When we make a beer for Noma for example, obviously the main reason is because I think it's extremely interesting to work with people from Noma because they can teach, I can learn a lot from them, they can hopefully learn a lot from me.

I'm also aware of the fact that it's a good thing for Mikkeller to be in Noma, for example, or to do a beer with Rick Astley, which we're doing as well. You can kind of call that product placement, I don't speculate in it, but it's obviously I know that when we do something with people that the world is looking at, obviously you get something out of it as a company as well. The main reason is that I think it's an interesting project, but for example, we would never pay to have our products somewhere. We would never pay.

We work very closely with Scandinavian Airlines, SAS, and all flights with SAS you can get Mikkeller beer. It's not something that we pay to, we have a relationship with them now, and we work on developing new beer styles on top of that, because they think we're interesting, and we think we're interesting, and we have a good relationship. It's not because we pay them a lot of money to get into the airplanes, or pay a lot of money to get into something else. We would never do that. Again, I don't want people to buy my products because I tell them to. I want them to buy my products because they feel like it's interesting and they want to be a part of what we do."

Malin Gardeström, International Marketing Manager, Carlsberg & Tuborg.

"Depending on what size your brand is. I would consider doing product placement. In the case of Carlsberg and Tuborg, as they have the size that they do, I don't really see the need for it. I know a lot of people who would like to use our brands to get some qualities and statements, but it's not adding that much value because we are there anyway and people might not notice as being in a video because it's so natural for us to appear that there's no need for me to pay any extra money to do so. I would say if you have a brand that's very unknown, it could be an idea in order to get someone to talk about it."

Asger Leth, Director & Screenwriter, DGA award winner. (Ghosts of Cité Soleil, Man on a Ledge, Five Obstructions, Move on (Telekom)).

"Good product placement, bad product placement ideas or examples? Look, there's no way in hell I don't want an Aston Martin. I only basically

know it because of James Bond. There's no way in hell. I want that car. That's the best product placement in the history of movie-making, then the Omega watches and all that stuff. Here, that's an example of where product placement can elevate the product, put it into a stratospheric level, but also, in a way, brand the movie. That's like a marriage that just makes both parts better. Similarly, you could discuss, and people would say bad product placement is when you notice the product, or whatever. I'm not so tough on that. I prefer that it's so elegant that you barely notice, that it's only subconscious, but I'm also like, "I get it. They needed more money. Actually, I wouldn't watch this good movie, great movie even, if they didn't have the money to make it." I'm like, "I'll let it slide. I don't mind that, as long as the movie is good and as long as the product placement didn't hurt it.

There are examples, and I'm not going to come up with some, because I'm not going to sit around bagging on colleagues' movies, but there are definitely examples of movies where the product placement is so in your face, where the deal that has obviously been made is so strict on how close-up you have to see this and that product, that it just destroys the scene and then destroys the movie. Ultimately, you're left with a movie that's so bad that people almost think it's cheesy, and they laugh about it. Then the product becomes cheesy and laughable, and that's not in anybody's interest. It's in everybody's interest to make a deal where it's like, "We don't have to write it down, second-to-second where it's going to be, but we trust you. We're going to give you this money. You're going to make a great movie, and I know you're going to help us look good while we're doing it." Those are the examples where I think it's absolutely great."

Cross Promotion.

Cross-promotion is a marketing method where customers of one product or service, are targeted with promotion of a related product.

Basic examples of cross-media marketing are when a buyer purchasing a shirt is shown a picture of a pair of trousers that coordinate with the shirt, when talk show hosts promote products such as books and magazines, when a buyer of a computer program receives an email offering a reduced price on a guide to using that program. When airline web sites shows that customers may earn mileage points towards free flights by purchasing air travel, or through many other actions or when a mobile phone network teams up with music artists to make ringtones.

The strategy may also involve a host of organisations working together to promote a service or product. For example when manufacturers of sweets or fast food tie their products to a feature film in order to create a mutually beneficial win-win situation.

Company B has access to the shared target group. Company A adds value to B's product in the shape of a cool film universe or hero. And in return B offers access or promotion to the target group.

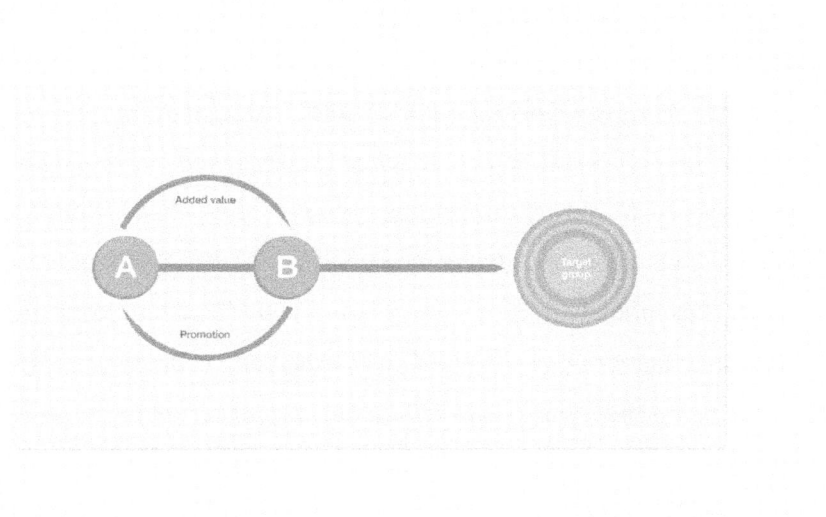

Figure 22.

Cross-promotion marketing has proven very effective due to the lower costs. However marketers must be careful to choose the right partner. You are placing part of your brand equity in the hands of another company so be sure that it's a brand you want to be associated with.[37]

Interviewees.

Ole Henriksen, Founder and Creative Director, Ole Henriksen Skin Care Brand.

---

[37] Kumar, D.S. (2012). The Dark Side of Cross-Selling. Harvard Business review, December issue. Gruner, S.L. (1997). The Secrets of Cross-Promotion. Different entrepreneurs tell how they have found marketing partnerships to be an effective way to stretch a budget.

"Cross promotion can work incredibly well when you do it with the right partner. Clarisonic being an example of a cleansing device that was created here in America and later sold to L'Oreal about two-and-a-half years ago. That is a device similar to what I've used at my skin care clinics/my spa over the years. So when they reached out to me and said they'd like to do a cross promotion, I jumped at it because not alone are they big, and we're certainly a nice sized business as well. And one of the claims they made was, that when you use your Clarisonic your products work on a deeper more effectual level, especially your serums. My Truth serum, being the number one selling anti-aging serum in the world of Sephora, again, many years in a row, and really my iconic product, was just a perfect partner there. Because the exposure it gave for my "Truth serum" with the five stable sources of vitamin C, and of course Clarisonic, was fantastic. We did it both in retail and on QVC Television. And QVC Television, of course, being the biggest shopping network in the world. That was a win-win.

I don't necessarily go out and seek it out as far as this thing of partnering up, but I do believe, absolutely, cross promotion is great, because it could be a fashion event. And we have done those many a time and around the world, and I'm sure more to come in the future. I think you must always leave your eyes open, your ears open, to any opportunity and when it's right, it can be a marriage made in heaven."

Lars Liebst, CEO Tivoli.

"Well, let's take the con first. If you have a rather strong brand, you have to be very careful. Are you diluting your own brand by going out and do something with somebody else? The pros are definitely that you can

reach much further than we can. You have to be very selective and you probably have to think twice before you do it. Have we done it? Yes we have, and I'll say that when we do Friday Night Rock, for instance, which we do, funny enough, every Friday night. We can do it with a beer company. I think it adds something to the value of Tivoli, because now we do our own craft beer, a Tivoli beer, so in that sense, it makes sense."

Petter A. Stordalen, Founder and owner of Nordic Choice Hotels
"Choose somebody you love because that's like in life. Somebody you really like to work with. That's the most important, but cross promotions, we do a lot of course. You can even have a loyalty card staying in my hotels, and when you go and you fill up gasoline or you go and buy your groceries, you get points. If you go with a particular airline company, you get points so you can use that either in my hotel or you could use it in the airline company.

So obviously that's also a part of the future. But more important, don't do it too difficult to understand. It must be like, "Keep it simple, stupid." It must be easy to communicate, it must be easy for the guest to understand. So I like that... obviously, hotel and airlines fit together. Rental cars, of course. And then you can add, but don't do it too complicated. Because the most important thing is to focus on what's important for your guest. And that's the rooms, the people, the service. So the three most important things for my guests is the people in the reception, the people cleaning the rooms, and the people preparing and serving your breakfast. Because that's hotels.

The GM, it's not that important. Don't forget the people that actually do the job. Ask them about cross selling. Ask the guest what they really need. And in my industry, they will tell you clean rooms, good breakfast, a good bed. Most of all, nice people.

Matthew Bagwell, Managing Director Naked Communications Europe.

"You're talking about essentially the opportunity of using someone else's channel in a timely way, to engage with that brand's customers. Again, I think that this is all about relevance. I can quite understand that if you've got incredibly high footfall into a chain of restaurants, or you've got an incredibly captive audience, who are in a football stadium or at a concert, you may perceive that firstly you have the permission to introduce partners, and secondly that you're going to have a captive audience. You may have reach, for example, or you may have high amounts of attention.

I can see why that might be attractive to brands. I think this is not about necessarily only considering the mutual benefits of the two brands, but to the impression about both, or multiple brands, for the consumer. Can they see some synergy that makes sense to them? Or do they become cognizant of the fact that they're really simply being exploited because they happen to be in a proximity, or they happen to have some kind of engagement, and then there is a partner.

I think it's always about thinking who are the right partners to bring into an engagement, and what are they doing that is unique for the customer that we have the relationship with. As it becomes increasingly unique and increasingly sort of related to the initial brand, I think it can become really very, very powerful.

For example, with the Flying Club at Virgin Atlantic, there are many benefits of being a member, not least the fact that there are offers from partners. For example, if you have a Virgin Atlantic credit card, then there are going to be particular offers from partners of Virgin Atlantic that are offered to the loyal members of that program.

We have to work hard that the offers themselves and the partners make some sense of the Virgin Atlantic brand, as well as obviously the brands that are involved in the program. If that makes sense, I think you have to take a view of, the take out still needs to be for the customer, and it needs to be consistent with what you are trying to achieve. Otherwise I think you're actually eroding your own brand equity."

Christina Bilde, Spokes person Roskilde Festival.
"For us it's very important, first of all, to stay an independent festival. We're non-profit and we're independent so we don't have as many partners and sponsors as you usually see especially outside of Denmark. I think, considering that also people from outside of Denmark may be watching this, that's important to tell. When we always work with partners in a way that... it has to make sense, not just for us and for them but actually it has to make sense mainly for our participants. When they're sponsoring, working with us, they have to create things at the festival, whether it be content or deliverances of different kinds that fits with the festival either as activities that they create or support in a special way or just basically food, for instance, has to be organic and stuff

like that. Even better, if they have values that we can, where we fit good together."

David Angelo, Founder & Chairman, David & Goliath advertising agency.

"Cross promotions, well times have changed. People are brands now, right? People are brands, as celebrities are brands, athletes are brands, as much as brands are brands. What we do here at David&Goliath, is that we take like-minded brands and we bring them together to create even more power.

For instance, KIA Motors is a challenger brand, right? They're a brand that's always challenged convention, they've always done things differently, because they had to. They were outspent, out-branded, and the many cases uplanded by the competition. They had to march to their own beat, to their own authentic beat.

Then you have an athlete named Blake Griffin, a very different basketball player. It's not the same sort of player that you see in supporting all these other brands. He has the same type of spirit, a scrappy, like-minded, hardworking spirit that Kia Motors has. When you put the two of them together, and you see the connection, it's a more authentic connection, a more believable connection. When it ends up happening is that they both become twice as powerful. It's not, it doesn't feel like a spokesperson that's trying to sell a car, it's more of a shared mindset that's just trying to connect with another shared mindset. That's how I see cross promoting. I know that there are other examples of products, product placement and all that, but I believe at the end of the day it comes down to like-minded values. You can always tell when there is a product that's in a movie that it's not supposed to be in, right? It's like, "Hello, what happened there?" That's why you always have to start with the core truth of that brand, and then find other brands, whether it's a movie or a person or whatever, that share those same truths."

Peter Holten Mühlmann, Founder and CEO, Trustpilot.

"Inherently, if you look at Trustpilot, we're offering businesses an opportunity to show what they're customers are thinking about them. We'd like to think that because we invest so much in the integrity of the reviews that if the visitor can see that these reviews are helped by Trustpilot... or collected by Trustpilot, then people will trust them more. In that sense, there's a cross-promotion between what we do, where our presence adds value; almost like a BMW logo on a car to that service. In that sense, we are a big cross-promotion. We're promoting, in a way, the merchants that are embedding our logo and what we stand for. They're promoting us.

I think my advice is you need... if you want to do these cross-promotions... Everybody intuitively thinks, "That's a great idea." You need to do something that really makes sense and adds a lot of value to the people who are doing it. I think way too many small companies are spending a lot of time talking about how they can cross-promote each other's products. It ends up not being very efficient."

Klaus Nørskov, Head of communication Red Cross.

"The question of which partnerships we enter into and say, for instance, partnerships with rock musicians like Bono, it's also a question of who

might be the right partner to choose. I think, to some extent, that partners might be too obvious. You end up in situations where everybody says "Yeah, well, it will be like that." What happens is, and again looking at target groups, you don't get any further. You don't reach anymore. You reach exactly the same people because it's exactly the same people that agree with us 100% up until now. The really interesting partners will be the partners that actually enhance our reach. I don't think Bono enhances our reach, actually. I think there would be more... Almost any other rock musician would probably be a better choice from that perspective. Maybe we should go for Black Sabbath, or we should go for some other big rock bands with a similar size, but a different target group."

PR and the art of writing a press release.

Public relations is the art of managing the spread of information between an individual or an organization, such as a business, government agency, nonprofit organization, media company, etc., and attempting to frame that information in a positive light.

If we look at Holk's Communication Platform left to right we have:

The organisation.

The communication platform.

Media execution.

Target group.

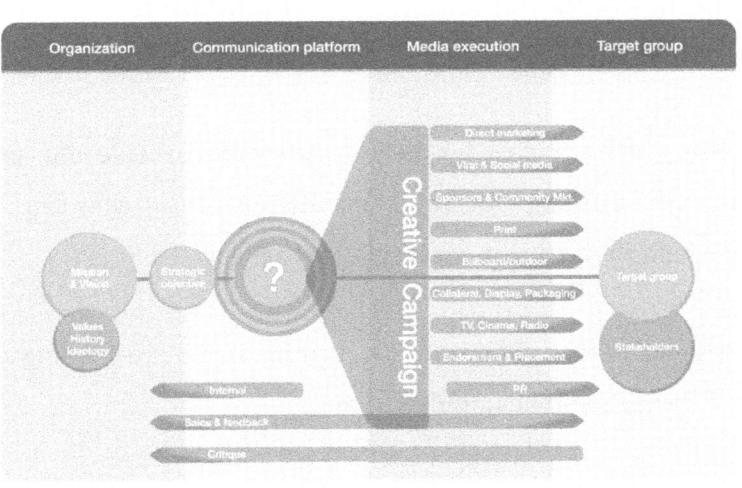

Figure 23.

Public relations is based on the idea of creating coverage for clients for free, rather than marketing or advertising. Thus an example of public relations would be generating an article featuring a client, rather than paying for the client to be advertised next to the article.

A press release is a written statement to the media. It can announce a range of news items, including scheduled events, personal promotions, awards, new products and services, sales accomplishments, crisis management, etc. Reporters are more likely to consider a story idea if they first receive a press release.

Two styles are the Amsterdam or Dutch style, and the Leicester or UK style.[38]

The Amsterdam style.

Make it easy. Make it easy for the journalists that receive your press release to put all the important information in first so they can decide if they want to read on, or contact the PR agency.

Keep it short. Keep it short and to th e point. If you are sending a hard copy, the text should be double-spaced.

Use the 5 W's: Who, What, Where, When and Why in the introduction because a journalist doesn't have time to read a whole press release.

---

[38] How to Write a Press Release.
https://www2.le.ac.uk/offices/external/news/publicising/how-to-write-a-press-release
Press release template.
https://www2.le.ac.uk/offices/external/news/publicising/how-to-write-a-press-release/template

Who is this about?

What is the actual news?

When does this event happen?

Where does this event take place?

Why is this news?

Some add an extra H: How is this happening?

The typical structure involves 6 steps:

1. Intro/lead, including the 5 W's.

2. Source.

3. Essentials.

4. Quotes.

5. Anything else.

6. Ends.

Remember to write a note to the editor and your contact info.

The Leicester style.

The Leicester or UK style starts with a very short introduction with a maximum of 20 to 30 words, as opposed to the Amsterdam schools five W's. In a way, it turns the process upside down:

1. Ends.

2. Anything else.

3. Quotes.

4. Essentials.

5. Source.

6. Intro/lead.

A few other key points to keep in mind are:[39]

• Understand what media you are aiming for.

• Find an interesting angle for that specific media.

• Conduct research on the journalist.

• Feed the story in two steps: A short press release and a longer press kit or package.

• Be available and quick to respond.

• Remember your target group and other stakeholders.

• Define the purpose of the press release.

Interviewees.

Christina Bilde, Spokes person Roskilde Festival.

"You have to make it relevant. That is one area where you really have to look. It's not enough that you find it relevant or exciting or the newest thing. You have to find that hook that makes it relevant for everybody else than yourself. Some of the things that we're dealing with are quite narrow, you could say, quite small topics. Upcoming art, for instance. You really have to find, to be aware, that even though it's, for instance, an artist that you yourself love, it's not necessarily enough to create an awareness from the surroundings. Maybe what you have to look at is what is that artist working with, what are the topics, or what is it that

---

[39] James, Geoffrey (2016). "How To Write a Press Release, with Examples". cbsnews.com. CBS News. Retrieved 19 May.
What is a Press Release? Digital Media PR, Public Relations/April 7th, 2015
http://www.5wpr.com/new/press-release/

makes him or her relevant to the surroundings and that's what you have to look in to.

Then I have to say, in working Roskilde Festival, it's very privileged also in that area. A lot of the times when we go out with something, it's interesting just because it's Roskilde festival, which is a privilege but it's also something that you have to be aware of because it could, it hasn't but it could, create some kind of laziness. That's another thing you have to be very aware of. Never take attention for granted."

Klaus Nørskov, Head of communication Red Cross.
"Obviously what you need to do is maintain good relations with whichever areas or corners of the press that you can think of you'd need later on to relate to. Stay in touch is basically the best advice you can give, and also maybe have a certain sort of two-way thinking about it, so it's not necessarily every time you call a journalist in order to get them to write an article or whatever, but maybe sometimes you call them just to inform them of stuff you know they might want to know. If you're dealing with politics, there's a lot of information that you have that they might want, and it might not be to your benefit immediately, but it's certainly going to strengthen your relation with this journalist. When you actually want to pitch, you can do this with a much more... They want to hear, listen to you, and you don't have to feel like you're troubling them, basically because you know that last time we spoke, I gave him something, gave her something that he or she wanted, and I got nothing in return."

Asger Leth, Director & Screenwriter, DGA award winner. (Ghosts of Cité Soleil, Man on a Ledge, Five Obstructions, Move on (Telekom)).

"How to use the media to get attention for your movie or for your product or for your commercial, or for whatever it is that you're doing? How to use the media outside. I think that's a great question. Actually, it's also a difficult question, because I think I always, not just me but everybody I work with always think about it somehow. It's like, who's the right media to invite first? Who should be the ones leading with the story, because then the right kind of other media's are going to follow up? I think how you seed the initial story of what you're doing, to whom you seed it, who are the first re-layers of your story, that's important. That sets a tone for where you want to go with it, in the same way that you have a target customer base for your product, in the same way, I think, you choose your media.

You have to choose the media that says the right thing for the target audience, or opens it up to the areas of perhaps potential future target audience. You have to think about, do we want to go out and sell this story about how we made this commercial or how we made this movie to the hip, inner-city, urban crowd, or do we want to sell it to the 45 to 55 suburban soccer moms, and whatever? Who we want to reach, not just with the product, but also with the story of how we told the product. Those things are something everybody has to think about, of course.

Once you've decided that, there's definitely ways to spin the story. You can just look at a movie like the Revenant that was out this year. It had an Oscar campaign that was so massive that everybody noticed. The story was, 75% of the time, how they were freezing their rears off and shooting this 200 days, and how difficult it was to almost survive the filmmaking. That was the story. That's obviously the angle they chose. It worked, at least to an extent. I think you have to choose your battles. Usually, it's about the unusual approach, the craziness of the original idea, or the difficulty in executing it that you manage to overcome somehow."

Peter Holten Mühlmann, Founder and CEO, Trustpilot.

"It played a huge role, actually. The 1st day Trustpilot went live, we were on the front page of national media in the country we started which is Denmark. That created a big awareness for us. Also, being a company where many consumers are using it... You have hundreds of millions of people that are exposed to our reviews and hundreds of thousands of companies. Of course, they care about it. In that sense, we've become something that people have an opinion about. For that reason, it's very important that we're part of the media landscape, that we have a voice and that we are participating in the debate. For people who are thinking about starting a company, I would say a little bit like my advice with viral media. Don't count on it. Don't have a strategy based on you getting a lot of attention or media.

For some personality types, it just comes across really easy. For others, it's very difficult. Also, for some products, it can be very easy to get media attention and impossible for others. Then, also I would say, don't overestimate the impact when it's positive but also when it's negative. If you're on the front page. That's fantastic. Congratulations. It's good. The day after, nobody remembers. In a similar fashion, if you get 1 bad story about you, it doesn't matter so much. There's a lot of content out there. Get back on. It's not the end of the world. Focus on the next good story."

Klaus Nørskov, Head of communication Red Cross.

"We do what we call "Core storytelling" or "Core stories," which means that when we want to pitch... Because whenever you have an issue that they want to raise awareness around, you need to straighten your mind. What we always do is we have a discussion, and then somebody sits down to write this core messaging or core story, and when you have this, you have it to share with journalists, you have it to use on your website, you can maybe extract to Facebook posts or messages on Twitter. You basically have one story that you use in all these different channels, variations of cause, short and long and everything, but basically you have a mutual story, and what's really important about this is that if you're having a complicated issue, and you have like 3 or 5 or 7 people from the organization involved, they will have the same story, as well, which is far more difficult than you'd think because everybody leaves meetings having their own conclusions. This is a way of sharing a mutual message and a way to make sure... Even if you want to involve volunteers, you want to have a local impact, you'd share this with 10 volunteers, 10 different places in Denmark, you have the same story. It's a very, very strong tool."

Leif Rasmussen. Strategic Branding. Lecturer, DIS – Study Abroad in Scandinavia.

"An advice could be that you should be thinking about working with media as handling your stakeholders because the media, well, in general, are your stakeholders, as well as other stakeholders. So what you should

be thinking about when you write such a press release or make such a press release, you should be thinking about how would they react. Is there anything in what you are writing or showing them, which they can use in their media? Can they use it for a news story, can they use it for something which is unusual? And don't make the same press release for all kind of media because they have very, very different interests in what to write."

Christina Bilde, Spokes person Roskilde Festival.

"It depends on what kind of press release you're writing and who you're writing it to. Are you presenting this to be in the news? Then you have to focus on what's new about this. If you're writing, and I'm working with culture, if you're trying to present something to a cultural magazine, someone who knows about this then you'll have to be more aware of the content of the presentation. Always use a good hook line, I would say. Never make it too long. I have one thing that I always work with is it has to be presented in a way that you can use it directly and it has to be presented so you can use only the first few lines and that's it. If you want to have a longer article then you can copy the rest of it. It's very difficult to say anything more specific than that. Never use too many blooming words. You have to rely on your content. If you have to tell someone that it's exciting then it's not exciting enough. It should be exciting in itself."

Peter Holten Mühlmann, Founder and CEO, Trustpilot.

"What I did, initially, was that I would always just call the journalists. Every newspaper has a publicly available phone number. You call them. You say you have a story. You can actually speak with a live, human journalist. They're pretty upfront in telling you whether they think that's

interesting or whether they don't think that's interesting. They're busy people; but you can always get ahold of someone.

I did that the 1st 10, 20 times. Then, that was a great way for me... I didn't realize it back then. It wasn't a conscious thing that I did because of this. I realized, after having spoken to 10, 20 journalists, then, I figured out what it was that they cared about. Then, we included those things in future press releases."

Part V. Digital marketing and social media.

Customer journey mapping.

A business must understand the stages and channels that consumers travel through to reach their destination. Customer journeys are multi-stage and multi-channel, and users require information at each stage to make the right decisions as they move toward their destination.

The customer journey map is a graph which illustrates the steps your customers go through, whether it is a product, a website, a retail store, or a service, or combination.[40] From initial contact, through the process of engagement and into a long-term relationship, the customer journey maps allow you to understand and improve your customer's experience.

---

[40] Richardson, Adam. (2010). "Using Customer Journey Maps to Improve Customer Experience". Harvard Business Review, November 15.
Srivastava, Apigee, Kumar. "How Data Analysis Drives the Customer Journey".
https://www.wired.com/insights/2014/01/data-analysis-drives-customer-journey/

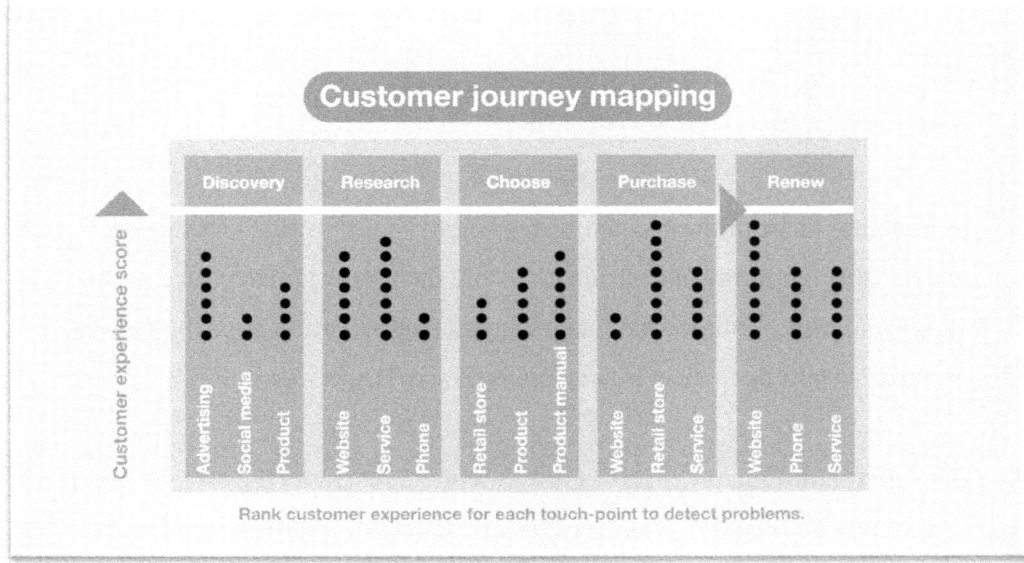

Figure 24.

It highlights the user's feelings, motivations and questions for each of these touch-points.[41]

---

[41] Compare: "Customer Experience Management: What it is and why it matters". SAS. (2015). Customer experience is defined as your customers' perceptions – both conscious and subconscious – of their relationship with your brand resulting from all their interactions with your brand during the customer life cycle.
Thompson, Ed and Kolsky, Estaban. (2004). "How to Approach Customer Experience Management". Gartner.com. Retrieved 2016-07-15. Summary: Managing the detail of customer experiences is an important part of any customer relationship management strategy.

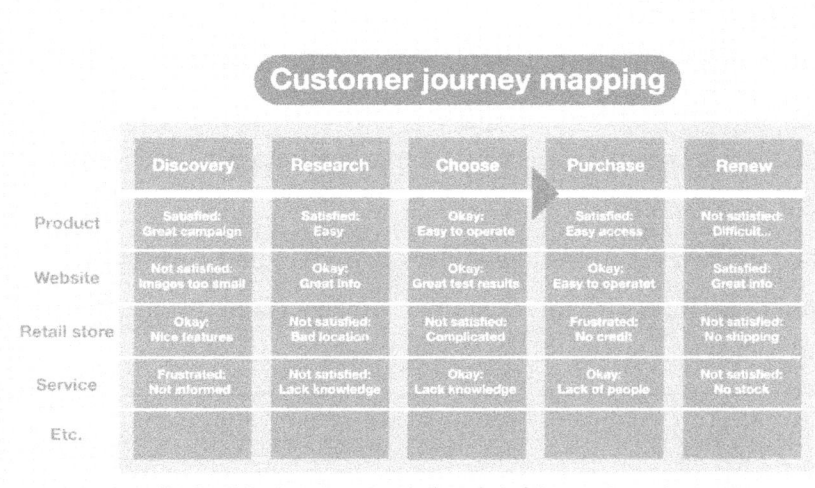

Figure 25.

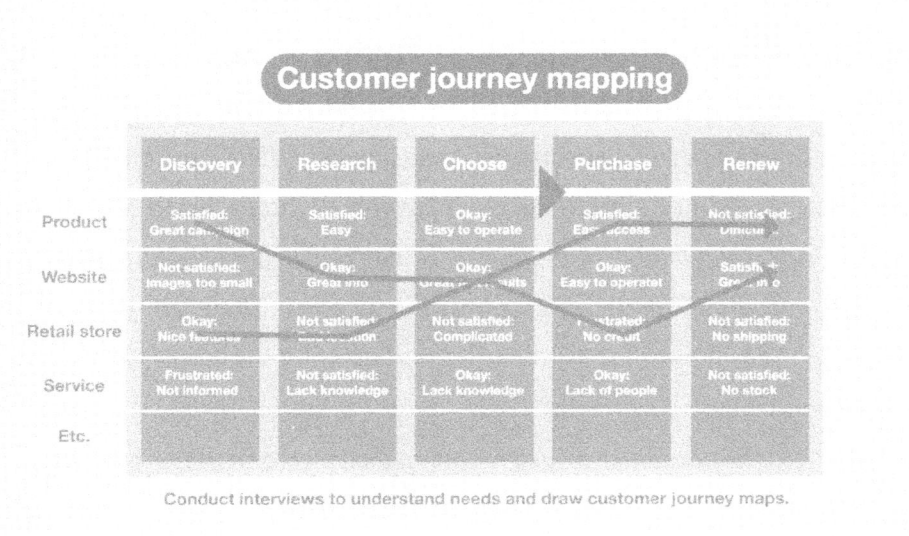

Figure 26.

227

---

1. Identify customers.

2. Identify touch-points (From discovery to renew phase).

3. Identify sources for data collection.

4. Conduct surveys ranking customer experience at each touch-point in order to detect problems.

5. Conduct interviews with stakeholders to understand customer needs and problems and draw customer journey maps (From discovery to renew phase).

Interviewees.

Johan Boserup, Global CEO of Trading at WPP's GroupM.

"The consumer journey mapping is incredibly open and it's been more important now where data is at the heart of what we do. So, both in terms of the communication industry and the sales side of the industry. Their both using data in a completely new way and that data can inform the customer journey and therefore it becomes an integral part of the map. I think that what is different now is that you've got this data glue that actually glues the two ends of the map together. Therefore, you can much more easily see that what you do at one end of the map impacts what comes out at the other end of the map. I think, partly, the consumer journey and the consumer driven mapping has been a strategic tool in the past whereas now it's much more of a tactical tool. It's a tool that can actually adjust the individual choices you make in communication and sales and you're price.

Amazon is a great example of that. Amazon does not distinguish between communication and marketing and sales. It's one in the same. They say that they will do both or a combination or the one thing that is just the... take care of the entire consumer journey. And you have things like re-targeting which has been very popular but without a proper consumer journey mapped out, you're almost shooting in the dark even with re-targeting. So, you need to know what your consumer journey is. You need to understand why people didn't do what they didn't do as much as why they did do what they did do.

So, yeah, I think the short answer is I think it's much more of a tactical tools now and it informs all the ways of the sales and the ROI on an investment where it's a more strategic tool in the past and therefore not seen as important."

Steffen Hjaltelin, Founder & Partner at Hjaltelin Stahl.

"What I think has changed completely in the last two or three years are the demands for the CMO. The way we see is the necessary to look at the world in different layers. We call it, "Platform Present and Peaks." And when it comes to... Because that's the way you have to sort of divide your thinking as a CMO.

First of all, you have to ask yourself the question, "Do I have the right, proper platform, the digital infrastructure to be connected with my audience?" That goes from your marketing automation system, to your CMS, to your app presence, etc., all the digital platforms.

On top of that, "What is my always-on strategy? How can I produce content to be relevant 24/7, 365, when people are actually looking for my product?" On top of that, when you have that in control, one of my peaks: "How do I attract new customers into this marketing system?" That's what you could call it. We call it the ignitions in large campaigns, but basically, how do I make the explosions that everybody will notice like the Momondo Digital, the DNA journey as it was called... Danish, long-form video reaching 400 million. Beautiful work. But you can only make that on top of having everything else in order.

When it comes to customer journey, that is the thinking about: How do we get people through this? And it's actually a contradiction in terms because in this world we know that ... we call it a fly-in-a-bottle purchasing process, because people... they go all different ways into the actual buying. In the old days, people were looking at a TV commercial. They picked up the information on the company's website. Perhaps they went to a store and then made the purchase.

For instance when it comes to buying a new kitchen, that was something that happened... installing it during Easter and then just going backwards. You had the campaigns in January in the old days a few years ago.

Now, the first time you just think about buying a new kitchen, you'll make the first search on your telephone, on your iPad in the evening enjoying a half-cup of coffee or tea, you'll put it aside. Two weeks later you might look at it again from another angle. You might have had a few brands that you were considering before you started. Your first searches will give you some referrals. You'll get pointed in different directions. You'll find out that what you were looking for might not have tested well on test sites. You'll be pointed in different directions. We can see from the diaries that we make that people are easily visiting 70 to 80 different diligent touch points just in this research phase.

At one point you just decide that you know enough to make a mental purchase, either going to a retail store or just thinking, "This is the brand that I'm going for," and going into a more traditional purchase mode for that particular brand. But when on earth is that going to happen? This whole process ... from the first time you think about a new car, a new kitchen, whatever... could be over two years, because it's that easy. And you get pointed in all different directions. And that is actually the case why you need to be present, always. And that is the thinking behind the "always-on".

We are trying to map the customer journey in this whole regard, but I just told you it's fly-in-a-bottle. How do you do that? That is actually... that's the contradiction in terms. The answer is that you just have to. You have to predict different possible narratives for people to go forward. And based on behavior at one place, you give them the relevant information the next place they're going to. We are trying to do what is not possible to actually do, to make order in chaos, because we had to do that. And then you try to describe the few possible patterns and journeys, and optimize towards that."

Petter A. Stordalen, Founder and owner of Nordic Choice Hotels.

"If I should say one thing, that makes a success and is an important part of success, it's culture. Most people think that it's money, and that the strongest always survive. That's wrong. It's even wrong that it's a misinterpretation of Darwin. If you think that Darwin said it's the survival of the strongest, it's wrong. What it's actually saying is, it's not the strongest that survive, it's the ones most adaptable to changes. So always be adaptable to changes because the world changes fast. Technology, everything. The future of the hotel industry is also about the digital guest journey."

Steffen Hjaltelin, Founder & Partner at Hjaltelin Stahl.
"To find and collect the actual data to be extremely efficient in the customer journey, you have to go to the source. That is why we see companies like Salesforce and the huge, huge IT companies that go into the marketing automation, because they have the actual transactional data.

When you look at IKEA, for instance, they have the swipe when people actually buy something. That means that when we know that people have bought a kitchen, the next thing they're going to be met with is all the things they need for the kitchen. But you need that. When you don't have that you see what some of the terrible retargeting that you see … that when you're looking for a pair of sneakers and you already bought them, then the next three weeks you're haunted by other offers that are extremely irrelevant for you at that particular point because you already bought it or decided not to buy. That is terrible.

The only place where you get the actual is when you get close to the actual transaction. So we see now strong, strong players coming from the transactional side, from the internal side, and from the companies' ERP systems and going outside into the media. That is one central place.

The other places, of course, are huge social media. You get closer with Facebook and the Google products because they're extremely good at having people actually giving you the right to use their information. The worst place ever is banners... Just traditional banners, and the whole banner-thinking, in our opinion, is close to being dead."

Petter A. Stordalen, Founder and owner of Nordic Choice Hotels.
"So why do you think I spend more money right now to invest in this than in the hotel? We spend actually 30, 40 million dollars in an app where you can find a hotel, or find a destination, find a hotel. You can book it. You can pay your hotel. You can check in. This is also your key. And then, you can pay, check out, everything. Then the reception doesn't need to do all this technical work. They can go and talk with you about other things.

I guess within the next six months, if you download this app, you'll also have after you've booked a room at Nordic Choice, you will just, a day or two before, or are supposed to check in, on your phone it pops up a picture of a new room. If you pay $10 we will upgrade you, and then you will have a small balcony, or a bigger room, or a king sized bed, or ocean view... whatever. And it's easy, just by saying, okay, you accept it. That's upsale. And we are doing nothing without, everything is done by this. This is the future. We are the first one in the world that launched an app *like this, and we will be the first one to have the best digital journey. Because this is the future. Not for you, because you and I, I'm older than you but, I'm 54. But when I asked my daughter, she's using this one. But she's using this one very different from me. And you need to understand that generation, because that's my future guests."*

Steffen Hjaltelin, Founder & Partner at Hjaltelin Stahl.

"When it comes to the amount of information a creative team will need before they can actually go into solving the problem and solving the brief, I think it's very different. When it comes to always-on, the very transactional creativity leading close to sales, basically as much as possible, because you need to understand the path in full. In that regard, it needs to be a lot. You need to have the strategic planner, the client service director working close to understand the business part of it.

I would actually say that when it comes to the peaks, to the explosions where you make, for instance, the long-form videos to be seen by hundreds of millions, it's not so important. In that regard, you have to be so broad. If you see the first 100 ideas, they are all over the place, and they should be because that's the only way you can get the span from where you can find the truly unique solution. And it needs to be truly unique. In that regard, it needs to be truly unique, because we need to get people's attention on the mobile phone. Everything is on the mobile phone. For me to get your attention on a mobile phone, it needs to be extremely relevant, extremely entertaining ... are coming from influences: your friends and family. You're giving me five seconds to decide whether it fills one of those criteria.

It needs to be extremely interesting, not compared to other commercials, but compared to anything you could see online on your mobile phone. Therefore, we need to... it takes a lot of time to find out something that is actually unique enough for that. You might not succeed. You have to be open to that. So very tight when it comes to always-on, very broad when it comes to ignitions and the campaigns that are going to attract completely new audiences."

Big data.

Big data refers to the ever-increasing volume, velocity, variety, variability and complexity of information. For marketing organizations, big data is the fundamental consequence of the new digital marketing landscape.[42]

Big data can deliver insight in terms of whom your customers are, where they are, what they want, how and when they want to be contacted. It can help you discover what influences customer loyalty, or determine the optimal marketing spend across multiple channels, as well as continuously optimize marketing programs through testing, measurement and analysis.[43]

Interviewees.

Johan Boserup, Global CEO of Trading at WPP's GroupM.

"Big data has become quite a buzz word. I think it's misused in a lot of ways. Undoubtedly it's incredibly important for our industry- the media industry and communication- but also for other industries. But, the funny thing is that we've actually, in the media industry, we've been using big data in a certain form for the last twenty to twenty-five years. The media agency industry was founded on the ability to suddenly track people's media patterns- readership surveys that were 100,000 people that were

---

[42] Boyd, Danah & Crawford, Kate. (2012). "Critical Questions for Big Data, Provocations for a cultural, technological, and scholarly phenomenon". Pages 662-679. | Received 10 Dec 2011, Accepted 20 Mar 2012, Published online: 10 May 2012.
[43] Hellerstein, Joe. (2008). "Parallel Programming in the Age of Big Data". Gigaom Blog.

being monitored about what they were reading. We had a millions of lines of data for ratings of TV programs that we would analyze and optimize on. Much smaller data sets than what we call "big data" today, but the same principles applied.

So, I have to think that big data is incredibly important. My company, my career, and everything we do in this industry is founded on that. The success and the value that we've brought to the table is founded on big data. But, I think that we could go a lot further on big data. Obviously, as the different parts of the consumer journey is now bound together by this data. We can extract a lot more value from it. Whereas, the traditional big data sets that we were working on- sort of ratings and readership, they were just media metrics. They were just "what happens in the media." There was no link to what the consumer thought; what they did; what they bought; and how they reacted to it. We can now make those links.

Big data is becoming incredibly important to inform the decisions that we make every step of the way. Therefore, obviously, at the end of the journey - in terms of the performance that we generate - and if you use big data right, it's not as much about the big data as it is about the analysis that sit on top of the big data. For example, we can measure modeling or machine learning. If the data set is big enough, it can articulate what does a choice in terms of media do for the return investment and the sales and the performance.

Once we do that, we can actually articulate to a customer, or client, or an advertiser- what is the value contribution that we bring from optimizing the individual plans. We can only do that through big data. Big data, you can argue, is the foundation of media agencies. It's the only reason that we can do what we do, it's because we have big data and we use big data."

Dr. Kate Stone, Director Novalia.

"I guess to me it means kind of an amalgamation of lots of data and lots of information that is somehow not personal. So, we don't need to know the details but if we can understand the trends, then we can use that to predict things and to create environment that benefit the detail. So, if I'm the detail in amongst that data and somehow that's obscured, but it predicts and creates a world that is better for me then I'm okay with that. So, big data should mean so big that I'm not known in it."

Klaus Riskaer Pedersen, Entrepreneur, Author, Founder of CyberCity and CopyGene. Fmr. member of the European Parliament (MEP).

"We all need it, we all use it, and we all hate it. That's it. Who loves big data? Nobody. I don't like big data. Why should they have big data on me? I don't want anybody having big data about anything, not all myself. But I love it. We need it. We do algorithms. We can spin over a lot of marketing tools, we can actually ... To be realistic, big data is the new editor of the internet. Instead of having editors sitting in some closed up newsroom somewhere, editing everything. Who cares?

We can do algorithms where we can do instantaneous editing and adaption to, profiling users so they don't waste a lot of time seeing a lot of stuff they don't want. It is a very, very, very useful tool. It is very good for marketing purposes. It will probably be very interesting when you combine it with block-chain. You can probably actually establish some very, very interesting algorithms in the field of political development and network democracy. Can get a lot of interesting possibilities here if you add these two things together."

Lars Seier Christensen, Founder and owner Seier Capital, Co-founder and fmr. CEO Saxo Bank.

"First of all, I think people talk a lot more about it than actually executing it. Big data's like a buzz word, and everybody's talking about it, but it's actually very, very few companies that are good at handling data, or even good at collecting data. We're not super great at it in Saxo Bank either, but what we focused a lot on in the last few years, we're getting a lot better at it now, and of course in the perfect world, it allows you to deliver in a timely and orderly way, your service exactly when it's required and exactly tailored to the individual client need. That's the theory, but in practical terms, it's very hard to handle very large data sets.

For example, on the trading platform where you have tens of thousands of people watching tens of thousands of prices and doing many trades, that is a huge amount of data that you generate there and really, structuring that, collecting it is a very, very important exercise. That's where you start. Afterwards, if you have done that properly, potentially you can then use that to enhance your service.

Of course, it is the big thing for the future, is ownership of data, no doubt about it, but there's still very many people that handle it extremely inefficiently, so I think there are big opportunities for people that focus intelligently on collecting the right data. Then from the outset, if you have a new business that you're starting up, make that a very high priority, what data am I going to generate here, what could it be used for, but initially, how do I at least collect it so I have it for the future and I can make those intelligent decisions later on, because actually, sitting with a whole bunch of unstructured data will get you nowhere."

Klaus Riskaer Pedersen, Entrepreneur, Author, Founder of CyberCity and CopyGene. Fmr. member of the European Parliament (MEP).

"My answer is from a technology point of view, from a business point of view, from a political science point of view, it's okay. Primarily, I basically hate my bloody iPhone, and I hate my laptop. I want to get rid of all that stuff, you know? It's taking too much of my time. It's always intervening what I'm doing.

I have started now, when I go out with my girlfriend, at eight o'clock at night I leave my iPhone at home. I don't bring it with me anymore, it's finished. Then I've got this one, which I'm using now. Its very cool, very, very cool. It's only for very, very short text messaging and calls. I have five kids, I want them to be able to call me. This is a private one, and my iPhone 5s, and I don't want to upgrade because the thing is more than enough than what I need, it's fine, I use it during the day. Unfortunately I have to use it, with all the messages and interaction with all my systems, I realize that's how it is.

My answer is, big data, digitalization, all that. I really want it to go a little bit back, I think it's going too far. Politically and privately I'm against it, I want to go more analog, I want to go back to the analog world where you can touch and feel and smell. Where things are more lovely, people's relationships are being developed much more, much more intensively directly, and what you eat and what you do is healthy and it's green and it is carbon neutral. I want things to be fine, you know, and a nice world we're living in. And all this stuff here is a little bit against it, including big data. What do we do? Well, business is business as we say, and Moses is Moses. That's how it is."

Stefan Kehl, Market Director Nordics (Norway & Denmark), SET, AppNexus.

"I associate big data with the enormous data explosion, which we have seen in the recent years. And I'm sure you've all seen this graph showing the exponential growth in data creation in recent years driven by the internet of things, social media usage and also increased internet penetration. But big data is not the same as smart data. And the ardent challenge has been to truly identify the data, which is valuable and useful for your business objectives and focus on that data. It's also that data is like a ... It's obviously more crucial than ever before as we are entering the programmable age and the programmable age is our way of describing a new era in which the once static internet of web browsers and email has become much more dynamic in customized, containing billions of interconnected apps and devices and users.

Each of them feeding a massive data loop, which allows for highly dynamic personalized digital experiences at scale. And my advice to future marketers would be to really understand like the immense value of data and don't just give your data away to vault guarding companies. You need to own your data and you need to own, have full ownership over the date loop in order to learn, enrich and train your data in order to drive more personalized more intelligent advertising decisions."

Social media & viral marketing.

Social media is the social interaction among people in which they create, share or exchange information and ideas in virtual communities and networks. Examples are: Facebook, Google +, Friendster, Linkedin, Twitter and YouTube.

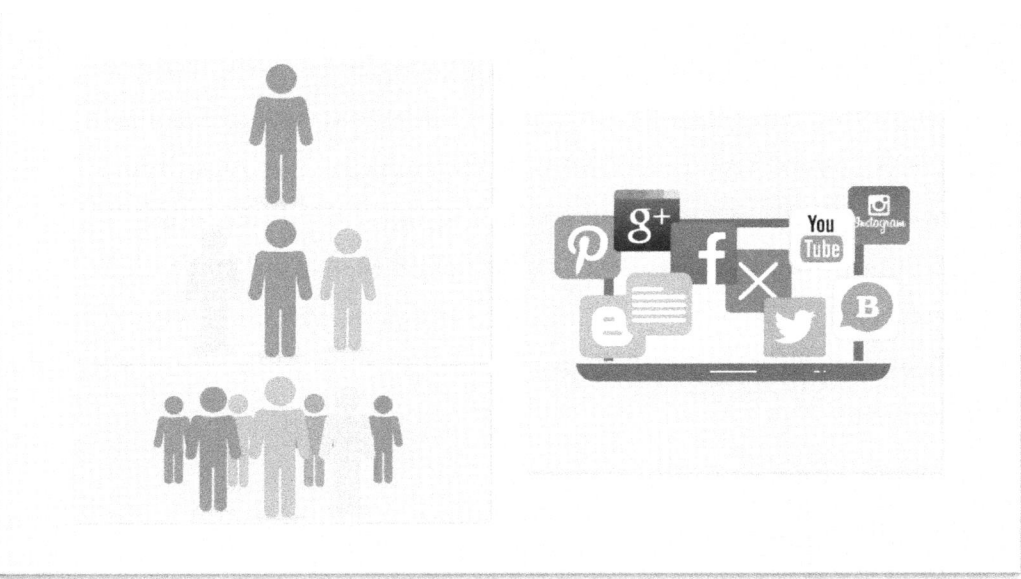

Figure 27.

The media is characterized by: Transparency, authenticity, decentralization of authority, collaboration and speed. It serves as an effective corporate tool in regard to:

Employee engagement.
Market research and product development.
Media relations.

243

Crisis management.

Customer service.

Community-building.

However it's important to monitor the situation carefully or develop social media guidelines, as transparency, authenticity, decentralisation of authority, collaboration and speed makes the media difficult to control in regards to brand consistency, rumours, complaints etc.

The terms viral marketing, guerilla marketing, or buzz marketing are buzzwords referring to marketing techniques that use pre-existing social networking services and other technologies to increase brand awareness or to achieve other marketing objectives through self-replicating viral processes[44]. It can be delivered by word of mouth or enhanced by the network effects of the Internet and mobile networks. The idea is that people will pass on, and share striking and entertaining content.[45]

Interviewees.

Klaus Nørskov, Head of communication Red Cross.

"There's a lot of interesting measurements about the digital reality, so to speak. I think ... Actually we were speaking about this yesterday at a meeting, the last 3 years, if you look at social media, have been a

---

[44] Surowiecki, James (2016). What happened to the ice bucket challenge? Derided at the time as "slacktivism," the social-media campaign has had surprisingly long-lasting benefits. The New Yorker, The Financial Page July 25, 2016 ISSUE.
[45] Worland, Justin (2014). ALS Ice Bucket Challenge Donations Just Topped $100 Million Time, Aug 29.

revelation, basically. To substantiate that, the digital strategy that we decided 3 years ago is very, very ... It's not like "Oh, Facebook. What's that?" It's that we knew about social media, but we knew nothing about the potential of social media, at the time. Over the last 3 years, I think it's been one very, very fast and steep learning curve for us, I think for everybody, actually. Today, without a doubt, Facebook is our most important channel of communication. We have reached with single posts that exceeds what even the most popular television program in Denmark can achieve."

Peter Holten Mühlmann, Founder and CEO, Trustpilot.

"The 1st advice I've given on using social media and viral marketing is to produce some content that you yourself genuinely cares about and that you yourself really think is cool content. Come up with something that you would love to read. I think way too many people think they have to be on Twitter. They have to be on Facebook. They have to do X tweets per day. Then, they end up doing some content that's not really interesting for anybody. They're just mass producing garbage."

Mikkel Borg Bjergsø Founder and CEO Mikkeller brewery, bars and restaurants.

"It comes from me. It's my personality. It's something that I guess my employees have learned. We don't control it. We don't control them. Obviously there are things that they're not allowed to do, which means that they cannot put up stuff that our company doesn't believe in, or that I don't believe in. It's pretty much, again, my personality that they have to show together with their own personality.

I think I have employees that know the basic moral of the company, and they show that in what they do, and on all our social media platforms. But it comes from me. They're copying my personality. Even though I give them a lot of freedom, I'm also very controlling in some ways, which means that they know. I don't have to say to my employees, but they know what I don't like to do, what I don't like to show for Mikkeller, so they kind of follow that."

Benjamin Holk Henriksen, Strategic planning & branding. Lecturer DIS and Copenhagen Business School, Author, Filmmaker "The Mind of a Leader", "Holk Master-class".

"I believe that social media campaigns and viral marketing campaigns have become increasingly important. Look at how many job postings you see for social marketing managers etc. And how much buzz we hear about user interaction, collecting data on social media platforms, big data etc.

Examples of social media campaigns varies from simple postings, I believe a musicians like Taylor Swift will get up to 230.000$ for just promoting a product, endorsing a product on her blog, to bigger large scale campaigns like one of the first, the ALS ice bucket challenge for Lateral Sclerosis which would create awareness to the cause and where people either had to donate or dumb ice water over their head. This went crazy viral on the internet, shared, shared, shared, shared and before we knew it Bill Gates, Oprah Winfrey, Cristiano Ronaldo were participating and supporting the cause

Another example is the Air Asia campaign. Where you could invite about 300 of your friends to fly for free from Australia to Malaysia all you needed to do was you needed to tag them in the campaign, where they would be seated in the plane, and if you were the one that actually got selected you could win tickets for all your friends to go flying and that also got a decent amount of attention.

But again at the end of the day it depends on the message I believe, what you have to offer. You need to offer something whether it's an emotional message, a connection with the audience, if it's just about creating ideas, I don't think that's enough, a lot of people are doing that but with no effect so I believe you need some kind of connection with your audience. Emotional connection."

Matthew Bagwell, Managing Director Naked Communications Europe.

"Sometimes we get asked, "Can you do us a 'Ice Bucket' challenge?" Can we do something which either a competitive brand has done, or someone else has done, and it's created incredibly powerful engagement. Whether it's become a meme, or whether it's actually generated an awful lot of revenue.

There's a tendency sometimes for people to sort of say, "Okay, there's a formulaic way that we could do this, and we could capitalize upon it." I think people are getting savvy to when something is true and less true. I think it's a real danger just to sort of say, "Please create us a meme, such that we can be perceived to be doing good, but actually what we're on is, we want cheap reach, or we want high engagement for little money. We want people to do the work for us, let's jump on this bandwagon." I think we always have to start with what is the purpose of your brand, what are you trying to achieve as an organization? How does that impact society and culture? And within that, we'll find the things which they can genuinely be involved in, and could be incredibly powerful for them.

I hate that shit where we literally get, "Create us," you know this because you're in the business of distributing your content through sort of engagements that, people sharing it, the virality of your content. We often get asked, these must be the constituents of a successful campaign, people must nominate other people, people must do something ridiculous, people must be able to Facebook it, and there must be some video, obviously, these days, because that's the only stuff that creates engagement. Then there needs to be some cats and some unicorns, and a rotund person, because that's funny. You kind of get this formulaic response, and honestly I've received them, "Please do me one of these." I can remember when, and this is not related necessarily to community marketing, but I think it's sort of adjacent to it. "Please create us a Felix Baumgartner." The number of brands who sort of said, "Okay, we want that moment," you know, most people have seen that piece of content, an incredible achievement as a piece of content."

Peter Holten Mühlmann, Founder and CEO, Trustpilot.
"Then, in regards to virality; if you're 1 of the 10 geniuses that can come up with something viral and you can do that consistently, great for you. Then, do that. If you stumble upon something viral, that's also fantastic. If I read a business plan and they say, "Month 3, we'll launch our viral

campaign." Then, I'm just smiling. I'm saying, "I'm looking forward to seeing the results of that.""

David Angelo, Founder & Chairman, David & Goliath advertising agency.

"I will tell you something that I'm part of now, that I believe is on the cusp of being one of the greatest things I've ever done. It was the culmination of all the things that I've created, that has now led to a certain point. All the campaigns I've ever created, whether it was a campaign I did in my first year in advertising, for the New York Lottery, to work that I did for a tequila brand, or for a car brand. I mean, all of those have contributed to where I am today.

I would say that one of my greatest aspirations is to take our agency philosophy of being brave and make it accessible to the rest of the world. Because it's not something that I own, it's something that's in all of us. If I can inspire, if I can put something out there in the world, that inspires people to believe in the power of their authentic core, if I can get them to just believe, and have the courage to be true, to be who they really are. If I can do that, I don't need credit for that, I would just love to be a spark of something really great.

I have something that we're working on right now, that I can show you, that is really starting to pick up a lot of speed. It's called, 'Today I'm brave' and it's a philosophy that started, or it's an idea that started in Sierra Leone, with a group of, a school of 300 kids, called the Muddy Lotus school. These are kids who are, for the most part, up against some pretty tough challenges in Sierra Leone. I don't know if you've ever been there, but it's, whether it's starvation or Ebola, they are up against challenges that we can't even fathom. As an agency we banded together with an organization called 'Shine On Sierra Leone' which created the school. Our goal was to take our brave philosophy and insert it into the school, and watch what happens when we do that. What's happened over the last six months, how it affected them and transformed them, and how they in turn inspired us, has been nothing short of amazing. Now it's going viral, now it's starting to move around, because it started in Sierra Leone and now it's going all around the world. People from all over, of all different ages and races and creeds and et cetera, religions, are all submitting videos, or pictures of themselves being brave. Whether they're up against cancer or dyslexia, or starting a new job, or taking a test, or whatnot. It started with this T-shirt called, 'Today I'm brave' and now the T-shirt is making its way around the world. The great thing about that is it's not an add at all. It's taken the power of authenticity..."

Klaus Nørskov, Head of communication Red Cross.

"The social media reality, basically also changed the scope of campaigning or the opportunities in your campaigns. Giving that everybody is their own communication manager, giving that everybody owns their own channels, and everybody is building their own network and their own target groups through Facebook and elsewhere, the more that you are able to tap into those channels, the better that you are able to inspire people to use their own channels to communicate whichever issue you want to communicate. The more you have success with this, the more reach you have. Basically, the third party, and the third party being everybody, being like employees, being volunteers, being friends, being family, the more third party endorsement, the more third part

communication, the more borrowing into everybody else's channels you can achieve, the further reach, the more impact ... Not only impact, actually because you reach, not only more people, but you reach different people. You reach people that you wouldn't have been able to reach in any other way, or at least you would find it hard to reach in any other way."

Paid, owned, earned media.

Social media is often referred to in relation to the model Paid, Owned and Earned media.

Paid.

Paid media are the channels an organisation uses to target so called strangers. Examples are Print, Television, Radio, Magazines, Cinema, Outdoor, Banners, Direct mail, SEM, Paid Search, in-store media etc.

Owned.

Owned media are the media channels an organisation uses to reach or correspond with its customers. Examples include brochures, retail stores, company website, Microsite, community, Facebook Fanpage, Mobile apps etc.

Earned.

Earned media are channels that an organisation uses to communicate or interact with its fans. Examples are word of mouth, Facebook, Twitter, Digg, Youtube, Flickr, blogs, forums. Brand content uploaded by consumers may also be referred to as "social currency".

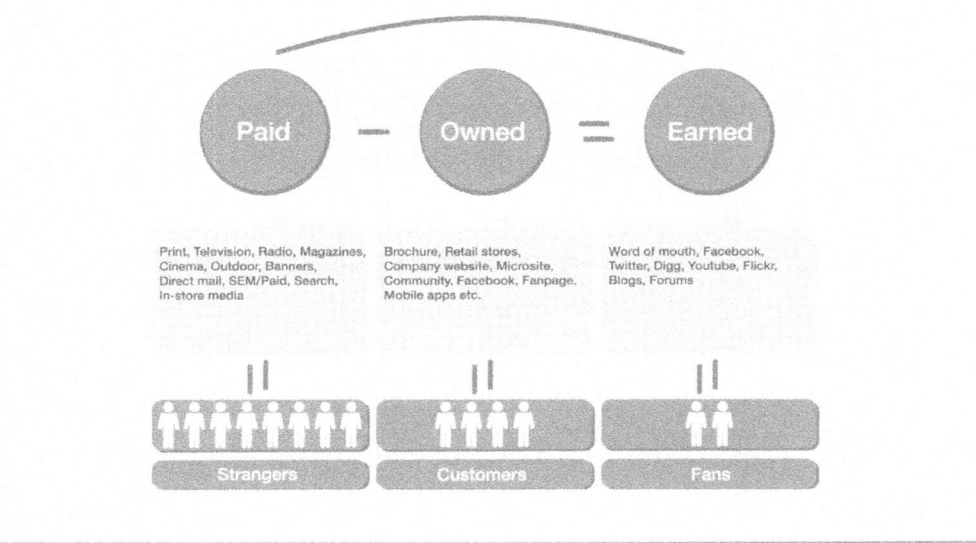

Figure 28.

The idea is to move the potential target group from being strangers to customers and fans.[46]

Social media is often used for content snacking. We take little bites here and there... share and like, instead of watching a full commercial or reading an article. Thus content must be intriguing and captivating.

Interviewees.

---

[46] Ceren Demirci, Koen Pauwels, Shuba Srinivasan & Gokhan Yildirim (2014). Conditions for Owned, Paid, and Earned Media Impact and Synergy, Marketing Science Institute, 14-101.

David Angelo, Founder & Chairman, David & Goliath advertising agency.

"Today's consumer has a megaphone that is bigger than ever before. They have the power to call bullshit on a brand, and they can help create a brand, if you share those values, if you're true to who you are.

One of the great advantages of social media is that you have the ability to turn people into fans, and then turn fans into ambassadors. I believe that is the great advantage of social media, that if you tell your story right, and you do it in a way that is authentic, inspiring and contemporary. Like you telling a story for the most part, that if you do that in a way that connects with them, connects with that on an emotional level, connects with that belief system of theirs, then they don't see you as a brand anymore. They don't you as a product, they don't see you as a brand, they see you as one of them. Then what happens then is they don't feel the need to be paid by you or anything like that, they don't mind sharing you, because you're true, you're just like one of their good friends."

Johan Boserup, Global CEO of Trading at WPP's GroupM.

"I think the Paid, owned, and earned Model has become very popular because it's simple and it's proven that it works. It's not just that the model is simple, it's also that the logic behind it is simple. What you do in terms of your consumer touch point, how you communicate to a potential and an existing consumer, obviously they don't see that as separate. They don't see that as, "Oh, this is the company's own website, so now they are talking to me in that context." Or "This is an advertisement from this company and therefore they're talking to me in that context." The consumer doesn't see it that way. So, in fact, the fact that we have these

three different components of the model that were invested by the people behind the curtain and not the consumer. I think it' ... when you just put those three together, you get so much closer to the consumer and also you're able to so much more efficient in your communication to the consumer because you can link these different touch points together. Obviously, you can take it a lot further and you can make it a lot more sophisticated than just linking those three together. But, a lot of advertisers still don't do that. So, I think it's a very, very good place to start."

Mikkel Borg Bjergsø Founder and CEO Mikkeller brewery, bars and restaurants.

"Our marketing is pretty much based on social media, which means it's free. Obviously we have employees, but we have a social media guy, but a lot of our employees actually have access to our social media accounts because what I think is most important and what we have done from day one, and we still do, is that you communicate in a very personal level to customize to your fans. If you try to use social media as a way of advertising, and as a way of selling your product, I think it's not going to be a success. You might as well put an ad in a magazine.

We communicate in a very personal way. We kind of have built a community on our social media platforms, where we communicate with out customers, and we show ourselves. I show my personality in what we do. People know what I drink, what I like to drink, what I like to eat, pretty much what my family looks like. I never put my kids on my social media, but I mean, there's a lot of things that, when I meet people, they feel that they know me, which is not common with a company of our size, that you communicate that way, but we hear that people love that way of communicating, because they feel they're a part of our world. They know what we do and what we eat for lunch at the office and where we go when we go out and stuff like that, and I think that's really important.

There are a lot of companies of our size that always take the perfect picture and it's always set up, and there are competitions and you win this and that, or buy this and that, and then you get this and that. It's not our way of doing things, and I don't believe in it."

Birgitte Mabeck, Head of fundraising and marketing Red Cross.
"We are very much in favor of social media, of course. We are strongly working with the media. Everybody would like to be in the earned media, but in order to be on the earned media, you have to make yourself earned to be that. Of course, we using both the paid because we can't really rely on people to find our sites if we don't also use paid media. We are on all, paid owned and earned. We were working all three levels. Doing that, social media is good. It's good to see how many people are raising their hands and so forth, but really what's most important for us is to make sure that they not only raise the hand but send us a text message or somehow leave a footprint so that we can re-contact them. For us, it's all about leads. We need to know more about people so we can re-contact them and tell them a little bit about more of our offer and basically make a sale to the people.

If we at the Red Cross were only to do petitions, we would probably not get the same result as we would wish for because when you do a petition you only get the thumbs up and the minimum of a footprint. You don't really get the phone number. You don't get the basic data to re-contact people."

Matthew Bagwell, Managing Director Naked Communications Europe.

"There is a bit of a myth that if you create incredibly engaging experiences, then you will not have to pay for it. I don't believe that, genuinely you are going to pay for people to be engaged with your brand, loyal to your brand. The question is where you pay for it, in my opinion. If you make a product that isn't brilliant, you are going to pay for it by advertising it.

I think advertising is the tax of bad product and service design, frankly. It's many things as well, but it certainly can be that. I think you're always going to pay, if you want create attention, you're either going to pay for something that's amazing, that creates natural, or earned attention, or you're going to pay to actually get the eyeball, because actually what you're trying to attract people to is not that interesting. Brands always pay. Frankly, the question is, "Can we pay less and earn more?" I actually think you need to pay more to earn more. We get the question, "We want to do something highly engaging in social, so that we don't have to pay for so much television advertising." Doing great things in social channels may not cost less, because you always have to pay."

Christina Bilde, Spokes person Roskilde Festival.

"I think we're quite privileged, we've always had a very engaged group and large group of followers even before social media and Facebook and that means, having social media and having Facebook is just giving us

even better opportunities of staying in dialogue and staying in contact, getting ideas and asking for inputs, nursing the relations that we have with our followers. We use that quite a lot. We use Facebook very much. We use Snapchat quit a lot. Twitter, not as much. That's a matter of resources actually. Then, Spotify and YouTube as well because it gives us different opportunities. But relation marketing and relation nursing, I think you could call it, is something that the social media are really helping us to do. They help us create and nourish that community that was already there.

We also have the pre-paid posts and, as I said, in Denmark that might not be as necessary but in other parts of the world that is something that will help us. It also depends on what issues that we want to put forward. When it's music, it's natural then people are really interested in. If we want to talk about equality, which was our main theme this year, we have a large group of followers but not as large a group of followers and they may want to interact with us in another way, then we work with Facebook in that area, in a way that fits with that kind of perspective. Something new for us in that is actually getting into a debate-like dialogue which is very interesting when you are also concerned with the more ethical issues or topic. Facebook is giving us new opportunities for doing that."

David Angelo, Founder & Chairman, David & Goliath advertising agency.

"I think you'd have a hard time connecting someone who is authentic with someone who isn't. You know what I'm saying? It's really, you've got to dig so deep to get to know, first and foremost, you've got to dig deep to

get to know yourself, and then bring that out. Then you have to dig deep to get to know the consumer base. Just making sure, when you dig deep, making sure you know what that cultural sort of conversation is going on in their head at that time. What type of music are they listening to, what type of music are they listening to? What type of movies are they watching? What type of trends, what type of furniture they're buying? All that stuff comes into play the more you dig deep. You start understanding a lot of nuances that most people just take for granted. Once you understand that, then you can shape your conversation in a way that it's less of you just trying to sort of engage with them and sell their product, and it's more of you just like saying, talking to them like you would a best friend over a few beers in a bar."

Malin Gardeström, International Marketing Manager, Carlsberg & Tuborg.

"We are working together with the media agencies to make sure that we have the right split and we spend the right money to get both paid, owned, and earned. To me, I feel like earned is getting more and more difficult. Of course a lot of brands out there, we have seen a lot of fun videos on YouTube, people are not as eager to share as we were just a few years ago. Of course, we are focusing a lot of getting the right split on those, and we are focused very much on social media."

Benjamin Holk Henriksen, Strategic planning & branding.
Lecturer DIS and Copenhagen Business School, Author, Filmmaker "The Mind of a Leader", "Holk Master-class".

"Of cause it has a lot to do with the content, your advertising, how you make you advertising but also the product in itself. Otherwise you cannot

be sure that paid media will turn strangers into fans. The strength in owned media is of cause that it's relatively cheap to administrate your own webpages and event and so forth and also that you have a lot of control over it. And of cause where you initially want to get is to the earned, where you actually have forums or social media fan groups where fans interaction with each other and support your message without you even have to do anything.

Examples will be of cause Star Wars, amazing brand and amazing what they have managed to create in terms of fan groups. Same goes with sport clubs, who would have thought that you can actually have people walk around as living billboards with club shirts advertising for companies, that is essentially quite interesting I think."

Johan Boserup, Global CEO of Trading at WPP's GroupM.

"So, I actually really like the Paid, Earned, Owned Model because the media is ... it's on the tin. Paid is what you paid for. The owned is what you owned. Most advertisers have had and done both of those. The new one is the earned media in the middle. The reason why I really like that phrase "earned" is because it's something that you have to earn. You can't just set up a Facebook page or a social media presence and expect consumers to engage with you. You have to earn that".

Strategies in an ever-changing media landscape.

Let's take a closer look at Strategies in an ever-changing media landscape.

Interviewees.

Johan Boserup, Global CEO of Trading at WPP's GroupM.

"The current environment is incredibly, incredibly difficult to navigate. The only constant is change. I can't remember who said that, but it's incredibly accurate for a lot of industries, but particularly our industry right now. I would go as far as to say that everything has changed in the last 10 years in the media industry. For media agencies, we've had to change the way we work, the clients we work for, the results we try to generate for clients, the people we hire, the tools we use, everything has changed. And it's become a lot more complex, a lot more complicated. A lot more difficult. But, also a lot more interesting and a lot more fun.

And one of the things that comes with all of that complexity is it's much easier for us to take the component parts of what we deliver to the market place and to our clients and show them the result of each of them. So, instead of just saying, "This is a good media plan because it reaches a lot of plan." We can say, "This is a good media plan because it will give you this business results." And it's not just about performance in terms of sales. It can be a lot of various different factors.

I think that has ... it means that the industry is much more interesting to be in right now. But, it's also tough. We have to... we've had to over the past ten years adopt a significant level of technology and that means that people who weren't ready to make that change, whether it was a mindset change or a practical change to simply learn new skills and take on a different job, they've had to exit our industry. And we can see that there are some players in the industry, particularly in the media vendor side, that have not been able to make that transition and it's because they haven't hired the right people. They haven't made the technology changes. They've been adverse to change and they haven't been successful.

As one example, I can say that, probably the most significant change in our industry was not the digitalization of media per se, it was the way we trade media. In the past, and still to a degree, you pick up the phone and you say, "I want to be 100 million impressions on Yahoo or whatever it was next month in this target audience and this context or whatever it was." We don't do that anymore. We have machines talking to machines. We have programmatic buying where we buy each individual impression individually. For that, we need a technical set-up that's able to do what we need. We need people with technical skills who operate that. We also need data that can inform those buys and people who understand that data. All of that is an entirely new discipline that we haven't seen before and it requires new people, a new corporate set-up, new communication to clients (who don't understand why we need to do it this way). But in order for us to create a competitive advantage for our clients and therefore for ourselves, we need to push our clients into this sphere.

So, there's been a lot of change in our industry and it's been very, very difficult to navigate. But, if I was to say it comes back to one thing, it comes back to people and it's about the managers who are willing to make the changes and also take some risks at going down wrong avenues some times. It's about people coming in with an open mindset, not saying, "I'm going in with a media buyer and this is what a media buyer does." If you want to be a media buyer, you may not be doing the same thing today that you'll be doing in two years and certainly not the same thing you did five years ago. So, if you have the right mindset, I don't think it's that complicated. But, you have to have the acceptance of change. Otherwise, you're not going to succeed in this industry. Or any other industry."

Dr. Kate Stone, Director Novalia.

"Don't only think about what you're actually doing. The individual thing you're doing or the medium you're trying to use. It's just constantly trying to deeply understand the message and the philosophy and being authentic; being genuinely authentic. And the medium... the changing medium, it's just a channel through which something can flow. And thinking about that, first and foremost, can I genuinely and authentically channel my philosophy and what I'm actually trying to do at the most fundamental level I can think about and not worry too much about the channel. Does the channel allow me to do that? Yes or no? And keep focused on that philosophy and authenticity."

Steffen Hjaltelin, Founder & Partner at Hjaltelin Stahl.

"When it comes to the changing media landscape, what we do is look at actual people's behavior. A leading trend in that, by far, right now is that

people use their mobile phone. If you cannot get people's attention on the mobile phone with the message you are coming with, then you will not get the attention. And you can get the attention either by being extremely relevant with the right email, with the right message, with the right Facebook post if it's for a product that we know you're actually considering. That's one way.

You can get it secondly by extremely entertaining in the regard of not funny-funny, but something that touches you. We see different examples from Dove and other companies like that, that are extremely entertaining.

And then the last part that is very relevant now, and is getting more and more, is the influencer part. That's because for me to have you open that message... if you see it's from your friends... And we see that people actually look at the influences, the YouTubers and the bloggers as their friends. And they actually open messages, and they look, and read, and understand, and act on the messages from them. So that's why we say mobile is going to be the winner. It is. To speak to people on their mobile phone... extremely relevant, extremely entertaining, or from friends and influencers."

Stefan Kehl, Market Director Nordics (Norway & Denmark), SET, AppNexus.

"Right, my advice would be to truly try and understand the ecosystem and try to have at least a basic understanding of the technology driving it. And it's obviously a really important to keep updated and keep learning and to try stuff and if you fail just try again. And it's also

important... It's also growing importance of data and machine learning. But the same time it's really important to remember that we still need human creativity and intuition in order to put all the different pieces together and achieve the best marketing results.

And I think for companies there's several things, which are of huge importance. On the one hand I think it's very important to companies choose technology, which allows them to leverage their consumer insights for their marketing needs while the technology at the same time also protects the consumer's privacy. And it's huge important for companies to invest in their people because in this very, very, very fast changing environment the marketplace it is now more important than ever to have knowledgeable people who are able to navigate through this changing space.

And I also think there's a lot of short term focus in the industry. A lot of like people are being blinded by the colors of their quarterly score cards. I think it's really important to kind of have a longer term perspective and take decisions, which setup your company for long-term success, not just for the next few months but like for five years and in ten years time.

And then obviously it's all about innovation and to innovate and I think to really like innovate in this challenging competitive landscape. It is kind of crucial to perfection the collection and use of data and embrace machine learning and at the same time I think also companies can get better at partnering with other companies in order to drive business innovation."

Molly DeWolf Swenson Founding member / CMO of RYOT.

"Well, I'm a bit biased because the strategy that's worked for us is harnessing new technology and I think that often there's barriers to entry because of price or perceived difficulty of use. I think all of those are perceived, right? You actually just start tinkering or you take a digital content approach to using virtual reality or augmented reality and all the sudden it doesn't cost that much. It just takes one person going and figuring out how to do it and sometimes it is that one evangelist in the organization who is doing it.

But, for us, you know, we've become obsessed with figuring out at Riot how to use technology in service of journalism and story telling.

In our case, virtual reality was sort of the first tool we've found that we thought was really going to help us fulfill our potential as an organization. Because we'd been connecting news and action for years and years. It wasn't until we started telling the same stories but with virtual reality that we saw reactions so strong from people that every single person took action. We'd been gaging our success as an organization not only on how many people were coming to the site and watching our films but also on how many people we were converting from passive reader or viewer into active participant.

Our VR films were doing that better than any other media- better than normal documentary films; better than photos; better than print. So, that's why we jumped in head-first to virtual reality. For us, that's just because that's a story telling technique and we're looking forward to exploring that in augmented reality and in mixed reality and in voice recognition technology and face recognition technology. All of it not because technology is the end goal in and of itself, but because it's a means to an end of communication and story telling and distribution and that's what we use."

Johan Boserup, Global CEO of Trading at WPP's GroupM.

"I think the key thing in terms of what makes the difference in communication and certainly in media buying is that it's not just one thing. It's never just one thing. So, people may say "VR is the new black" or "it's all about programmatic buying" or "it's all about this, that and the other thing." Even... at some point in time, the pendulum, might swing over and it becomes very much about one thing. It will never be completely about one thing. But, the pendulum will always swing back.

And one example is, that... In programmatic buying, for example, it tends to become all about the audience and all about the price. And what we're seeing right now, in the first part of 2017 is a huge what we call "brand safety crisis" across the entire world. Where, we have advertisers whose advertising is showing up in ISIS videos on YouTube because Google does not have brand safety measure that are strong enough. And that happens because we buy audiences. We do not buy contexture, we do not buy the ISIS videos from Google, we buy the audiences that watch ISIS videos and therefore we end up in ISIS videos. Which is, obviously, completely unacceptable.

It happens because the pendulum has swung over so it's all about audiences and all about programmatic buying. Sometimes there will be a counter-reaction, so the pendulum will swing back. Sometimes it will just swing back over time. And 10 years ago, we were all saying "content is king." That's not true either. That's the pendulum too much in the other direction. The truth is somewhere in the middle. And I think on that particular example, the pendulum is swinging back and we'll reach a much better balance.

But, then the next thing. From client's eyes... since the financial crisis we've had procurement departments taking over the communications with agencies. Not just the media buying agencies, but the creative agencies as well, essentially killing creative and killing the good ideas; killing the strategies that we've put in because they just want cheap raw material. Which is not the best for any company either. But, it was what the industry needed for a little while and now the pendulum needs to swing back. That's been harder for the pendulum to swing back from that one because everyone likes cheap. But, cheap is not always right."

Stefan Kehl, Market Director Nordics (Norway & Denmark), SET, AppNexus.

"I think a lot is up to the individual I mean obviously you learn a lot by doing it and working for the right kind of companies. But at the same time I mean I think it's very important to kind of follow like a relevant industry publications and websites and keep up to date. And just like try out stuff as well I mean there's a lot of like, kind of modules about machine learning and artificial intelligence, programming and so forth. I mean you got sites where you can kind of learn to code for free and you can learn a lot of like those things if you have just have the interest and the curiosity.

So I think it's a lot of... Up to like the individual while at the same time I mean it's also like... Obviously for the companies to kind of put the right framework and the right kind of environment for people to learn and to innovate kind of by having the right kind of environment regarding diversity and having cross function and teams so... At our company for example, we have regular Hackathons where we have a lot of people, also non-technical people who kind of try to come up with new ideas. Some, which I think is very good and I think it also needs kind of to be embedded in the culture of the company. Again, like an example from my company we have like three key values. One of them is to see and improve the whole system. Then the best idea is to do so, there being recognized and rewarded, which is also an important aspect. Then again after the idea creation process then it's like a lot to kind of have like a structured follow-up and implementation process of the selected ideas in order to... We kind of also make that innovation come out in the real world and doesn't get lost somewhere along the way."

Part VI. Global management.

Reflection on business development and Ansoff's Product Market Growth Matrix.

Ansoff's matrix is oftentimes used in regard to strategies for growth. It's was first published in the Harvard Business Review in 1957 in an article called 'Strategies for Diversification'. How do we define our growth strategy in terms of new or existing products in new or existing markets?

There are four main categories for selection.[47]

1. Market Penetration.
Marketing our existing products to our existing customers.

2. Market Development.
Marketing our existing product range in a new market.

3. Product Development.
Marketing a new product to our existing customers.

4. Diversification.
Marketing completely new products to new customers.

---

[47] Ansoff, Harry Igor (1957). "Strategies for Diversification". Harvard Business review.

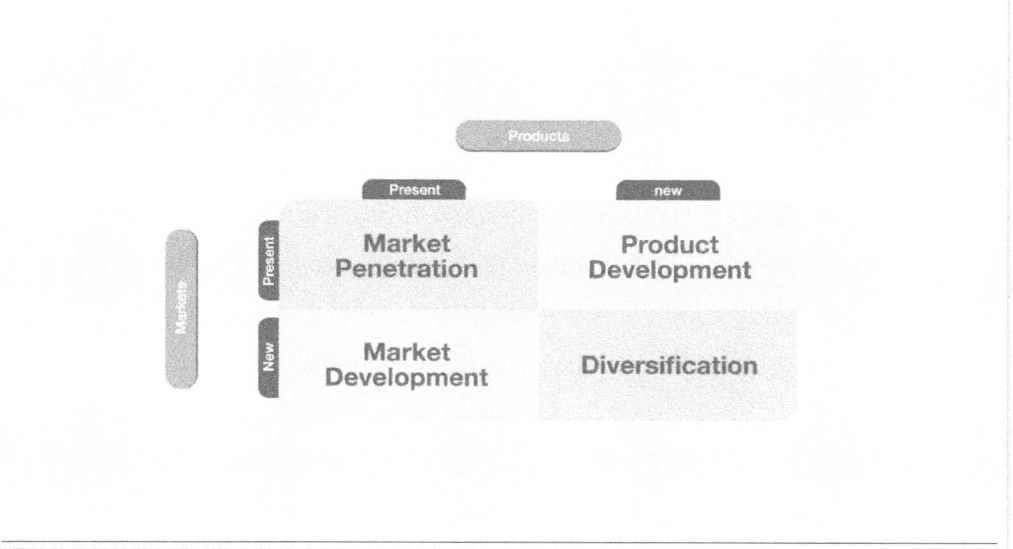

Figure 29.

Useful terms when discussing strategies and making sure everybody is on the same page.

This work presents marketing & communication abstracts. For more details about the theory please view the authors' own works.

Interviewees.

Ole Henriksen, Founder and Creative Director, Ole Henriksen Skin Care Brand.

"Well, when I got the opportunities to bring my products out there into retail, needless to say it was an amazing opportunity, because for one, it was a matter of spreading the Ole Henriksen wellness philosophy. But

271

also it allowed me to travel. Quite frankly, I've always dreamt of travelling and conquering the world, because growing up on the Danish countryside, I didn't get to go anywhere. There was not the money to do so. But, what I did initially was, when the opportunities came in from New York at the time, Henri Bendel who was very big on Fifth Avenue in beauty and fashion, I jumped at that opportunity. I got discovered from there by Harvey Nichols in London. Well I jumped to London, and then I got discovered by companies in Asia, Lane Crawford, a very elegant department store chain in Hong Kong/China, I jumped there.

So initially, I actually didn't have a specific strategy. My attitude was, hey, they want me, I'll be there. I'll be there in five minutes. And I'll do my very best. And I loved the challenge of going into these foreign territories, because not alone did you have to go and train the staff in the stores, you had to work with the media because it goes hand-in-hand. If you don't have the media behind you and spread the message, then you won't get anywhere."

Benjamin Holk Henriksen, Strategic planning & branding. Lecturer DIS and Copenhagen Business School, Author, Filmmaker "The Mind of a Leader", "Holk Master-class".

"...if we look at the four classifications first and there disadvantage and advantage I would say that market penetration involves the lowest risk because you know your market, it's close to you, you know the culture and so forth as long as you increase you advertising budget or your sales force you can have an impact until the market matures and you have to look for new usage of your product or for alternative opportunities.

272

The second one market development is way more risky. Most companies start out by partnering up with a local distributor that knows the culture and the barriers to entry. If you think you can build on your core product and enter a new market setting up a new subsidiary, you need to be aware of the local habits the culture and the restrictions and so forth. So many start with a local distributor, and as they become more successful they will buy back the rights for that market from the distributor which is seen by Pandora, which is seen by Bang & Olufsen the Danish brand.

Then you have the option of developing new products for an existing market which is also risky. That implies that you build on your brand equity and you kind of extend that into new categories. We have seen many examples of how that can be extremely successful, but also less successful if you don't have the same quality and know your target audience. And lastly Diversification which involves two unknowns. That you both build a new product and to a new market that of cause is highly risky and take lots of knowledge and research, but if you can hit it and do it right you can really hit a homerun I would say."

Lars Seier Christensen, Founder and owner Seier Capital, Co-founder and fmr. CEO Saxo Bank.

"I think it's very wise to test the viability of whatever you're doing in an area that you understand. Because if you cannot making it work sitting in the market where we're sitting now, what are the chances you'll make it work in Taiwan? It might be an easy way out, to say now we go international, whatever, but at the end of the day, you need to get your product to work. In my little bit old fashioned way, that means it has to be profitable. I know this is not really a buzz word anymore, you can

build something and if you get a lot of users, you can probably sell it to Facebook or Google or something like that. I respect that that's the dynamics of certain types of business, but for most of us, you basically have to be profitable. That's not a bad strategy.

Before you expand, usually, this is a necessity for the first products to be profitable, I would say prove in the hard way that your product actually adds value to somebody, that you can actually sell it and ... Sometimes I sit with even some of my own portfolio companies and they're really proud about some new functionality or something like that, and I have to ask, did we sell any of this stuff, and they're like, "No, but it'll come with this one."

At the end of the day, you have to sell it. It's got to be, at the end of every PowerPoint, of every process, of every discussion, of every consultant that comes into your company, which I would advise not happens too often, at the end of that process, there's got to be a dollar somewhere because you got to pay the rent, you got to pay your employees and hence, simply try to verify before you ... If it doesn't work in Denmark, or wherever you're situated, I think that the probability it's going to work in America or in Russia or in Taiwan, in Australia is probably very limited.

The more you can prove the viability of your product and the stronger you can actually identify what can improve it further before you go out and scale it big time, I think is very solid advice for most types of businesses. Obviously if it's one where it's only the number of users that count, maybe the dynamics are different, but if you have an unprofitable product, you don't really want more users because you're just going to be

274

even more unprofitable. Make sure it works before you think that you can teach the Americans or the Japanese anything. They probably know their markets better than you do."

Dennis Balslev, CEO IKEA Germany. Fmr. CEO IKEA Denmark.

"We are working with, you can say, the existing markets is number one for us, to grow in what we call common units, is the most important and then we add the expansion to Ikea because if you only built your future on expansion, you have a short future you believe in. I think, I'm responsible for Ikea in Denmark and we can be very proud of going ... We have tripled Ikea Denmark in say turnover and numbers of people the last ten years so it's really something to build on the foundation you have in the different countries. In small Denmark, we put over 2020 ambition so we want to almost increase our turnover 60 percent from 2013 to 2020, which means we really believe in growth in the countries we are in. We can do that through more stores, the way we are working with the range, the pricing, how we meet our customers so that's a lot of opportunities in the countries we are working in today. It's not only about expansion.

We have to be a very healthy business in the existing stores. That's the only way we can pay for the expansion for the company. It's a huge focus on the going units at Ikea in not only Denmark but worldwide."

Peter Holten Mühlmann, Founder and CEO, Trustpilot.

"What's happening in the world is what's called the trust economy. That's enabling services like AirBnb, Uber, just the reviews that you know on Ebay or on Amazon. The way we see it is that's a human foundation.

275

You would not care less about what other people think if you're living in China or you're living in Turkey compared to the people who live in the Netherlands. Also, if you're a business, it would be as important for you to show that you're ... that people can trust you no matter where you are.

We think that the opportunity in front of us is a global opportunity. However, we also know that we don't have unlimited resources. 1st, we're going after some key markets that we very deliberately picked out. As we win those markets, we expand internationally.

Of course, you always make the product stronger. I think, in our case, being an online service; I really believe on the internet that you are successful if you do few things really well. I'd rather just focus on doing the things that we do today and just doing them better, rather than becoming a big conglomerate."

Ole Henriksen, Founder and Creative Director, Ole Henriksen Skin Care Brand.

"So I loved all these things that suddenly came my way. However, as the business grew, and I created a stronger infrastructure as far as management, I realized "Ole, you cannot make five dollars here and ten dollars there". Of course we did make a little more than that. But you began to realize, "Wow, why not stay tighter, more structured, and put your focus where you do the most business and then spread your wings?". So I pulled a little back. And then in the USA and in Canada and Australia and other territories, my focus became the world of Sephora. Sephora being the biggest purveyor of beauty in the world. And what I loved about the Sephora model was that they also ... When they wanted you,

they said, "Hey, let's partner up, but let us help guide you to be successful. If you want a part in all our marketing initiatives, invest your money, it's going to pay big dividends long term". So I did that. And the fact that they also have the biggest website in the world, and very state of the art, it became a win-win for both Henriksen and Sephora.

In northern Europe, I stayed true of course to the established brands like Matas in Denmark, Magasin, and Salling. In the UK, I again, since Sephora doesn't sell there, I did my business there. But I definitely tightened the belt, stayed more focused. And I think that's very, very important. And that really also goes back to this thing of maybe spreading your wings into other areas. Me doing fashion? No. That would be a mistake. And it also, by the way, it doesn't overwhelm you. You have, of course, a tighter grip on things. And why not be profitable that way, and don't stress out? And I think that's very important in this journey towards success. Enjoy the journey. Don't get overpowered, uptight, a control freak. You only have one life to live. And for me, I want to live the life I tell the people to live: have fun, laugh, be celebratory. And you can actually bond the two together: hard work, success, and just having a great life."

Barriers to entry.

Barriers to entry are obstacles that make it difficult to enter a given market.

There are various barriers to entry. Some are a natural part of the environment or given circumstances, whereas others are created to protect own interests.[48]

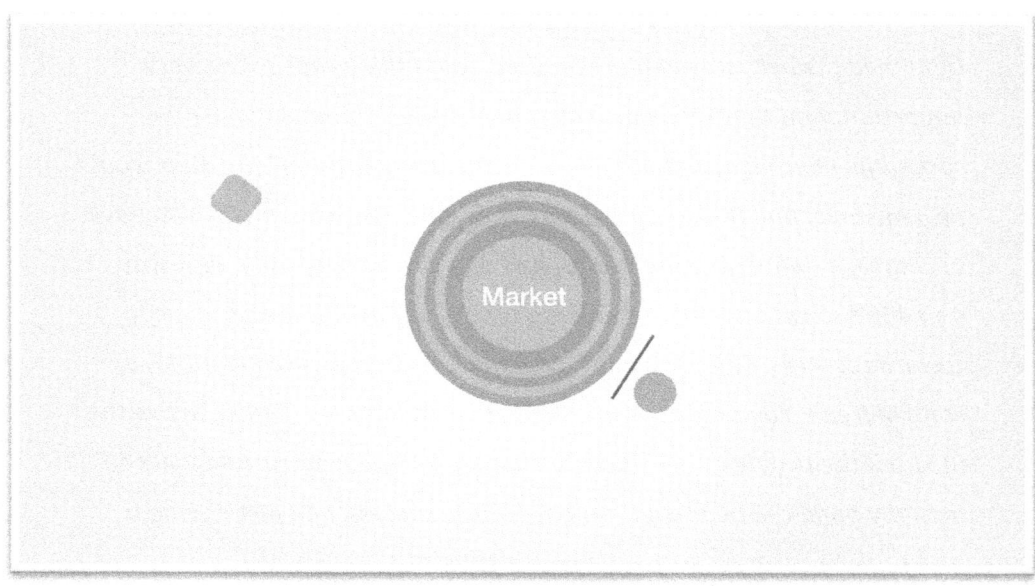

Figure 30.

A few examples:

1. Advertising.

---

[48] Lazaroff, Daniel E. (2006). Entry Barriers and Contemporary Antitrust Litigation, Posted Monday, December 4.

Massive spending on advertising may exclude others from entering a market.

2. Resources.

Control of capital or resources may limit others from entering an industry.

3. Customer loyalty.

4. Know-how.

Geographic limitations in terms of production or distribution.

5. Exclusive distribution agreements.

6. Economy of scale.

7. Government regulations, such as licence requirements, permits, zoning or statutory monopoly.

8. Religion or culture.

9. Intellectual property restrictions.

Issues that should be taken into consideration when entering a new market.

Barriers to entry can force you to adapt or change your business model or strategy. For example restrictions, or a ban on advertising alcohol, may result in the use of brand symbols or logos instead of brand name and text.[49]

Interviewees.

Dennis Balslev, CEO IKEA Germany. Fmr. CEO IKEA Denmark.

"...to be a worldwide company who have done business to be create a better everyday life for the many people, then we want to be in many countries but it's very difficult to go into a new countries. Even in looking around the world, there are many different laws. There are many different interests. India will be the next country. We are now preparing the first store in India. It's took like 15 years to come in. It was discussion from ownership, it was discussions of where to be located. So it's not easy. South America, we would like to go in, but what about sourcing, what about distribution? There are many questions for a company like Ikea, where do we want to go in the future because it's not easy. It was easier 25 years ago when you could more or less come in everywhere. Everybody was open and interested to get you into the country. Ikea still has a strong brand so many countries really want Ikea to be there but it's a lot of laws and regulations that make it difficult.

Also, for us to look into distributions, factory supply, how can we supply as close as possible to the location we want to sell it, to think about sustainability. How do we do it in the smartest possible way? Where do

---

[49] Demsetz, Harold (1982). Barriers to Entry, The American Economic Review Vol. 72, No. 1, pp. 47-57.
Barriers to entry, exit and mobility, The Economist, Jul 13th 2009.

we have the raw materials so there's a lot of things for us to think about when we go into new markets. That's why Ikea has worked out what we call a market penetration plan so we have a big picture of where do we want to be and how do we do that for the next many, many years. Even in Denmark, it took 25 years to get allowed to open a store in Odense on Fyn, we have a very small store but the Danish regulations said no to a bigger store, It took 25 years.

Peter Ålbæk Jensen, Producer, Founder & fmr. CEO, Zentropa.

"Of course there will always exist barriers in terms of exploiting a specific product. Times are changing constantly. Right now, it's almost impossible to get an actor to perform topless. Twenty years ago, we always had to pay them not to take off their bra. Nudity, any kind of sexuality is the most difficult thing to handle. On the other hand, there's both nudity and sex in almost any film. It is a goddamn hypocrisy. Especially the total hypocrisy that there has to be restrictions for what type of film that has to watched in the cinema. Then everybody can wank off watching any kind of porn on their computers. Why does it have to be, that they can take control it in a cinema and not on the internet? That will probably also change."

Malin Gardeström, International Marketing Manager, Carlsberg & Tuborg.

"While Tuborg is a music focused brand, Carlsberg is focusing very much on sports, which might be in some ways more visible as we can have the logo on the shirt. However, legal restrictions making it more and more difficult to have alcohol brands on your shirt. You see us less and less on actually a name sponsorship. But in terms of people of course, having

your brand very close to you, it does make a difference. People are much stronger ambassadors, and have a much stronger relation to your brand."

Kaspar Basse, Founder, CEO Joe & The Juice.

"There are tweaks on different markets and various difficulties on different markets. One of the things that's interesting about our company is, we're tremendously, internally recruited. This means, of course, that we have, on rather high level of management, less experience than many others would have. We also have less traditional ways of thinking and tremendously more ignition and interest and enthusiasm. This means that we actually, honesty do not recognize that there should be any barrier in any country that we cannot over come. We would just go there and deal with it.

This is not talking about Russia or markets where ideally you need to have local partners for various reasons. In the free economy, like we just did in New York, we go there and prepare ourselves as much as we can, and we deal with whatever happens.

There are obviously markets where you can say the total of things are more challenging. Competitiveness. Profitability. A sense of how much do you pay in rent, versus the price level, etc, etc. Ultimately, when you become stronger in a market, you end up, if you are so fundamentally strong and solid, you end up with more or less the same profitability in most markets. That may be also because we are, at the end of the day, a high quality café on high street. That's something the most urban cities have a strong relationship with.

I think we see that penetration might take longer time in some markets, than others, but eventually it will work very well, and at more or less at the same level or lower. Typically where it's very tough, and where penetration takes longer, you ultimately have stronger foundation for more stores and more businesses, because they are larger cities. We will not do anything conceptually to adapt. Unless it's for cultural or religious reasons or whatever. We believe that our products are so random and so high quality, because we do them on the order very fresh, that the taste in that is a very universal appeal."

Petter A. Stordalen, Founder and owner of Nordic Choice Hotels.
We have always had respect when we've entered new markets. Right now we are sitting in Copenhagen, in Denmark. First time I entered Denmark I did everything wrong. I lost more than 100 million dollars in cash. We survived. But the same day I sold my business in Denmark, after taking all the losses, on my way back on the plane, I decided, I'll be back.

That's a quote from Arnold Schwarzenegger, "I'll be back." We will go, and know we have learned. So when life teaches a lesson, like it did with me in Denmark, you learn all your failings. And now I'm sitting here, and we've just taken over the huge Hilton hotel at Copenhagen airport, which nobody believed was possible. Hilton. How is it possible that the strawberry seller can take over the Hilton hotel?

And we just bought a post office here, and we will convert it into a hotel. It's a beautiful building. This hotel we are sitting in right now, it was owned by my competitor. The one that bought my Danish operation. And what happened to that guy? He ran out of cash. And I bought his debt. That's why the hotel is mine today. So today I'm sure that the Danish operation will be a profitable and a strong operation, and we can grow the Danish market at least for the next decade. We have 90 hotels in Sweden, it's been a huge success, but even in the Nordic it's cultural barriers, it's cultural differences between the Nordic countries. Even though we can understand the language, the culture is different in each country. So we work with local people, we work with Swedes in Sweden, Norwegians in Norway, Danes in Denmark. Then we tend to take some Swedes to Norway, so we have this inter-Scandinavian culture. And that's the magic word: culture.

Anne Marie Bülow, Professor at Copenhagen Business School. Dept. of management, society and communication.

"Obviously there have been many models of barriers to entry and there have been models that have been used in the academic world for years like the Uppsala model that meant incremental growth going abroad a little bit and then a little bit so that you've shifted your comfort zone as slowly as possible so that the sole was still in it. It is no longer the only model in the sense that when they talk cultural distance now, it's more complicated. You would expect as many people do expect who haven't tried it before, that if you're out of your comfort zone, it means that the distance is further.

If you go to a country where you are South America for example, you expect the distance to be very great and it could make a difference to the kind of commitment you make. That you would prefer to start with a joint venture rather than a direct foreign investment for example. Fair enough, but research will show that it's blurred, it's not just black and white. It's a series of shades of grey. For example that the distance from here to there is not the same as the distance from there to here. For example, there is research that show that Germans, this group of Germans that they followed that settled in Canada, had a much easier time than the corresponding Canadians who settled in Germany.

Why is that? Distance should be the same? It isn't. We're going to have to talk psychic distance, that the Germans were simply better prepared. They knew about Canada from knowing about cultures in a way that the Canadians did not know about Germany."

Peter Ålbæk Jensen, Producer, Founder & fmr. CEO, Zentropa.
"It is strange that actually our world is pretty free, we are allowed to sell and export practically to everybody except Russia right now because there's an embargo on films. They can only import twenty films and can promise you that is not twenty Zentropa titles that's for sure."

Malin Gardeström, International Marketing Manager, Carlsberg & Tuborg.
"There might be some markets where there are very strong players, and of course we do evaluate all the markets before entering. Of course there's no need to enter in a market where the only reason to be there is to fight head on head with the local very big competitor. So we might take in another brand from our portfolio.

Dennis Balslev, CEO IKEA Germany. Fmr. CEO IKEA Denmark.

285

"When you can go in huge respect for the size of the company and the volumes we will do so when we go into a new market, we should really be sure that we can deliver to the customers what we promised them. For us, we just don't go in and hope the best. We really have to secure the distribution, secure the low price, secure we will be the right place to work with the right laws and regulations. So we prepare ourselves quite a lot today before we go into a new market.

If you take India, there was a lot about ownership, so you can't be owned together with another company. We said no, we want to own it by our self. What is it about the distribution, should it come from Indian suppliers? They cannot distribute or supply a lot of different groups of products so why and how should we do that? That's a lot of questions when we go in. Of course, the idea for Ikea is to come as broad as possible in the world. That's also why we work as a franchise system. We have lot of franchisees who open Ikea in countries where you can say the original old Ikea have difficulties so that's a very strong business model for the last 30, 35 years, the franchise model. This means we can open in more markets and we can do it much quicker and we can again, create a better everyday life for the many people that we can offer them good quality products in a different way than in the market already. It's not easy. It's really a challenge for Ikea with the new markets to come for sure."

Reflection on sustainable competitive advantage, strategy tripod and PEST analysis.

A competitive advantage is defined as a condition or circumstance that puts a company in a favorable or superior business position.[50]

"Control your expenses better than your competition. This is where you can always find the competitive advantage".

Sam Walton founder of Walmart.

"An organization's ability to learn, and translate that learning into action rapidly, is the ultimate competitive advantage"... "If you don't have a competitive advantage, don't compete".

Jack Welch fmr. Chairman and CEO of General Electric.

The strategy tripod.

Three leading perspectives in strategic management are the industry-based view introduced by Michael E. Porter in 1980, the resource-based view advocated by Barney in 1991, and the institution-based view described by Pen in 2002.

---

[50] https://en.oxforddictionaries.com/definition/competitive_advantage

The industry-based view.

The industry-based view focuses on the industry. In relation to his five forces model, Michael E. Porter, list three potentially successful generic strategic approaches to outperforming other firms in an industry:[51]

1. Overall cost leadership.
2. Differentiation.
3. Focus.

The focus strategy rests on the premise that the firm is thus able to serve its narrow strategic target more effectively or efficiently than competitors who are competing more broadly. As a result, the firm achieves either differentiation from better meeting the needs of the particular target, or lower cost in serving this target, or both.

The resource-based view.

The resource-based view advocated by barney focuses on the organizations internal aspects, strength & weaknesses. It is often associated with the VRIO framework, a tool used to analyze firm's internal resources and capabilities to find out if they can be a source of sustained competitive advantage. It starts with vision and objectives, continues with internal & external analysis, strategic choices and implementation.[52]

---

[51] Porter, Michael E. (1980) Competitive Strategy: Techniques for Analyzing Industries and Competitors. Chapter 1. The Structural analysis of industries. Chapter 2. Generic Competitive strategies. New York: Free Press. (Republished with a new introduction, 1998.)
Porter, Michael E. (1996) What is strategy? Harvard Business Review November issue.
[52] Barney, Jay (1991). Firm resources and sustained competitive advantage. Texas A&M University, Vol. 17, No. 1, 99-10.

Value: "Is the firm able to exploit an opportunity or neutralize an external threat with the resource or capability?"

Rarity: "Is control of the resource or capability in the hands of a relative few?"

Imitability: "Is it difficult to imitate, and will there be significant cost disadvantage to a firm trying to obtain, develop, or duplicate the resource or capability?"

Organization: "Is the firm organized, ready, and able to exploit the resource or capability?"

It can be argued that a notable difference between the industry-based view and the resource-based view is, that the industry-based starts from the outside and work it's way in, whereas the resource-based view works inside out.

The institution-based view.

According to Mike W. Peng, the institutional-based view conceives strategic choices as the result of the dynamic interaction between organizations and the formal and informal institutional environment. Peng and his colleagues argue that an institution-based view, in

---

Barney, Jay, Wright Mike, Ketchen, Jr. David J. (2001). The resource-based view of the firm: Ten years after 1991. 20 September.

combination with industry- and resource-based views, will help sustain a strategy tripod.[53]

PEST analysis.

The PEST analysis describes a framework of macro-environmental factors that can be used in the environmental scanning or marketing research. The concept creator thought to be Harvard professor Francis Aguilar, as he included a scanning tool called ETPS in his 1967 book, "Scanning the Business Environment."[54]

The analysis includes Political, Economic, social and technological factors.[55] It is a strategic tool for understanding market growth or decline, brand position, and business direction. The analysis is also referred to as PESTEL or PESTLE, which includes Legal and Environmental factors.

Interviewees.

Mikkel Borg Bjergsø Founder and CEO Mikkeller brewery, bars and restaurants.

"We have advantages but those advantages are built on the fact that I've lived and slept and dreamt about beer for the last twenty years. I've met

---

[53] Peng, Mike W., Li Sun, Sunny, Pinkham, Brian, and Chen, Hao (2009). The Institution-Based View as a Third Leg for a Strategy Tripod.
[54] Aguilar, Francis J. (1967). "Scanning the business environment". New York, Macmillan.
[55] http://www.businessballs.com/pestanalysisfreetemplate.htm

so many people and I have a huge network in the beer community all over the world, which means that we work with a lot of people, we work with the right people. I mean, if you're a small Danish brewery, which we were when I started obviously, and you go and brew with the brewery in Chicago, which is named the best brewery in the world, obviously that's a big advantage because you get your name out, and I actually did that the first year of Mikkeller, because I've got to know those people.

Our advantage is based on our network pretty much. I think networking is extremely important. We're talking about breweries now, it could be other kinds of companies, but if you run your brewery everyday, and you think that you make the best beers in the world, I don't see how you can ever get better, and how you can get your products out. You need to go out and meet people, and learn from people, and network with people, and talk with people, and teach them and get feedback and all that stuff.

I'm very open-minded. When I'm asked who is your biggest competitor, I always say, it's the ones that make shitty beer, because I don't see great breweries as my competitor, even though I know that if the customers see my beer on the shelf next to another beer, they will pick one of them. It could be the other one, if it's a good beer, but I think that's only to my advantage because the more people that we get to drink good beer, the more customers and the more recognition we get. If somebody who normally drinks a Carlsberg wants to try a craft beer for the first time, and he buys a beer and it's really bad, he will never buy another craft beer. I'm very open-minded and I think it's a force that I'm actually sharing recipes and sharing ideas with competitors and colleagues, and again, it comes down to networking."

Henrik Fisker, Automotive designer and entrepreneur (BMW Z8, Aston Martin DB9, V8 Vantage, Fisker Karma, Mustang Rocket, VLF Force 1, Destino V8).

"A sustainable competitive advantage means that you to keep on, first of all, innovating in your company. You also have to understand your own brand. What is it that makes people buy your product versus another product. Where is our core strengths? It can be in different areas. It can be in safety. It can be in usability. It can be in design. It can be in the way the car drives, if you're talking about a car. You have to understand where is our strengths. I do believe that is very important, that once you understand that strength, you have to take that element and keep on innovating and being ahead of the competition, in particular, that area.

I think of course you can look at other areas of your product, in this case, if it's a car and say, "We want to move forward and get a competitive advantage by going into another area of our product and improve it so much that not only do you get this from our product that you already know it's better, but we have added something and therefore have gone in on the competitor's territory to become better." This is usually where a lot of times, things go wrong because a lot of times, the competitive area has been created mainly because you have dedicated first of all, a lot of time and money but also sometimes sacrificed something else to get this. For instance, two examples would be in the car industry, to get an amazing handling of a car, goes around corners amazingly, you sacrifice the comfort. If you now later say, "Well, I want to go into my competitors territory and make better comfort." Now, you're taking away from the sportiness of this car and you're maybe losing some of your core customers.

You might gain some over here but you're start losing some of you core customers. Maybe you gain more customers than you lose, which looks really good short-term. What happens long-term is that suddenly you don't have a competitive advantage anymore because now you're just like everybody else. You actually end up with customers who are not loyal to you anymore.

Another example would be, again, a good-looking car usually sacrifices some interior space because you make a sleeker roof etc. Again, you may want to gain some market share and appeal to more people. You keep increasing the interior space but eventually, the car doesn't really standout as being beautiful anymore. It's pretty like all the other cars. You've gained a lot of customers. Now, the customers don't have to be that loyal because as soon as they see a car that looks slightly better than this, and maybe a competitive have gone in on your area and said, "Well, we're going to make our car nice too. Now, we can easily do it because the other guys don't really have an advantage anymore. So I think it's very dangerous to stray away from your core strengths."

Lars Seier Christensen, Founder and owner Seier Capital, Co-founder and fmr. CEO Saxo Bank.

"Saxo Bank's core product is a trading platform, and there's a lot of trading platforms out there. Actually, when we started out, we pretty much invented our own market together with a few handfuls of other companies, because our main focus initially was on foreign exchange

trading, which used to be a territory for large clients that would be on the phone and being treated in very manual ways. We kind of democratized that by taking it online, so you had a much more efficient process really, but also a process that was scalable. There's a limit to how many phones you can have in your hands at the same time. The activity in the foreign exchange markets is very much in bursts. You have the US trade figures, bang, something happens, everybody needs to trade inside a 30, 60 second time span. As you can imagine, if you have a lot of clients, that's highly inefficient, if you have to sit and talk to them on the phone all at the same time, which in effect led to a nondemocratic, much better service for the very large client and a much worse service for the very small client. So much so that there were not really small clients in foreign exchange. We changed that, and hence because the big boys could not at all adopt to that, for a long time, we together with a handful of other companies, we had the lower end of the foreign exchange market pretty much to ourselves, the big banks never really got involved. Also because there wasn't that much business from the outset, but over time, it turned out that actually, people liked to trade this as well. As long as it was made accessible to them, also if they were not billionaires, there was quite a big market there. You can say that's a classic blue ocean, that are more or less created ourselves.

Of course, as it turned out, that was a good market and a profitable market to be in. A lot of competition has shown up, and I would say pricing is no longer, if you're not very competitive in your pricing, you're out of business, because it's very easily comparable. It's not like, I like the Audi or I like the Mercedes, the price of Euro versus a dollar is what it is. You have to be very competitive to even be in there.

You can't really differentiate yourself from pricing. What can you differentiate yourself on, on smart, on the intelligent platform, I would say that platform that goes beyond just giving you a price when you want to trade, but actually assist you in making informed choices about when to trade, what to trade, how to manage the risk that's implicit in your trades, and also having a good personal service, because some of this stuff is fairly complex and sometimes, you need to speak to somebody about it. In contrary to many traditional stockbrokers where you, if you have an inquiry about this, press one, if you have an inquiry about this, press two. When you call us, you get a real person that actually speaks to you and try to sort out your problems."

Johan Boserup, Global CEO of Trading at WPP's GroupM.

"The three different roots from Porter, I think, are very interesting. But, there's a lot of focus at the moment on procurement and on driving down cost or extracting costs from the system and perceiving that as a sustainable competitive advantage. In fact, I'm not so sure that I agree. At least not in our industry. In the media and communication industry, I don't think you can ... if I'm better at extracting value ... First of all, it's easy to replicate it. So, if I'm best at that, I will only be best for a set amount of time. Which means that it's not sustainable necessarily. So, if that's all I offer to my clients, then someone else is going to offer more of that.

But also, you know, it's a race to the bottom. I can only go so far, literally, because I can't get free media for our advertisers. They have to pay for it. So, if my only value delivery to our client is to get it cheaper and cheaper,

295

than I'm going to hit rock bottom at some point and, obviously, that's not sustainable either. So, I'm not so sure that where the industry is going right now is sustainable. So, we work with this term that we want to move away from extracting value, we want to create value instead. The key word in sustainable competitive advantage is to create value. You can obviously do that by aligning to your customers or you can do that by innovating and creating new value all the time. I think that the latter, the innovation, is the most difficult one. But it's also the most reward one. If you create innovation... If you have innovation that will create genuine value, that value will continue to pay off. So, as long as you have something that is genuinely innovative, because things don't necessarily continue to be innovative over time. As long as this new thing that you're doing, for your client, or with your client, is innovative, it will continue to deliver value to you and to your clients. So I think innovation is the most effective way to generate a sustainable competitive advantage."

Reflection on strategic planning and Michael Porter's five forces.

Porter's five forces analysis is an industry analysis and business strategy development formed by Michael E. Porter of Harvard Business School in 1979. The analysis identifies and analyses five forces that determine the competitive intensity and therefore attractiveness and profitability of a market.[56]

Porter's five forces.

Three forces from "horizontal" competition:

1. Threat of new entrants or barriers to entry.

2. Threat of substitutes.

3. Threat of established rivals or competitive rivalry.

Two forces from "vertical" competition:

1. The bargaining power of buyers.

2. The bargaining power of suppliers.

---

[56] Porter, Michael E. (1979). How Competitive Forces Shape Strategy. Harvard Business review, March Issue.

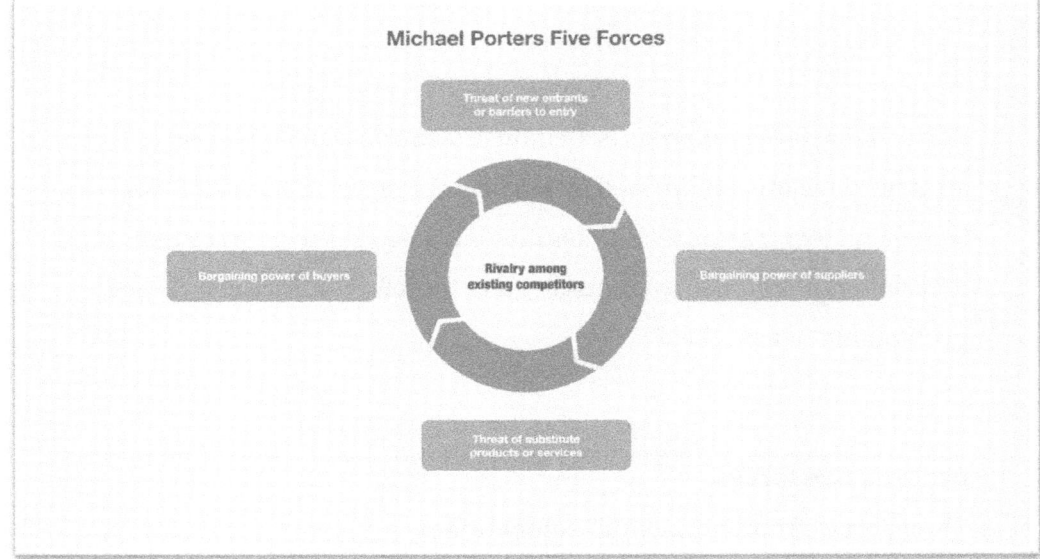

Figure 31.

This "five forces analysis", is just one part of the complete Porter strategic models. Other elements are "the value chain" and the "generic strategies".

This work presents marketing & communication abstracts. For more details about the theory please view the authors' own works.

Interviewees.

Ole Henriksen, Founder and Creative Director, Ole Henriksen Skin Care Brand.
"For me, when I start the process of bringing a new product to life, of course a lot goes into it. First, you reach out to the suppliers. And there

are lots of those around the world that I've built relationships with over the years. You start the model their of indeed saying, "I need X amount of ingredients. What are the cost of these ingredients?". You do your budgets. You start, again, to build in... What are the margins going to be? And we have a model we work from, of course, so that there's room for all of it. And I can still arrive at being a very affordable, attainable brand, which is very important for me.

But, a lot of it is also just an organic, natural process. I have not been overly analytical... I mean, yes budgets. Yes, for sure. Business plans, yes. I learned early on when I created the board in my company from one of my great ladies Karen Boyt, A graduate from Yale University, she came in and taught me a lot of those ropes. And the importance of, for instance, doing a five year business plan. Of course, we do it all. But I think, again, a lot of it is still in that playful mode that we don't become too analytical. As long as the budgets are in place, that's what matters. As long as the marketing model is in place for the launch of the product, that all these things are thought through. But I hope that we never lose the playfulness, the fun, and the creativity. Because you can also lock yourself into a situation where it just becomes, "What happened here?". Where you become cookie-cutter. And I think that sometimes happens with businesses, and as such, they lose what made them successful, the authenticity. And that's dangerous."

Karim Jabbar. Entrepreneurship & Innovation specialist. Industrial PhD Fellow. Lecturer, DIS – Study Abroad in Scandinavia.

"Porter's Five Forces, is actually an interesting model because when I went to business school, this was in the early '90's, it was already the main established model that we were taught, in order to talk about industry analysis. Actually today, it's pretty much still valid. It's a timeless model, I think, that does the basics but of course, there are things that it does not do and it's not a unique model, that basically tells everything about everything. As is the case with most models, it is for something specific and it should be applied with a certain element of rigor.

As a teacher, I've been trying to use this for a number of years now, with different types of students at the Copenhagen Business School, as well as Danish Institute For Study Abroad, with mixed results but mainly positive, if applied properly. I can just go into the details about what I think of the model.

As I see it, students often tend to misunderstand what the purpose of the model is. As you mentioned, figure out what the profitability of an industry is. Basically understanding that this is actually an industry that we're talking about. The main challenge here of course, is to figure out how do you then define an industry? What goes into the central box of Porter's Five Forces? How do you delimit the box? What goes into it, what does not go into it? What is a competitor? What is a substitute product and so on? For students to actually understand that, a lot of diligence needs to go into establishing the scope, both geographically. Essentially, we're talking about a global industry. Are we looking at a regional part of that global industry because the competitive situation might be different, in different geographies. You might be up against different competitors at a global level, versus if you'd begin into a specific market and so on and so forth. As well as the intersections with other industries might be different. The important thing is, making sure that you understand how to actually focus on the central box. Usually students will start... Maybe it's because the way we write. They will start from left to right and they will fill in the box, which is according to me, I think the wrong way of doing it. You should zoom in on the central one, establish who are the essential players. Then try to view it as a supply chain almost. These people, where do they get their input from and where do they actually sell their products, so their finished products? Here again, there are some common mistakes that I maybe could elaborate on. One of the mistakes would typically be to say, "The buyers is the people who use the product." Obviously the buyers are not the people who use the product. It's the people that send you the bill or that you send the bill to. Most often, most companies in most industries, are business to business.

Your buyers are going to be wholesalers, they're going to be retailers, distributors. Usually the users of the products, are going to be down the supply chain and that's important for you to take into consideration when you do your analysis. Understand that the next step in the supply chain, is actually the ones that is the buyers. The same goes with some of the other boxes. Overall, if you use some diligence in making sure that you delimit the model correctly, that you're aware of your place in the supply chain because in essence, if I can put it this way, you could move to the left or to the right of the model and make a similar Porter's Five Forces. If you move down to the buyers, for example, let's say it's wholesalers, they have their own competitive situation. They have rivalry among wholesalers and they would also have a Porter's Five Forces that you could apply to them. They would be selling to retailers and they would have certain barriers to entry. There would be certain substitute products, maybe not using a wholesaler, for example and so on and so forth. Placing the model into the broader picture, is actually quite important for people to understand. That's the first thing that sometimes people get wrong."

Birgitte Mabeck, Head of fundraising and marketing Red Cross.
"I think the increased competition for us has a lot to do with a combination of the social media, to be honest. What happens now is that a lot of well-meaning people, one person deciding to collect, I don't know, shoes, clothes, money, toys, something for a case or a cause in India somewhere, before would never be visible. Now this person is suddenly visible and could become just as huge on the social media as the Red Cross. Suddenly it's not a case of how big your organization is, but it's a case of how good are you at getting your message out there.

I think that is really what we can see as the biggest threat in terms of our competitors. Maybe they have always been there, those well-meaning people, but we didn't know about them. Now they just have a channel to enter where we are more equal in competing. That's for sure one thing. Generally speaking, there is just more organizations starting. There are more well-meaning organizations, NGOs and so forth establishing, getting established out there. They are getting into the social media channels as well, so we have more organizations and standalone people competing about the same message."

Leif Rasmussen. Strategic Branding. Lecturer, DIS – Study Abroad in Scandinavia.

"Most companies, and believe me this is actually the truth, most companies tend to make one specific analysis before they start on a new campaign, a new market or whatever it can be, and that's the SWOT analysis. That is know by everybody, but that's not good enough, because it does not cover all the competitive areas, which actually Porter's Five Forces does. It is I think very good at finding out what is this new market or this new segment of the market that you are going into to describe the different things, not only seeing in your own perspective, seeing through the glasses of your own company, but actually seeing in a little bit more overall, little bit more objective way so that you get different competitive powers into your analysis."

Peter Ålbæk Jensen, Producer, Founder & fmr. CEO, Zentropa.

"First of all, I thought it was fun to make porn movies. We read a research quoting that twenty five percent of all Danish couples, at that time, watched VHS tapes with porn film together. That's why we then made a porn division focused on a female audience. It was extremely fun to do, but it was also fun to stop it again. But this still the best selling Scandinavian porn films ever. We got any kind of promotion since it was us, an art-house company, suddenly making porn film. In our cantina it was fun having ten porn models sitting in bathrobes having lunch together with all these art-house directors. The porn models didn't care but the art-house directors was quite uncomfortable about the situation. It made us laugh."

Karim Jabbar. Entrepreneurship & Innovation specialist. Industrial PhD Fellow. Lecturer, DIS – Study Abroad in Scandinavia.

"The second thing is, actually seeing this as a dynamic thing. It's something that changes over time. It's not something that's static. Students typically will say, "Well, I've checked out the boxes. This is Porter's Five Forces. What's the next assignment?" They will present it as some sort of appendix, rather than actually seeing it as something that is ongoing. It's only when you add on the element of the dynamic changes that are taking place in the industry and trying to anticipate that for every element, that you actually get some use out of the model.

For example, a lot of industries over the past decade, have completely changed because of integration maybe. Maybe some companies will buy up other companies, so you would have horizontal integration, you would have vertical integration. They buy out the suppliers of the distributors and all that effects the competitive situation in the central box. Being aware of how these trends are and trying to translate them as they happen, into the Portes's Five Forces, makes it a very good steering tool for you to understand where this industry is actually going. Based on that, as a company, you would then be able to say, "This is the direction of the river," so to speak.

Now our job is to figure out, where do we position ourselves, versus the other guys that are also floating down this river and here other tools are going to be more useful than Porter's Five Forces. You need to think about models that explain competitiveness between firms. You would need to look at the business model itself, which is internal. How does the company actually generate revenue and so on, which is not a model that looks at the context. These models together, you need to patch together as pieces of a puzzle, in order to make them useful for your particular case. Porter's Five Forces, is hard to escape because it's the background that you would use in any situation."

Peter Ålbæk Jensen, Producer, Founder & fmr. CEO, Zentropa.

"We could just see that since all of the titles was more or less addressed to men, why not try to address them to woman. That was quite easy and it took five seconds to analyze, especially because the research was done properly before. Like all good boys, we have watched a lot porn movies, we know it of course. How they look like and how the language was, so that was easy."

Benjamin Holk Henriksen, Strategic planning & branding. Lecturer DIS and Copenhagen Business School, Author, Filmmaker "The Mind of a Leader", "Holk Master-class".

"Porters acclaimed work grew out of the "positioning school" in the late 70s, start 80s. The wave consisted of the systematic empirical search for relationship between external conditions and internal basic generic strategies.

As such the positioning school favored management consultants. Massive research was conducted in order to find one basic solution as opposed to the tailor-made solutions practiced by the "design school". Despite it's generic nature, Porters Five Forces strategy serves as an excellent tool to analyze the competitive intensity and therefore attractiveness and profitability of a market."

Centralization & Decentralization.

The communication platform defines what a company, organisation or specific product wants to stand for or be perceived as, internally in the organisation and externally in the market. It's important that there is a link between the two.

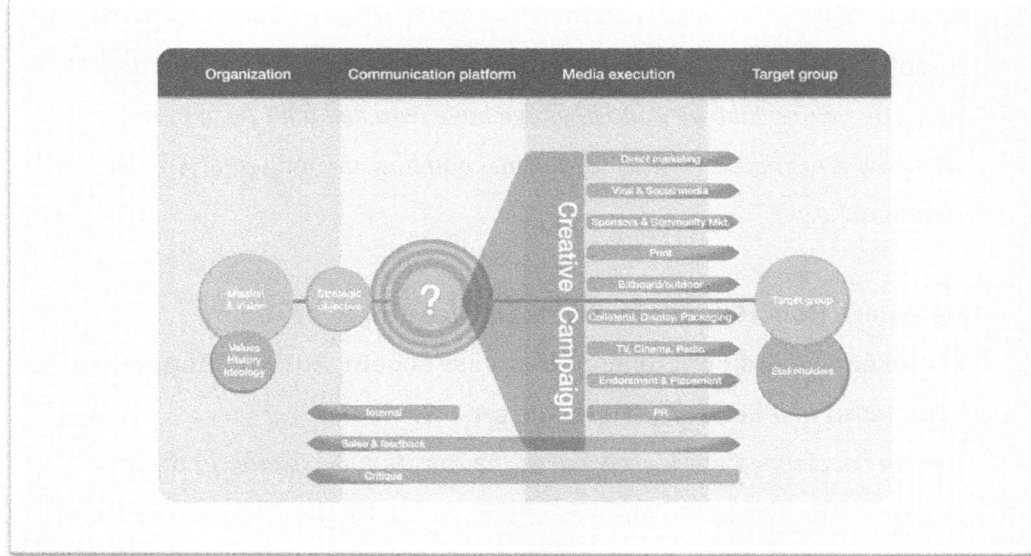

Figure 32.

In this episode we will develop this concept in relation to export markets. Who makes the decisions in external markets and who defines the local communication platform? Headquarters or local management?

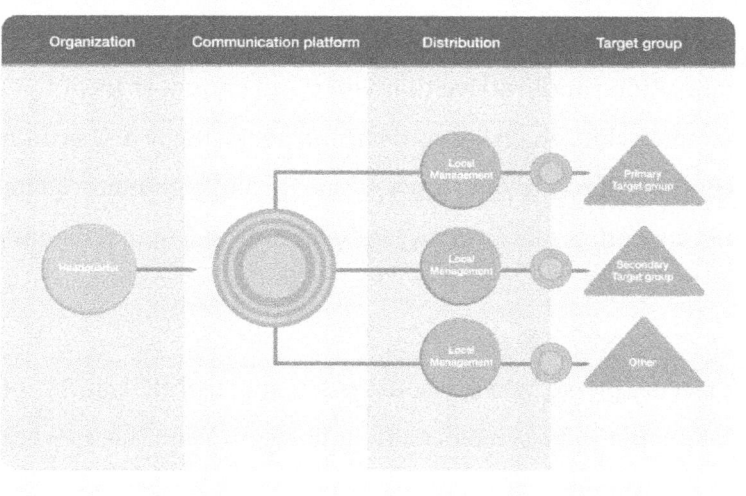

Figure 33.

This is very important from a branding perspective. A centralised approach favours brand consistency and economy of scale. The headquarters has full control over the brand and can ensure a uniform identity in all markets. A decentralized approach favours flexibility and local know-how.[57]

In 'The Mind of a Leader series' marketing guru Philip Kotler likens the empowerment issue to a swinging pendulum. Power is delegated depending on a company's current needs. He stresses the importance

---

[57] Hatch, Mary Jo and Schultz, Majken (2002). The dynamics of organizational identity. SAGE Publications.
Gouda, Dr. Islam Gouda (2014). To Centralize or Decentralize your Marketing. American Marketing Association. Warton.

307

of listening to local markets. Companies may be global but markets are local.[58]

An organisation should strive to involve and empower local management while ensuring some brand consistency and economy of scale. One solution is to develop a range of campaign material based on the communication platform and then let the local management choose from it.

In the start-up phase, when resources are short, organisations often use local people such as agents and importers to run the operation instead of setting up a corporate subsidiary but adopt a more centralised approach as the organisation grows in order to secure brand consistency.[59]

Interviewees.

Peter Ålbæk Jensen, Producer, Founder & fmr. CEO, Zentropa.
"We definitely prefer a decentralized marketing because it is very difficult... if you see all different posters it has you know, so we're selling the film to a local distributor. They know the market and they know how to attack their audience, so we never interfere in that."

Dennis Balslev, CEO IKEA Germany. Fmr. CEO IKEA Denmark.

---

[58] Lassenius, Fredrik & Holk Henriksen, Benjamin (2011). The Mind of a Leader I based on Niccolò Machiavelli's 'The Prince'. Episode 3. Astromax Entertainment.
[59] Lassenius, Fredrik & Holk Henriksen, Benjamin (2010). Sådan tænker ledere/The Mind of a Leader. L&R business. 2010.

"The way we are working as a global company, one part is global and the global part, we try to adapt to most countries so it fits all but of course you cannot fit everything to all countries and then you have to work locally in much stronger. In the marketing sense, we are working very locally and the decisions, inside the frames of the concept, we are working very locally. Take the global part and it's getting more and more difficult because when we talk about the Ikea catalog, we have seen examples from Saudi Arabia where we try to adapt the global catalog into a market where you have a law, what you are allowed to do and show and you have other countries where you are allowed to do something different. Then, we see today that it is getting more and more difficult with more than 40 countries we operate in today, what does it really mean to get global and we are very aware of it as a company and see how we can secure that we operate in the best way. We have to respect that there's different laws in different countries and how do we adapt our products to those countries."

Benjamin Holk Henriksen, Strategic planning & branding. Lecturer DIS and Copenhagen Business School, Author, Filmmaker "The Mind of a Leader", "Holk Master-class".

"It makes sense to develop a centralized cost saving production and purchasing system of raw material, marketing material etc. in order to negotiate low prices.

And I do believe it makes sense to have a centralized product portfolio and marketing approach in order to keep a strong consistent brand and customer experience.

However while companies are global, all markets are local. If companies are not willing to adapt to local cultures in terms of distribution, employee incentives, motivation, customer preferences etc. they risk missing out on major markets opportunities. This leaves us with the classic conflict... the battle between brand consistency and local adaption.

Take the fast food industry. Take McDonald. They have managed to keep a pretty consistent global brand image, but still adapted both menu and marketing material to the local markets in for example China, Singapore etc.

And take Pizza hut... if you visit Pizza hut in China you will see and find an alternative business model, offering a kind of fine dining atmosphere with knives and forks, and an expanded menu catering to Chinese."

Kaspar Basse, Founder, CEO Joe & The Juice.
"I would do it if we were entering and seeing ultimately difficult times. I would do it. With all due respect, I think that some of the concepts that you mentioned here, are also from a fundamentally point of view struggling to keep being contemporary. They are very well embedded, but old concepts that, perhaps, would have done some alterations anyway if they were only in their home markets.

I don't necessarily see the necessity for us to do it. Also we are ultimately less product focused than many of these companies. We are tremendously more than products. It's important to understand that appeal. I think that the identity, the relationships we create, the intimate ambiance and

310

atmosphere in our stores is a stronger force than any relationship between a product and a person.

Of course, it creates the best of both worlds that we have a very honest approach to the products. We have absolutely an uncompromised approach to the quality. We also recognize that eventually you will convince yourself that the juice you drink where you have the best relationship is also the healthiest.

That ignition between our juicers and guests and the store and the neighborhood is something that is fundamentally more important than the product by itself. This means that, that, as we call it, that combination of health and entertainment that we hope to deliver is tremendously universal. It's something that China craves. It's something that the US invented. It's something that even Scandinavia with the Jantelov (the law of Jante) seems to appreciate now and then. I feel we are as we are right now, based on something that two mega trends would charge tremendously strong. There's no need to start thinking about salads or, even though we have it in some stores. You got to watch out, becoming to much of a product focused adventure. In our company, it's more important to make sure that we have a relationship with you over the next fifteen years, than it is to up sell a double espresso, or find out if you want a salad, or ... Most companies end up trying to be too much for too many people. There's a very strong force in having the self confidence to limit your offer, because you believe in it as being the strongest."

Fumiko Kano Glückstad, Assistant Prof. PhD in Cross-Cultural Communication & Cognition.

"Yeah, actually centralized marketing strategy or decentralized, localized marketing strategy, actually I support both indeed. Mixed method I would say, but in a way... actually currently I have been, I'm interested in identifying actually more about intercultural marketing strategy. Because some segment, consumer segment are actually universalizing, some people are more influenced by the global culture. Some specific segment in Japan or China, they might have this quite similar values and identities, for these people we can really advertise in the same way, maybe different language, but still in the same way, say in Asia, say in music or something like that. But for some segment in some country that is, there must be some culture specific."

Matthew Bagwell, Managing Director Naked Communications Europe.

"We at Naked have been very involved, Virgin Atlantic, for example, is a global ... It's a global airline and the work that we do is global, which means in many markets, it means transatlantic and it means in each and every market. It's not the only, for instance, many of the brands that we work with have to consider this tension between what does central create, the central marketing organization creates, and how do they empower and enable local markets.

Ebay we're working for Europe, but we're also working for the markets within Europe. I think our role is to help the local markets articulate their requirements, such as they're reflected in the strategy of the central marketing organizations. We're also trying to help the markets understand how they can best leverage the assets that central marketing creates.

In a sense we're kind of trying to create an osmotic potential between these two fraternities. There's a tension in practically, if you're not in a single market, as soon as this becomes, a part of the challenge, there's a tension between control and consistency with empowerment, and sort of a local adaptation. I think agencies have to work hard to support clients understand the best way to achieve that fine balance, to understand how to absolutely get the economies that are possible in both, frankly, we want work that works, and there's nothing worse than a sort of, a decentralized market creating work that is inconsistent, or a central marketing team creating work that won't be relevant."

Dennis Balslev, CEO IKEA Germany. Fmr. CEO IKEA Denmark.

"I think it's very strong to work locally with marketing because in Denmark, we have Danish customers who live in a specific way, who have the Danish values and how do we want to adapt our marketing to the Danish customers. How do we want to adapt the meeting with the customer, in a Danish way? That's quite important. We don't want to be a big international global company. We're a Danish company in Denmark and we have 2,300 Danish coworkers who meet our customers in Denmark so it's very important for Ikea to adapt as much as possible.

What is interesting in that question is the home furnishing part. Nobody believed that you could sell the same product in 42 different countries in the world but we can do that. The only country we can laugh of a little bit is the U.S. because everything is bigger in U.S. The kitchens are higher and deeper and the couches are longer and deeper and the dining table is much bigger. It should be for the turkey and not for the chicken, so that's something which is a little bit different. We have to home furnishing houses for 25 square meters in Hong Kong to maybe two or three hundred square meters somewhere else, so it's a big difference in culture and way of living and we have to adapt to that."

Ole Henriksen, Founder and Creative Director, Ole Henriksen Skin Care Brand.

"There has to be a certain degree of centralized approach to the messaging. However, one thing is that ... It's sort of like you learn the A's and the B's and the C's in school, but if you don't allow that student to build upon that, and put their own personality into it, then something is wrong. So actually I've always felt that you should bring out the message, but do it in your tone of voice. Put your personality into it, and then you arrive at something incredible, because that way you've respect the talent of the people that work for you to shine in their own way, and we arrive at something successful."

Matthew Bagwell, Managing Director Naked Communications Europe.

"I think one of the things that I've seen firsthand is that it's actually about not just the marketing objectives, but the alignment of business objectives from central, where it's normally the headquarters and the C-suite, and the local market objectives.

You may have a global marketing director and you may have local marketing directors, but they may not actually be managed by the same

CEO, and they may have different market objectives, different business objectives and different business challenges. Sometimes it's very difficult to get one size to fit all, because each market has its own business objectives. In one market you may be dominant, in another you may be just emerging, or in a very different competitive situation.

Again, it's about people who support these brands being cognizant of all of the different dynamics, and actually empowering local markets to be able to do the things that they need to do in a way that's consistent and on brand."

Klaus Nørskov, Head of communication Red Cross.

"...you need to extract the neutral core of the Red Cross, Red Crescent and communicate that, which is why in one sort of way it's very simple.
You need to have very few and very clear messages, which is thought of the common values, and then you need to leave the rest to the different part of the organization because if you don't do that, you're going to leave a very confusing picture of the organization to the public."

Benjamin Holk Henriksen, Strategic planning & branding.
Lecturer DIS and Copenhagen Business School, Author, Filmmaker
"The Mind of a Leader", "Holk Master-class".

"I remember discussing the topic back in the days with Anita Roddick, founder of the Body Shop and also Stan Shih, the founder of Acer computers. They both started that with a decentralized approach you can empower the local management. But they changed to a more centralized approach as the organization grew, and the need for a uniform brand grew stronger. One of their key conclusion was however

to remember to invite local management into the decision making process. You might be centralized but you should involve your managers so that the ideas and that consistent brand is carried through by the whole company, the local management too."

Reflection on Hofstede's cultural dimensions and Hall's High- and low-context cultures.

Professor Geert Hofstede's cultural dimensions theory is a framework for cross- cultural communication. It's one of the most comprehensive studies of how values in the workplace are influenced by culture.[60]

The theory defines culture as "the collective programming of the mind distinguishing the members of one group or category of people from others".

The six dimensions of national culture are based on extensive research done by Professor Geert Hofstede, Gert Jan Hofstede, Michael Minkov.[61]

1. Power distance.

"The extent to which the less powerful members of organisations and institutions accept and expect that power is distributed unequally." A higher score on the Index indicates that hierarchy is clearly established, executed and accepted in society.

2. Individualism versus collectivism.

This index explores the "degree to which people in a society are integrated into groups." Individualistic societies emphasize the "I". Its

---

[60] Hofstede, Geert (1980). Culture's Consequences: International Differences in Work-Related Values", Sage Publications.
Hofstede, Geert. Dimensionalizing Cultures (2011). The Hofstede Model in Context. Universities of Maastricht and Tilburg, The Netherlands.
[61] Hofstede, Geert, Hofstede, Gert Jan, Minkov, Michael (1994). Cultures and Organisations: Software of the Mind", Profile Books, London, 1994; 2nd edn, McGraw-Hill, New York, 2005.

counterpart, collectivism, describes a society in which integrated relationships tie extended families and others into groups.

3. Masculinity versus femininity.

Masculinity is defined as "a preference in society for achievement, heroism, assertiveness and material rewards for success." Its counterpart femininity represents "a preference for cooperation, modesty, caring for the weak and quality of life."

4. Uncertainty avoidance.

A society's tolerance for ambiguity," in which people embrace or avert an event that is unexpected, unknown, or away from the status quo.

5. Long term orientation versus short term normative orientation.

The concepts address the different ways cultures view time and the importance of the past, present and the future. Cultures demonstrating a short-term orientation will be more concerned with the past and present and will focus their efforts and beliefs on matters related to the short-term, while cultures demonstrating a long-term time orientation will be more concerned with the future and will focus their efforts on future-orientated goals.

6. Indulgence versus restraint.

This dimension is essentially a measure of happiness. Indulgence is defined as "a society that allows relatively free gratification of basic and natural human desires related to enjoying life and having fun." Its counterpart is defined as "a society that controls gratification of needs and regulates it by means of strict social norms."

A few general assumptions when studying Hofstede's research and country indexes are that Western countries are more individualistic and have low power distance while Asian and Middle Eastern countries are more collectivistic and have high power distance.

Latin countries in general seem to rank relatively high on power distance and masculinity as opposed to Scandinavian countries.[62]

Another interesting work is the "high and low context concept" introduced by anthropologist Edward T. Hall in his 1976 book Beyond Culture. It refers to a culture's tendency to use high-context or low-context messages in communication.[63]

In a higher context culture, many things are left unsaid, letting the culture explain. The choice of words becomes very important. since a few words can communicate a complex message very effectively to an in-group. Thus high context cultures rely on traditions, very deep personal relationships, and established hierarchies.

In low context culture, the communicator needs to be much more explicit and the value of a particular word is less important. Low context cultures do not have the same depth of tradition and have shallower, short-term relationships.

---

[62] De Mooij, Marieke (2016).Global Marketing and Advertising. Understanding Cultural Paradoxes (Fourth edition).
[63] Hall, Edward T. (1976). Beyond Culture.

Examples of high context countries include: China, Japan, and the Arab countries. Examples of low context cultures include: USA, Germany and Scandinavia.

This work presents marketing & communication abstracts. For more details about the theory please view the authors' own works.

Interviewees.

Klaus Nørskov, Head of communication Red Cross.

"What we experience is huge differences when we meet in international forums. If, for instance, we get together with Germans, the Austrians, Italians, the British, we're going to look at very different ways of communicating if you want to achieve a certain goal. What works in Denmark definitely wouldn't work in Austria. This is very important learning when it comes to an organization such as Red Cross because we have this... If you have kind of a headquarter as we have in Geneva, you will have a headquarter that will try to implement mutual solutions, campaigns that works, if not around the world, but then, for instance, at least in Europe. The reality is that they hardly ever do. We almost always have to either adapt them or just run our own campaigns basically. Why? Because the target groups of Austria, Germany, Britain, France, and Denmark are very, very different."

Anne Marie Bülow, Professor at Copenhagen Business School. Dept. of management, society and communication.

"Hofstede has had an enormous impact. The quotation rate is out of this world and that means that a lot of people think that that is gospel truth. That perhaps is not the case in the academic circles anymore. He has gone out of fashion because the idea of static cultures has gone out of fashion. However, some of the parameters that he uses are still relevant."

Tue Walin Storm, Director, Screenwriter, Founder Storm/Hansen (Nielson, Ford, Pirelli, The Raveonettes).

"Yeah. I'll definitely say there's a big difference between various countries and how they interpret commercials and what kind of storytelling is needed. Denmark is much more subtle and refined, I would say, than the United States. United States have, obviously, a tendency to paint with broad strokes. I mean, they do big, epic visuals. They enhance music. Comedy is very different. I produced a commercial for some Russians and the comedy in that I personally didn't find very interesting or funny, but there's comedy. Denmark, which is to me, again, is a cultural thing, is far more interesting because it's much more subtle and humorous. The comedy in America, at least in the commercial sense, tend to be more slapsticky or broader.

There's no question in terms of content. There are big difference, but also in terms of visuals. I think What makes my directing duo interesting in the United States is that we have this mix between a European or Northern European, Scandinavian style and taste that then can be infused into American commercials. So, it becomes this sort of hybrid between beautiful aesthetics, but with an understanding of culture that is uniquely American."

Anne Marie Bülow, Professor at Copenhagen Business School. Dept. of management, society and communication.

"One of the objections is of course that what counts as a national culture? Denmark, we have a population of Maryland, but we are treated next to the United States of America, it simply doesn't make sense. India is a really big place and there is one count for India. That sort of thing really doesn't make sense. There is another thing and that is that it has moved with the time that all investigations will show that young Chinese react differently from old Chinese managers, and that they're much more focused on a different kind of dynamic where the power hierarchy has moved and the loyalty structures have moved. Therefore to count it in terms of what it was like in the 80s no longer makes real sense."

Dennis Balslev, CEO IKEA Germany. Fmr. CEO IKEA Denmark.

"I think culture is very interesting and especially you can say leadership culture in many different countries, even in Scandinavia, we are different. We always in Denmark talk about the Swedes want to sit around the table and agree about everything. In Denmark, we're a little bit tougher but if you come to the Middle East or North America, it's a different culture of course in leadership and how do you put that leadership into the company. As long as we have the Ikea culture and values with us, then I think we can be very proud as a company to see how we can change culture in many different countries. That Ikea's culture and way of thinking, moving, you could say more in the Swedish way of thinking, even in Middle East, Ikea seems as different from many other companies because they have brought in the Ikea values and culture into the companies.

That's something that's quite important but of course, that's a different. We cannot change every culture to be the same as our culture and we don't want to do that but we should be aware of the differences in the culture and all of this adopted into what does it mean in the way of thinking at Ikea.

One good example I think is in Japan, when we started in Japan. Women was not really in managerial positions and Ikea decided of course, we want a mix of women and men in those positions. It was a big thing in Japan, even for the government to listen to how it's possible for you to have a culture you allow women to have manager positions and of course it was a huge success for Ikea. I think the Japanese culture start to look into what is opportunities for the future and thinking in a very different way. To bring in our culture in many countries, we believe is strong. We will not change the local culture but we can move it maybe from our point of view in a different directions."

Anne Marie Bülow, Professor at Copenhagen Business School. Dept. of management, society and communication.

"Of Hofstede's dimensions, the one that has had most literature dedicated to it is definitely the scale between collectivism and individualism. I have a sense that particularly in America, they sort of take it to heart that they're individualists and it's somehow bad. On the other hand, if you look at the way that collectivism functions, it is a hugely complicated concept. Mostly because it functions not as a scale between individualism and collectivism, but as several dimensions. When they talk about the difference between vertical collectivism and horizontal collectivism, that gives you a whole new picture.

If we talk vertical collectivism, it means that a culture that you would associate with collectivism again like China, means knowing your place in the hierarchy, respecting your elders et cetera, et cetera. If you're not to make the decisions it means somebody else whom you respect will make the decisions and you're fine with that. However, horizontal collectivism means that group harmony is important and often people think that group harmony means that a negotiation will be easy because we are a group. Wrong, wrong. If we talk about the in-group that you represent at the moment, people fight for collectivism, how many in that group? It will mean that there is no social loafing, that people really try to do the best they can for the group and not be individually famous. If you don't represent that in-group in the group assure, you will get fierce competition."

Fumiko Kano Glückstad, Assistant Prof. PhD in Cross-Cultural Communication & Cognition.

"About low context and high context culture, I think this is also a tricky issue in way, because it's also again it depends on the context, not to high context or low context, but also the scenario. If you are in a Japanese, what do you say, let's say that for example European businessman is communicating with a Japanese distributor together with other Japanese colleagues in Japan somewhere, Tokyo or somewhere, then this is completely Japanese context. You have to really follow in a Japanese way, then you really have to understand this high context culture in a way, the way they communicate in that Japanese context. If you meet with Japanese businessman who is Westernized and who can speak English in Europe or somewhere, this is another issue I think. They are more,

actually they could be more direct in a way because they also know the low context culture, they also over react, they have to really be direct. I can also, I have been here for almost fifteen, eighteen years in Europe, and I can also be very direct."

Lars Liebst, CEO Tivoli.

"A very good question and I think for the future we have to pay much more attention to what we do to who and where they are coming from. Actually right now we are, later today, we are going to hire somebody who will start up a Chinese website and we will be targeting the Chinese in a different way than we target Europeans. I think the Americans, we have a pretty good grip on those guys but we don't understand the Chinese way of doing marketing and doing all of that. That is why we are trying to focus much more on getting people at our team that knows much more about it."

Part VII. HR management and innovation.

Reflection on mission, vision and the golden circle.

Mission & Vision.

Mission and vision are a set of guidelines. A Mission frequently defines what the company or organization aims "to do", whereas a Vision is a state of being, "to be".

"That business mission is so rarely given adequate thought is perhaps the most important single cause of business frustration."
Peter Drucker, management consultant, educator, and author.

Some companies add a motivational "ethical" purpose to the Mission & Vision, or a sentence that describes the corporate culture, defined as a mission statement.[64]

The golden circle.

Author, speaker, and consultant, Simon O. Sinek, has developed an interesting concept described in his 2009 book, "Start With Why: How Great Leaders Inspire Everyone to Take Action".[65]

---

[64] Campbell, A., Yeung, S. (1991). Brief case: Mission, vision and strategic intent. Pergamon Press plc.
[65] Sinek, Simon (2011). Start with Why: How Great Leaders Inspire Everyone to Take Action. Penguin.

Simon reflects on what he says is a naturally occurring pattern, grounded in the biology of human decision-making, that explains why we are inspired by some people, leaders, messages and organizations over others. Using Apple as an example, The Golden Circle shows how some leaders are able to inspire action instead of manipulating people to act.

The concept builds on a why, how and what.

Why:
The core belief of the business. It's the leaders vision and the reason "why" the business exists.

How:
"How" the business fulfills that core belief. Senior executives are inspired by the leader's vision and know "how" to bring this vision to life.

What:
"What" the company does to fulfill that core belief.

The "How" are the actions and the "What" are the results of those actions.

Partridgeon, Andy (2014). Executive Summary: The Golden Circle with Simon Sinek. Written. http://enviableworkplace.com/executive-summary-golden-circle-simon-sinek/

Sinek found that most companies work backwards. They start with their "what" and then move to "how" they do it. Most of these companies neglect to even mention or know "why" they do what they do.

When organizations or people think or communicate they do so from the outside in. From "What" to "Why". They naturally go from the tangible to the intangible. However this is not the case with the inspired leaders and companies. They think, act and communicate from the inside out. If you hire people who believe what you believe, they'll work for you with blood, sweat and tears.

Let's take a closer look at how successful modern leaders formulate their purpose or objective.

This work presents marketing & communication abstracts. For more details about the theory please view the authors' own works.

Interviewees.

Kaspar Basse, Founder, CEO Joe & The Juice.
"The most important thing is to see yourself as, or for us, is to see ourselves as more than the juice and the coffee and the sandwich. That also means that, coming back to your mission, vision, we call it why, how, who. That's Simon Sinek altered model.

The who comes in because of what I call the people brand side of things. There's a big difference between being a big company full of people and a people company. In the very early days, I was lucky enough to see the value of people. Also, just down to the very fundamental revenue side of things. Going to the bank, showing budgets, etc. This learning meant that at an early stage, we could start defining the principles for doing what we do. One of these principles is that we will do everything to work with people. We will not do anything that makes the job easier for them. We will not do anything to prepare stuff that makes it easier to do transactions, but creates a boring job, or less demanding job."

Mikkel Borg Bjergsø Founder and CEO Mikkeller brewery, bars and restaurants.

"Thinking back, I didn't think too much about it in the beginning, but I had certain ideas and certain ways I wanted to do it. Which, I didn't write it down or anything, but today, when I look back, if you look at Mikkeller the company today, we have some unwritten rules which is something that I founded back in the days. An example is that I decided never to spend money on marketing, because I started the company because I wanted to make good beer. I didn't start the company because I wanted people to believe I made good beer. I decided that instead of telling people you should buy my beer by doing marketing, I wanted people to find out themselves, because they tasted it, because they heard it from friends, or something like that.

That's something that we still work this way. We never spend money on marketing, because we don't want to tell people to like our products. We want them to find out themselves because I believe if you do it this way, you get more loyal customers. We have our fans, our customers, are people that see Mikkeller as a lifestyle, not as some brand and then the next day they move on to a new brand. Which is something that I think I've built because I chose to do it this way.

There are other things obviously we do a lot different than a lot of other companies, especially a lot of other breweries. Again, it's not something that I've thought too much about, or that I've wrote down. I just did what I felt was right back then, and I still feel the same things right. Even though we have grown from a company with one person, me, to now having, I don't know, maybe four-hundred employees worldwide. I still have the same ideas and the same way of doing things."

Dr. Kate Stone, Director Novalia.
"I think what I do is developed over time. Looking back, I think it's all about curiosity, so just being curious. Just thinking what if? What if I can do this? What if I can do that? Just kind of... the pursuit of curiosity. What all of that curiosity unfolds starts to add up, layer by layer by layer and build me. That's just who I am. That's who we all are, right? We're a collection of all the things we've done. All of the people we've met. All of the ideas we've shared. All of the ideas we've listened to. Layer by layer like in coal. That's who we become."

Henrik Fisker, Automotive designer and entrepreneur (BMW Z8, Aston Martin DB9, V8 Vantage, Fisker Karma, Mustang Rocket, VLF Force 1, Destino V8).
"When I jumped out to become an entrepreneur, my vision was that I wanted to design some amazing different cars and create a bit of

disruption in this industry which has been very traditional for a very long time. I think my mission or I would say my life sentence that I go by is never give up. That's something that you really has to follow when you're an entrepreneur I think because there is times when everybody says, "You're not going to make it," or "This isn't going to work." You just can't give up. You got to keep on going. Even if you go down, you got to stand up again and keep going. That is really what makes difference between an entrepreneur that's successful and somebody who is not. It takes a lot of persistence.

My vision was always to do something that was innovative, different and really create an emotional connection between the customer and the product that I create."

Lars Seier Christensen, Founder and owner Seier Capital, Co-founder and fmr. CEO Saxo Bank.

"I think it's very important. I agree that people understand where we're trying to go, and you do that through regularly setting out the direction and the vision for the company. We always spent quite a long time speaking to our colleagues and making them understand where we're trying to go, and set up again a set of values that they could adhere to and a set of principles for how we would want them to interact with each other and develop the service and the products.

We were never very detailed, because I don't believe in that because again, you cannot predict what the market wants, you cannot predict what's going to succeed or not succeed. You have to give people a lot of room to get from A to B in the way that they think is right, and you can

331

never know better than your employees that are sitting with the product every day and speaking to the clients. It's very difficult to sit in an ivory tower as a CEO and know better than them. It's quite common among strong CEOs to want to regulate the detail, but I think it's very dangerous because actually, the creativity and the innovative spirit people have, if you set that free and let them actually come up with the solutions, you'll be very surprised how much better they are than yourself many times. I think this is critical that you give that room, but inside a set of principles and inside a mission that you're trying to pursue.

We only had an explicit mission statement about 10 years in to the process, but because we were a very small company at the outset, I think it was implicitly understood where and what were our values. I would nevertheless recommend for people to do that much earlier, because again, you will for sure have a value set in a business, and if you're not very explicit about it, much of it will be fine I'm sure. It's very wise to be very, very explicit about what you really want, because then people will do their best to give it to you and if they feel uncomfortable with the set of values, for example, we always saw ourselves as a very capitalistic organization, we told people if you do well, you're going to get paid well, if you don't do so well, you're going to be paid less well, or we're going to say goodbye to you, which is not a very Danish way to do things, but we felt it was fair to let people know that that's the way we look at it, and that we wanted people with a capitalistic mindset in our business. If they have a different mindset, there's lots of public institutions they can work for in this country."

Henrik Fisker, Automotive designer and entrepreneur (BMW Z8, Aston Martin DB9, V8 Vantage, Fisker Karma, Mustang Rocket, VLF Force 1, Destino V8).

"When you design something, it's very loose. Nobody really knows until it's on the market and somebody else says, "Wow," and buy it or somebody says, "I don't like it". What I've found is that when most products, especially when it comes to design, you can obviously create something that is not polarizing and is in the middle of the road. If it is marketed really well, if it's priced really well, it can be really successful in terms of volume. It can also be a complete failure even if all these things have been done correctly. There is examples of products that has been gone through many product clinics etc. and they have become failures and nobody knew why because everything was ticked off. It just didn't really have that connection with consumer. What I found is if you do something very extreme and you really do get that emotional connection with a consumer, you can have a niche where it becomes really successful and you can charge a very good price which allows you to function as a specialty company. You will also have to live with some people really hate it or don't like it."

Peter Holten Mühlmann, Founder and CEO, Trustpilot.

"I think you motivate people by giving them a strong, "Why." Why are you here? Why is it that you go to work every day? What is the goal of the business. I don't think that people are very motivated by, say, giving a 7% annual return to shareholders or increasing the bottom line with 10% or whatever.

Of course, it's fun if you can have really big growth targets. But I think a lot of people will also care about you being able to explain to them what difference your company is making in the world.

2nd, I think if you can create an environment where people genuinely care about each other, want to get to know their colleagues and feel that they trust their colleagues, and conflicts are solved in that light... If you do something that I think is wrong, then I'll just walk up and tell you."

Kaspar Basse, Founder, CEO Joe & The Juice.

"Everything comes from putting everything into the recruitment, the training, the social relationship our employees create outside the stores, etc, etc. It's really an American term campus. I've referenced to that. We've built what we call the Joe & the Juice campus. Which is partly working a lot with what goes on in the stores, but also giving the guys opportunities to create clubs and mutual interest outside and nurture that. So, that they get the same kind of attachment to our company as people typically have if they go to Harvard or UCLA for four years.

The fundamental thing is much more about creating a tremendously attractive and admirable youth culture, then it is about how many stores we do. Of course you can't do a youth culture by having ten stores in Scandinavia. It's just a fact we need to do a lot of stores. To a certain extent, the more stores we do, the more people we will touch, and the more cities we have to send our employees to, creating a stronger and broader culture.

We will do a thousand, five thousand, ten thousand, twenty thousand stores. It's a tool to create the bigger purpose. Funny enough, our vision, in that sense, we typically formulate as our wish to come on the cover of Rolling Stones magazine. That's something that might be difficult for somebody to relate to, but it's not randomly defined. It's really because the day we are on the cover of Rolling Stone magazine. It is because we succeeded in not becoming just another sandwich concept. It is because we became so big that they noticed us. It does contain the quantifiable success criteria. Hopefully, less boringly formulated than when you see the typical."

Career Planning.

Benjamin Holk Henriksen, Strategic planning & branding.
Lecturer DIS and Copenhagen Business School, Author, Filmmaker
"The Mind of a Leader", "Holk Master-class".
"Career planning is actually one of my absolute favorite subjects. And I think we are very privileged that so many interesting industry professionals actually wanted to contribute to this episode.

Career planning share some of the ideas that we have seen in corporations meaning the mission and the vision, what is it that you actually want to do, and what is it that you want to be and become.

So before we actually start move in to this interesting area and listen to our interviewees, lets take a quick look at the corporate terms vision and mission."

Mission and vision are a set of guidelines that indicates what an organization wants to do and be.

In the entrepreneurial startup phases it's often dreams and desires that motivate a team. Smaller organisations are flexible and adaptable, and there are many examples of very successful companies that started out doing one thing and ended up in a different direction. However, as the company grows it becomes increasingly important to have a specific vision and mission that guides and motivates the employees.

A Mission frequently defines what the company or organisation aims 'to do', whereas a Vision is a state of being 'to be'.

Interviewees.

Asger Leth, Director & Screenwriter, DGA award winner. (Ghosts of Cité Soleil, Man on a Ledge, Five Obstructions, Move on (Telekom)).

"Wow. Damn, that's a tough question. Do I have a mission, vision in life? Did I have a vision in life from the get-go, and what's the advice to give to other future directors? I think it's a tough question. I had a vision. I'm not going to share it. I think a vision is something that's always a work in progress. You reach it. Then you have to redefine your vision or it redefines itself, because you're moving along. You're calming your way, so your viewpoint in life is constantly shifting. I think, because of that, your vision changes. It becomes a matter of reaching just one step at a time closer to your vision that keeps drifting ahead of you and changing where it's going. Those mission statements, how do I get from here to there to there to there to there is important. There's just so many roads that lead to Rome, that it's difficult to put down on paper.

I think it has to do with, at least as a starting point, a certain 'take no prisoners' attitude to make sure that you put yourself in a place where you're going to pursue your dreams, even though it's difficult. Finding your dreams as a director is nothing's easy. This is not one of those freebies. You go to school, and you get a diploma, and now you're a director. This is a lifelong struggle from movie to movie to movie to movie, you are constantly working and proving yourself. For instance, I studied law for three years, trying to delay my decision to become a director. I already knew before I got into law school, basically, that that's what I wanted to do. At some point, I got so far into law school that I was going to end up becoming a lawyer if I didn't stop myself. The sensible parents would have said to me, "No. You have to finish law school."

The sensible student, who's worried about life and so on, would have said to myself, "I have to make sure I have a safety belt. I have to get my degree. Then I can experiment in filmmaking," but I already knew I wanted to be a director, so I was facing a choice where if I took that next exam, I was going to be a lawyer. I knew myself enough to know that if I did that, I was going to make money being a lawyer. The filmmaking would become a hobby, and the hobby would dissipate and dissipate and fade out and never become. I knew that as a director, you have to give yourself 120% for years and years on end, where you make no dime, where you're questioning everything about yourself. Am I ever going to make it? Are people going to see what I'm doing? Do I even know what I'm doing? Those years are long and hard, and if you have something to fall back on, you're going to do that.

I needed personally to not have something to fall back on, to be able to do that, to put myself through that, but I did. I think I succeeded to get to that point and then the next point. Now, I'm here, and I know that getting to my next movie is another struggle, but I learned that struggle from going through those years. That's something, you grow a thick skin. You've got to move ahead, and you've got to be doing that comfortably, so you're not nervous, so you can still create a new vision for the next *thing you're going to do. Apart from that, the best advice I was ever given was, someone told me that Bette Davis told a young actress who was going to Hollywood, "Do you have any advice for anybody who's going to Hollywood as a young actress?" I know I'm a director, so there's not really directional or it's not proportional, but her advice was, "Yes. Always take Fountain." That's a street in Hollywood that cuts through everything.*

I love the advice, because it's like she said many things at the same time. She said, "There is not one piece of advice. On the other hand, if there's an easy way through where you don't have to waste a lot of time, in this case, it was traffic, but it was a parallel for life in general. Take that so you can spend valuable time on your craft. I think that's a good lesson."

Dennis Balslev, CEO IKEA Germany. Fmr. CEO IKEA Denmark.

"My career has not been planned from the beginning. My career has been planned step by step in the sense that, when I look back, I have never asked for position myself, only the first one when I entered the company and then I think with hard work and delivered what I should deliver, and I've been asked throughout almost 30 years now, to take on different positions so it has not been a plan from the beginning. I want to be retail manager in Denmark or I want to do this and that. It has been step by step and for me, it's more important to have interesting challenges than have a specific goal to go for. That's a little bit how it happened. Also, the next position could be something very different, inside Ikea of course, but it's not planned for me what the next position should be, no."

Malin Gardeström, International Marketing Manager, Carlsberg & Tuborg.

"I come from CBS where I studied for 5 years. I've been with some big companies, Novo Nordisk, L'Oreal, and Carlsberg now.

I have never seen myself as a career person, even though I know I can appear that way from the outside with a great responsibility throughout many years. To me, it's never been about title, I have worked quite hard to get where I am today, but I haven't worked hard in order to get where I am today. To me, it's more about having fun where I am at the moment. If HR and managers wanted you to make a plan for your career, that's not my way of doing it. I want it to be, to have fun and to be inspired where I am today, and I have no idea where I am in 3 years. My career has taken me based on my performance and the people I've met and to me, integrity is very important. I'm a marketeer at heart, so I do what's best for the brand."

David Angelo, Founder & Chairman, David & Goliath advertising agency.

"Absolutely, and it all started when I was a little kid. My father came from a very poor environment, he was a truck driver, a "Teamster", and a marine. He instilled these values in me, two very important values. One is, never forget where you're from, which means always honor your story, be true to who you are, no matter who you are or where you're from. Always give 100% of your heart and soul.

As a kid I always believed that challenges were a fact of life and if you take them head on you'll be better off for it. I'd say the biggest challenge that I've ever encountered was when I got kicked out of High School a month before I graduated. It was at that point I didn't really care about what I was going to do for a living.

My father got me a job as working the graveyard shift for a large spirit distributor, where I drove a forklift truck and loaded spirits on trucks and all that. It was at that point that I realized that I didn't want to do that for the rest of my life. I wanted to something that really used my strength to the best of its ability.

I heard a voice that said, "You're better than this." From that point on I just was determined to succeed at all cost. I went back to college, I went back to school, went to college during the day, while I worked the night shift. Eventually I graduated from college and the Academy of Art college, after 10 years, after working the graveyard shift.

It was right after I graduated, I received a postcard in the mail from someone. I know who it is now, but back then I didn't really know who it was, but I know who it is now. It read, "Do what you fear, watch it disappear." I thought to myself, "That quote is so inspiring and so true and so profound." All you have to do is just follow it. Do what you fear, watch it disappear, and you no longer have anything to fear once you take it head on.

I put it on my refrigerator and when I thought about where I was going to work after graduating, the first place that popped in my mind was the place I feared most, and that was New York City. I picked up my bags and moved to New York City, with just a ten speed, a basketball and a sleeping bag, and I got a job on Madison Avenue, working at a place called DDB Needham.

It was from that point on I found myself in a position where every single time that I was presented with a challenge, I would just follow the postcard. That gave me permission to be fearless. From there I produced a lot of great work for a number of agencies. I even worked on the '92 election for Bill Clinton, with my writing partner."

Peter Holten Mühlmann, Founder and CEO, Trustpilot.
"Yeah. No. I've definitely never had vision or a mission with a career. It was always what felt right. I recall being in university. Then, a friend came and invited me to join his company. Then, suddenly I found myself immersed in that. Then, after a while, that stopped being as engaging. Then, I started doing Trustpilot. Then, Trustpilot felt right.

I think decisions are taken more based on what feels right. I just go into a life a little bit like water running down a hill. I find that sometimes when something is not working out, then just slowly stop doing that and you start doing something new. It's actually the fear of that thing happening that's much worst than when the transition happens."

David Angelo, Founder & Chairman, David & Goliath advertising agency.
"After being in the business for like 10 years, I decided to take some time off and sort of asses what I wanted to do, what my next move was going to be. After looking, after working for various agencies around the world,

who all for the most part, aspire to do great creative work, I never got a sense of who they were or what they stood for outside of the work.

I really wanted to create an agency that best reflected my own outlook on life. One that would enable to me to go up against challenges, to live my brand 24/7, and inspire others to do the same. That gave way to the name David & Goliath.

Since then, it's been 16 years, we are an agency that is designed to inspire people and brands to take on their biggest Goliaths, and achieve greatness. Because we believe that if you are willing to do that, and willing to sort of step outside of your comfort zone and go up against the thing that you fear most, then only greatness awaits. Because before you can do anything great you have to be brave first.

Which is a good Segway to our philosophy. Our philosophy is called brave. Brave is a very, it's irrefutable truth that's in all of us. It's one single word that gives us permission to be true to who we are. I really believe that that's what's missing in the world, it's what's missing in today's branding, is that you see a lot of brands trying to be something they're not, when all they have to do is embrace their authentic self and just tell a more contemporary story.

That's David & Goliath for you. There's a David in all of us, that's the way I look at it. It's not just me, I'm just the person who, I guess, the person who pays the bills around here, but at the end of the day it's 200 of us and my philosophy has always been that no one is greater than all of us."

Reflection on HR management and Maslow's hierarchy of needs.

Maslow's hierarchy of needs is a theory in psychology proposed by Abraham Maslow in his 1943 paper "A Theory of Human Motivation" in Psychological Review.[66] In management theory - motivation relates to 'job efficiency'; but the tool may also be used in regard to consumer habits and preferences. The theory is often portrayed in the shape of a pyramid with five interdependent levels of basic human needs. Motivators that must be satisfied in a strict sequence starting with the lowest level.

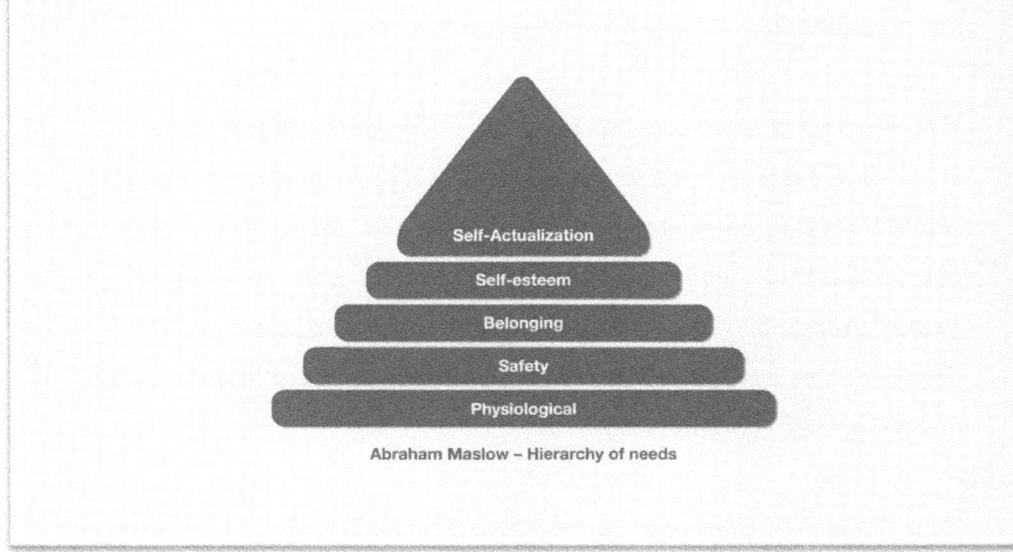

Figure 34.

---

[66] Maslow, A. H. (1943). A theory of human motivation. Psychological Review, 50(4), 370-396.

Physiological needs.

Physical requirements for human survival such as to stay alive and reproduce. If these requirements are not met, the human body cannot function properly.

Safety needs.

Personal security, financial security, health, and safety net against accidents or illness.

Love and belonging.

The third level of human needs is interpersonal and involves feelings of belonging such as: Friendship, Intimacy and Family

Esteem.

Esteem presents the typical human desire to be accepted and valued by others.

Self-actualisation.

The realisation of a person's full potential.

The theory states that once a need is satisfied, it stops being a motivator of human beings. In personnel management, it is used in the design of incentive schemes. In marketing, it is used in designing promotional campaigns based on the perceived needs of a market segment which a product satisfies.

This work presents marketing & communication abstracts. For more details about the theory please view the authors' own works.

Interviewees.

Asger Leth, Director & Screenwriter, DGA award winner. (Ghosts of Cité Soleil, Man on a Ledge, Five Obstructions, Move on (Telekom)).

"Wow. That's a big question. We were talking about the perfect work environment, or what I consider important in a work environment. I'm a film director, so my area of expertise and the area where I move, also, in terms of employees is a very particular one. Usually, filmmakers are extremely passionate people about filmmaking. The hours that we work once we are shooting are almost inhuman. We have, we could easily go six months with 16 hour, 18 hour days. That's not a normal environment. You know probably it should be shot down by all kinds of laws, but that's the only way they can make movies. This particular environment demands that I know and I'm aware that the people working for me on a movie are passionate about making this movie. That goes all the way down and in front of the actual hiring process.

I need to make sure that I hire people that are not only the best at what they do, but that they also are very passionate about this particular project, because it's only the passion that's ultimately going to carry them through, not the paycheck. There are other movies they could be on, so it's not the paycheck that's going to make them go 16, 18 hour days. It's the passion for the project and the passion for their colleagues that

346

they're working with, and sometimes even the passion for working with this particular director. Those are extremely important things to get in place first. After that, when you work with people who you know mostly are showing up for passion, that means that you have to treat them right in every other aspect. That means, when I hire somebody, I hire them because I think they're the best at what they do. That means that I'm not going to micromanage everything that they do. I'm going to trust them to come up with suggestions."

Ole Henriksen, Founder and Creative Director, Ole Henriksen Skin Care Brand.

"Well, the thing that's been so amazing over the years of building a brand is the talented people I get to work with. Creating that family, that extended family that I began developing, or creating rather, decades ago. Valuable people that bring so much to the table.

When I interview a potential employee, I want to hear about them, their personal lives, their interests. I want to get to know them as a person. And yes, then I want to learn about the professional know-how, and credentials, and, at the same time, I really weigh both the personal side as much as the professional. Because, at my company, it's very much about taking time for each other, visiting with each other. Yesterday, I made the rounds in the offices. We chatted about how was the holidays and New Year, how are the kids, whatever it may be. And I think it's very important that when you have that relationship, not alone do you work more effectually in a happy environment... And our business is really... Beauty is something very positive, and that way you bring out the best in everyone. And I'm the first to applaud and recognize.

Just like the other day up in Edmonton when I had to give a speech at night, I visited all the top stores up there in Canada. And that night there was a dinner for the twenty-four top performers, and I looked at the room, they were midway through the dinner, and took inventory of all these beautiful women and men, and first and foremost it was about celebrating them in their personal lives as the kind of amazing people they are. And there was a perfect stepping stone with the New Year. Recognizing that, and then recognizing them, of course, with their professional contributions as well."

Peter Ålbæk Jensen, Producer, Founder & fmr. CEO, Zentropa.

"We're trying to educate a lot of young people to have a career in the film business, and the first thing we learn them that is to shut the mouth do what they're told and be on time. We are really a fucking fascist company in that way. But if you can manage to take your ego down for a period in your life when you are a young trainee, then you can learn to endure and you learn that it is a funny glamorous business, but the backbone is extreme discipline and big precision of, a portion of hard work.

Because of that, you start as a trainee out here working for free for six months. Otherwise, we don't feel that they have that right devotion if the come in and get a salary from the first day. We have, we call it the trainee smother, which means they are midgets or something that. So they have an inferior title. But they're very much in some kind of military camp where they have to work, obey the stupid sergeant, which is me, for so long a period, that they can hit back at certain time in their life. But that's very fun and I educated around three hundred youngsters and they

are all in work and almost all of them are in the film business, so it
works."

Dennis Balslev, CEO IKEA Germany. Fmr. CEO IKEA Denmark.

"My advice for future leaders is focus on your people around you. It's a
big focus for me. It's a big focus for us as an organization because
without the right people around you, you will never, never succeed in
what you are doing. The people focus is so important. Engage people,
give responsibly to people and of course have the right people around
you means that you can deliver much more than you can deliver yourself.
We talk a lot about, that common people can reach high quality and high
deliveries if you do it together, and there's cooperation of working
together. Ikea talk a lot about do it together, work together so I think
from a leadership point of view, it's very much put the team around you
and secure you can deliver what you want to deliver. Make clear goals of
course, expectations and so on.

For me, it's important, as responsible for this company, it's not to talk
about what I'm doing. I have so many people around me who do the big
different and I think that's what count today. Very few people, you can
have fantastic people at the top of the company but they create maybe
the face outside the company but they don't create the value inside the
company. That's the people who work there. That's very much my
leadership to focus on my people around me and secure that we're
moving up as a company with clear goals and ambitions, yes."

Molly DeWolf Swenson Founding member / CMO of RYOT.

"There's a couple of things that to me have kept me at riot and have made me want to invest all of my time and energy into this venture. One of them is the fact that it's at this intersection of industries that I really wanted to work in. So, that was technology, entertainment, and social impact. So, sitting very squarely in the middle of those, I knew as sort of a career was a great combination. But, the more important thing was my co-founders and the team that we've built and so it's taken a long time, but the team that we have now finally feels like family. I wouldn't want to go into work every day, I don't think, if I wasn't working with people that I liked this much."

Kaspar Basse, Founder, CEO Joe & The Juice.
"It's very fundamental, old model you chose to use. Let's use it. Look at retail. Fundamentally you have some requirements. Water and drinks. Pay to pay your rent, etc, etc. Most people in our part of the world is covered by that. If you take retail and the position that most retail concepts put their employees in, then I don't see any self esteem or self realization opportunities there. That's the one fundamental thing that we do differently. We really try to create the most demanding, ambitious, celebrating culture and workspace. We do a lot to make the job more interesting. It's more difficult. It takes more training with everybody else to have the speed that it takes to pay the rent, etc, etc. We also put them in a situation where they get a lot of training. They have a lot of social connections. They have the opportunity to show what they can do. The fact that they are by far the fastest and most precise juicers in the world. That they can pour the juice while they look a guest in the eye, etc, etc.

If you take most of the retail concepts around, the requirements as an employee is nothing. You just need the key to open the store and push the cash register. How would you ever create anything special from that person? You may tell the person, "Listen, please, sell more than this today, and indexations." If you're very, you'll get a good Christmas gift. That's not intrinsic motivation. You need to be honest about the position you put your employees in. Also, because you can be more demanding then. Listen, we're doing a lot for you. Give is something back. Don't call in sick Saturday morning, because you were out drinking ten beers Friday night. Show up hung over and kick some ass. I think that approach to creating a people company where this mutual respect and hard work and level of interest is inherent in all levels. Just create something that sparks something you can't predict, as opposed to doing stupid service concepts, where you're telling people how to say hello and goodbye to customers."

Christina Bilde, Spokes person Roskilde Festival.

"For us it makes sense because, you have to remember, we are creating a city. We're building it up from a bare field every year. Without thinking Maslow's pyramid, we are thinking about those basic needs. You could imagine having a city where those needs are not fulfilled or you're not working with them consciously then I believe that city really wouldn't function."

Benjamin Holk Henriksen, Strategic planning & branding.
Lecturer DIS and Copenhagen Business School, Author, Filmmaker
"The Mind of a Leader", "Holk Master-class".

"This theory provides a useful summary of human needs, which can be used to create an efficient work environment. But the theory is also associated with marketing disciplines such as product design, product positioning, pricing, and retail outlets' designs. It helps marketers to focus their advertising appeals on specific needs shared by a large segment of their target market.

Some of the disadvantages that have been pointed out are: It can't be tested empirically. There is no way to measure precisely how satisfied one level of need must be before the next higher need becomes operative. The model lacks empirical support for the rank-ordering of the needs. The model is too simplistic, meaning the same product or service can satisfy several needs at once. The model is too culture-bound. It may be restricted to Western cultures. Fore example "self-esteem" or "security," has a different perception depending on where... which culture around the globe you look at. The hierarchy also fails to take into account individual differences. There is not much evidence indicating that every human being experiences the needs in the order Maslow suggests. Finally Pamela Rutledge has pointed out, in an article from Psychology Today, that it also lacks the interaction and the bond, and the interaction between people. But despite this disadvantages there is no doubt that Maslow's hierarchy of needs still stands as one of the great masterpieces."

Leadership & job motivation.

Interviewees.

Benjamin Holk Henriksen, Strategic planning & branding.
Lecturer DIS and Copenhagen Business School, Author, Filmmaker
"The Mind of a Leader", "Holk Master-class".

"Leadership and job motivation are essential factors in regards to creating a positive and efficient work environment. Abraham Maslow once wrote a paper called "A Theory of Human Motivation" where he list some of the basic needs that needs to be fulfilled, human needs that needs to be fulfilled in order to create an efficiency work environment. Needs such as: Physiological needs, Safety needs, Love and belonging, Esteem, and eventually Self-actualization.

In this episode we are going to look at some of the key questions in terms of leadership and job motivation. Questions such as how do you behave as a leader, how should you behave, how much should you associate with your employees, how do you get great ideas without loosing status, and how do you eventually create the best work environment for the company."

Lars Seier Christensen, Founder and owner Seier Capital, Co-founder and fmr. CEO Saxo Bank.

"I think basing yourself on facts and facing up to reality also when it's unpleasant, I think is very important and that's actually a message we emphasize very, very strongly internally that you have to be rational, you have to live in the real work and accept what the real world throws as

you. That being said of course, if people don't see a mission or a vision or that you're doing something here that actually benefits some people, that makes it easier for them to trade, makes it more likely that they're successful, that takes out some of the big banks because they didn't do the same thing. You need to build of course a story where people feel inspired and feel that this is really worth for getting up for in the morning.

I think we managed to do that quite well in the bank, that people working there are pretty excited about being part of Saxo, so much so that they themselves invented the term Saxonians, which is not something we put on them, but actually see themselves as Saxonians, and part of this is this great moving, move that we made of the past 25 years. I think people need to be inspired, they need to trust that you're doing something better than the rest of the world, and that you'll make a difference. Because otherwise, it's very hard for them to really be fully engaged and put in the extra hours when it's needed. I think you as a leader or the CEO or the entrepreneur, it's very much your responsibility to make sure that people understand innovation and understand why we're doing this and why it's exciting and why it's really groundbreaking. But, you cannot move away from reality still. Somebody out there got a better product, but the customers don't agree that your product is great, then you got a problem and you need to fix it."

Asger Leth, Director & Screenwriter, DGA award winner. (Ghosts of Cité Soleil, Man on a Ledge, Five Obstructions, Move on (Telekom)).

"I come from Denmark, where we have a different work structure than they do in the States, and I work mostly in the States. In the States, I feel that it's, the hierarchy is stronger and the amount of time that the boss listens to the employees is less. Basically, I invite the people working for me to bring their ideas, as crazy as they are, much more to the table than I think that they're used to. I actually invite it, and I consider it, in reversal, as a requirement for me. I'm not interested in working with them if they don't offer up both good and bad ideas. The American structure, the people are too afraid to come up with bad ideas. I think, in filmmaking, every day and every hour is a brainstorming process. Every brainstorm only really truly works if all ideas are welcome, good and bad. That's very important for me.

This means, also, that I have to become, not a friend, because we're not going to be friends. I am the boss, but friendly. I will socialize, as much as I can, with my film crew. I will hang out with them as much as I can. I can do it less than the others, because I'm usually the director that works more hours than anybody on the set, but I try as much as I can, because I think it's important to create a safe environment where everybody feels, he actually means this. I can throw off my crazy, goofball idea, and I'm not going to be looked down upon because of that. On the contrary. In this environment, I actually think it's important to get rid of also the bad ideas. The only way to get rid of them is to air them.

Instead of just walking around being cautious about only walking this tightrope of great ideas, you have to get rid of all the bad stuff. It makes everybody more sure that the great idea is actually the great idea. You're absolutely more sure that this is the right path when you have examined *all the wrong pathways. That's an important environment to create. Look, when I make a movie, whether it's a $50 million movie or whatever it is, I have 400 people on my payroll working under me. Basically, I'm doing that from nothing to 120 miles an hour, creating within six months to a year a product that's untested and unseen, that nobody's seen before. You're creating everything from scratch. You have to work with people who are going to kill themselves trying to get to that place, but who are passionate about it and who will throw everything at it, good and bad ideas. Then, ultimately, you have something."*

Lars Liebst, CEO Tivoli.

"I don't know, I think coming from a creative background with the theater and concerts and all of that, education, by the way, I think maybe I'm a little bit more open to never say no, because that I have learned the hard way, because even though you have been here for many years, there might be somebody who have a better idea than you have. That is something that you have to remember. It's not always that it just goes down the line like this year, maybe you have to take another direction. I think one should be more than open for that. Secondly, I think letting your employees come up with ideas, whoever they are, wherever they are, that is always a good idea, because the satisfaction among the employees is going to be higher, meaning they like their job, they would like to stay here for a long time, that is much better. You create loyalty among your employees as well."

David Angelo, Founder & Chairman, David & Goliath advertising agency.

"I always look at it this way, I always say, "All right, who's running that company?" Who's running that organization? Who's running that agency? Who's running that government? Everything starts at the top, so if you are a person or a brand that is living your authentic truth, like you're being true to who you are, then chances are you're going to inspire everyone underneath you to do the same. Chances are you're going to inspire your chief marketing officer to un-tap or unlock the authentic truth of the brand.

It starts at the top, look at every organization, Phil Knight, Nike, Richard Branson, Virgin, Steve Jobs, Tim Cook, Apple, it starts at the top. Here at David&Goliath it definitely starts at the top. To be honest with you, calling yourself David&Goliath is not an easy thing, because it means I am, you kind of have to live up to it. Because of who I am and where I'm from, and how I was raised and the challenges I went through as a kid, I don't know any other way but to live my authentic truth, which enables me to live the authentic truth of David&Goliath and inspire others to do the same."

Henrik Fisker, Automotive designer and entrepreneur (BMW Z8, Aston Martin DB9, V8 Vantage, Fisker Karma, Mustang Rocket, VLF Force 1, Destino V8).

"One of the things I'm doing now is I'm really paying attention to wanting to be in most of the job interviews, even if it doesn't really matter who it is, what level they're at. I'm creating a leaner organization. It does have a certain negative impact. You can say that more people are reporting directly to me, which means that it demands slightly more work. It means that I can make quicker decisions. I think it's very

important that if you get many of the managers or leaders to report to you, they start really understand how you want to run the business. You start communicating together. It becomes then I think easier to hand over something at a later stage because they're more integrated with the way you think the business should be ran. I do believe it's very important to find people that are self-drivers, that are taking initiative. You don't want only to have yes people around you."

Lars Liebst, CEO Tivoli.

"We encourage people to stay here and try to get a career in Tivoli. We think it's great. In different fields, somebody is... We have a lot of chefs and those people, they think they almost look at the watch and say, "Hey, I've been here for 2 years, it's a lifespan of time, I have to go." That is the way it is, that is their nature. Others would say, "Hey, I've been here 10 years, I love it, I will have 10 more years"."

Ole Henriksen, Founder and Creative Director, Ole Henriksen Skin Care Brand.

"Yes, in order to bring out the best in your fellow human beings and, in this case, in the coworkers in your company, take time for them. Listen to them. Learn from them as they learn from you. And that gives you a platform for them. They obviously want to blossom. And really let them be the best at what they are best at. And don't be a control freak. Let them bring it out there, and then you can have, of course, the dialogue, because there's a give and take. Certain times you have to compromise to arrive at the right product, in this case.

But for me, it's the people and the fact that I now, as the mature guy in the company... I used to be the 23 year when I started the business now I'm turning 65. And now I'm the old guy on the block with the young energy, and I just love to see these young people blossom and bring all their creativity and talent to the table. But that deserves recognition. Don't take anyone for granted. We all like a little stroke. And everyone deserves it."

Malene Torp. Executive Director, DIS – Study Abroad in Scandinavia.

"When I think of strategic planning I think you, as a leader, need to be very aware that it's a process and I think the biggest mistake you can make is to think that you have the best ideas and that you already have a strategy in mind and then you're just trying to get everybody to buy into your strategy. I think that's the wrong way to go about a strategic planning. I really think you want it to be an open process and actually really mean it when you say that you want input from people. I think it's been an advantage for me that I know that I'm not the smartest person in the room. I used to play golf and I was a pretty decent golfer. I also used to play tennis and I was a pretty decent tennis player, but I was never the best player on my team, but I was always the captain and I think of that when I think of strategic planning as well, that I don't enter a room thinking I already have the best idea for the strategy and now I just want other people to buy into my idea, but that I actually go into the room expecting that other people will have better ideas than I have myself."

Asger Leth, Director & Screenwriter, DGA award winner. (Ghosts of Cité Soleil, Man on a Ledge, Five Obstructions, Move on (Telekom)).

"In the meantime, you have to be the boss. I have one thing to say that I think is a lesson not just for other directors, but also maybe for CEOs and so on. I think CEOs should learn to use the word director and almost use it as a subtitle to their title, because there's something within that word that tells you everything. It's something I learned from my father, who is also a film director. He told me once, when I was a little bit afraid of executing my job, he said, "Son, remember that a director means someone who gives directions. You only have to point that way. You're the one who knows, this ship is going to go that way. Then, your job from that point on is to hire people who make sure it goes in that direction. If the ship starts steering in the wrong direction, you say, 'Wait a minute. It's a great idea you came up, but I feel the ship is drifting a little bit too much to the right. Let's take that idea, and put it into the folder and get back on track.'"

It's only a matter of pointing out the direction, and making sure everybody follows it, but there's many ways to get to that direction, to get from A to B. I think that's a great example of the workspace I'm trying to create."

Henrik Fisker, Automotive designer and entrepreneur (BMW Z8, Aston Martin DB9, V8 Vantage, Fisker Karma, Mustang Rocket, VLF Force 1, Destino V8).

"That's why our leader is there, to take that risk, to try and understand what's going on and move on.

360

I have usually found even if you make a wrong decision, it is sometimes better than no decision because at least people start working and you create something. Even if you slightly have to change it, you have created something rather than stagnating.

If one area of your organization is stagnated because of a lack of decision, it usually has a domino effect on the rest of the organization sooner or later. Sooner or later, everybody uses the argument that these guys haven't moved and that's why I haven't moved. I think you got to keep that constant speed within your organization to really make it function and also today, I think the pace is very important of an organization because everything comes faster to market. We don't even have the time to take years and years before we put a product to market. The competition is too strong. You have to have an agile culture and an organization that can move fast."

Code of conduct and CSR.

Code of conduct.

A code of conduct is a set of rules outlining the social norms, rules and responsibilities of an individual, party or organization. Many apparel companies have adopted codes of conduct setting labor standards for their contract factories. However, factories are also under contradictory pressure to lower prices and increase production speed and volume. Both companies and factories often find it convenient to ignore codes of conduct. And workers may not even know that a code exists unless it's posted on the wall in a language that workers can read.

Nike is an example of a company that has been accused of using sweatshops to produce footwear and apparel. Nike denied the claims, suggesting the company has no control over sub-contracted factories. During the 1990s, Nike installed a code of conduct for their factories called SHAPE: Safety, Health, Attitude, People, and Environment.[67]

---

[67] Locke, Richard M. and Romis, Monica (2010) 'The promise and perils of private voluntary regulation: Labor standards and work organization in two Mexican garment factories', Review of International Political Economy, 17:1, 45 – 74.
Fair Labor Association. Nike, Assessment for reaccreditation, October 2008.

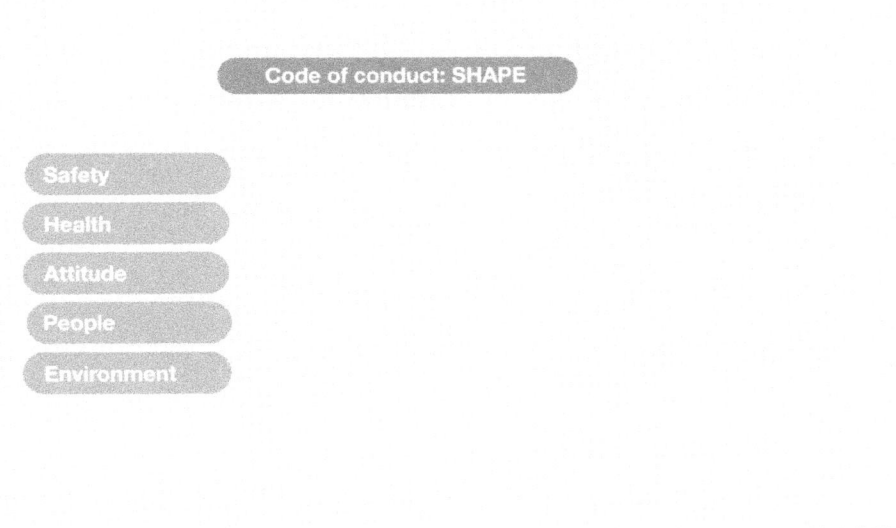

Figure 35.

Apparently Nike spend about 10 million dollars a year to follow the code, adhering to regulations for fire safety, air quality, minimum wage, and overtime limits.

Corporate Social Responsibility.

The code of conduct is frequently listed on corporate websites together with Corporate Social Responsibility, or CSR. CSR is a form of corporate self-regulation integrated into a business model.[68] A statement that supports the organisational mission. CSR strategies encourage the

---

[68] Friedman, Milton (1970) "The Social Responsibility of Business is to Increase its Profits", The New York Times Magazine, September 13.
Friedman, Milton (1962). Capitalism and Freedom. The University of Chicago Press.

company to make a positive impact on the environment and stakeholders including consumers, employees, investors, communities, and others. The aim is to increase long-term profits through positive public relations and high ethical standards. To reduce business and legal risk, and gain shareholder trust by taking responsibility for corporate actions.

Interviewees.

Lars Liebst, CEO Tivoli.

"Well, why we do it is clearly because we are a large company, we have to show responsibility in different ways. All the way back until 1999, I think, we started up, we had our own windmill, we do a huge program for changing light bulbs to LED. We try to look into all of this here in a certain way that we help, hopefully the environment. It is good for the environment but it's also good for the bottom line. Those 2 things can go hand in hand. We have a huge recycle program and we do, on a different scale, we welcome refugees as part of our staff. We think that is important that we open our gates, taking in people who might have some problems, and trying to get them back to work."

Karim Jabbar. Entrepreneurship & Innovation specialist. Industrial PhD Fellow. Lecturer, DIS – Study Abroad in Scandinavia.

"Back in 1970, Milton Friedman wrote a seminal text about CSR and of course, those of you who know Friedman, would know that he's pretty much an opponent of corporate social responsibility. For him, corporate

social responsibility, is a slippery slope towards communism essentially. It's mixing up things that are the realm of business and things that is the realm of government and essentially, making decisions on social issues, through the vehicle of corporations, which is mixing two things together, which do not need to be mixed together. In his view, people who claim corporate social responsibility and what it is that they do, he would say, "It's an act of shameless window dressing" Essentially you take something, which you are doing for the purpose of profits and you try to package it, as if it is for the goodness... Out of the goodness of your heart or whatever that you are doing it. That would be one case that he makes against it and another case would be, that when you're doing it, without it coming back to you, essentially charity, if that is what you're doing, then essentially you would be taking away money from your employees, from your customers because essentially, you take it from the bottom line. That's the only way you can take it up. Essentially his take would be, corporate social responsibility, is this left wing construction that has been created, which essentially obstructs the free functioning of the market.

If you fast forward a little bit to the world of today, CSR is embedded in most companies. All large corporations around the world, if you go onto their websites, they're going to have tabs that says, responsibility or code of conduct or corporate responsibility, corporate social responsibility, environment, what have you. If you click on to that, you're going to see a nice report, about what it is that the company does and why they are a responsible company, socially and environmentally and on other aspect as well. Essentially things that are not just about finances and making money.

It links a little bit to the idea of the triple bottom line, people, planet, profit. That you are actually doing something, that you envision yourself as being embedded in the broader scheme of things. You are a company, that cannot work in a detached fashion from everything else. You are connected to a society that enables or gives you the work force that you're need. You're offering back to the society and the environment that you take resources form, you have a certain responsibility, to make sure that you don't deplete those resources. Kind of a connected sick little kind of view of things.

There has been a big shift in that time and part of it might be, the way people talk about corporate social responsibility because in its old days, in the times of Milton Friedman, CSR was essentially charity. CSR was the division of let's say, the wealthy business man in the US, that had established a company. Become very rich, sets up the foundation and then gives something to charity. Which is a different take than what CSR is today. Today people will typically say, "It's creating shared value." A term that has been coined by Michael Porter and Mark Kramer. These two authors have actually written two papers in Harvard Business Review, a few years apart about corporate social responsibility and creating shared value. In a nutshell what they say is that, corporate social responsibility or creating shared value, depending on which one of the two articles you look at, is actually about making sure that you do something, which is inherently good for you as a company. It should be a sound investment. It should make money back but in the process of doing that, you're actually contributing positively to society and to the environment."

Petter A. Stordalen, Founder and owner of Nordic Choice Hotels.

"It's a different world. Everything has changed and it will change even more. For the hotel industry, in the old days they had either a one star, two star, or five star hotel. That's gone. That's like how it was. Still people ask, "How many stars?" You know? The reviews today is done on TripAdvisor. If you're at the top of TripAdvisor, doesn't matter if you say, "I'm a five star hotel." But on TripAdvisor, you are number 75. So the guest thinks you're a shitty hotel, but you think you're a five star. But not in the head of your guests.

So in the future, the most reviews will be on social media. And they will... you need to be transparent. To tell them why they should pick you. And you need to be honest. You need to be honest if you worked with environmental things. If they caught you using child labor, cutting rainforest, using chemicals, whatever, they will send it and tell it to all their friends. If you don't pay your taxes, you will end up like Starbucks did in UK."

Andreas Rasche, Professor at Copenhagen Business School. Department of Management, Society and Communication.

"If it comes to the concept of CSR I would say the history of CSR goes actually back to philanthropy, to charity, and it dates back many, many years. The first companies engaged in such type of charity were for instance, Cadbury's in the UK. and they for instance, financed houses for their employees. That is from the history where CSR is coming from.

In the 70s and 80s, the concept was popularized and became more of a management task and so, it got a management angle and it move a little way from charity. Although in the US. it still being understood as a charity to some degree. Nowadays, a modern understanding of CSR is of course more concerned with businesses practices and rather than philanthropy giving.

Code of conduct is a little different. Code of conduct, you view it internally the concept, and so, code of conduct for your employees. This emerged largely due to risk management reasons I would say. Firms were very concerned with getting into trouble, and so, they developed this concept of legal compliance and tried to formulate code of conduct to keep themselves out of trouble. Lawyers were the main players in order to enforce these codes. This is the history of both.

Why they got popular. Code of conduct was popularized largely for risk management purposes and it still is today. It depends a little bit on what kind of code of conduct you talk about. There are those code of conduct that are for internal employees, and so, you manage the ethical behavior of your employees. For instance, in a sense that you specify what kind of gifts the can and cannot accept and how they should treat each other. There are also code of conducts in which, often emerge in global supply chains. The code of conduct that for instance, IKEA has developed for suppliers." And this will also be a code of conduct however it is applied outside of the corporation."

Dennis Balslev, CEO IKEA Germany. Fmr. CEO IKEA Denmark.

"Ikea have decided to work with CSR and we have called it sustainability so we include a lot in that word. We believe that's a respect you need to have as a huge company today and you need to be part of society and working with sustainability in all areas. I think it's very natural because all of us are a little bit worried for the planet and the world and what can we as big companies do to improve our influence.

I think what people sometimes misunderstand is that you do it to paint yourself green. No, we don't. It's a good business to think about sustainability and take social responsibility. We cannot show one bad business case when we have taken decisions to renew energy, the way we invest in windmills in many countries, the way we are working with LED lighting in our stores, the way we handle our waste. I think as a big store, as we have in most countries, we are earning money on our waste today. Before, we paid a lot of money to get rid of our waste. Taking that approach in many many aspects from we develop the products, how we run our stores, how we work with social responsibility inside our buildings and outside our buildings, that's the future company way of thinking. You cannot allow not to do that.

I think we from Ikea, are very very proud of the way we are thinking and working as a company and our coworkers appreciate it very very much."

Birgitte Mabeck, Head of fundraising and marketing Red Cross.
"Companies, they are getting far more aware of their surroundings. They getting far more aware of what's happening not only in Denmark but also out in the world. The ones who are on the stock exchange they have to have a CSR documentations and work in that sense. Not only because

of they have to, but we can see that companies they would like to. They would like to take that social responsibility and be part of that. They would like to do it because of their brand. They would like to do it because of their employees. They have sort of a twofold reasons for doing it. They also have a bottomline. They would like to do it to earn the money. We are realizing that and we are finding that we need to be one of the partners that they could work with. We need to be the preferred partner for them to work with. We need to be the channel where they can get increase bottom... their revenue, get more happy satisfied employees, and improve the brand. That's not cheap so of course we need to do it in a manner where it helps the Red Cross and it helps the organization that would like to work with us."

Andreas Rasche, Professor at Copenhagen Business School. Department of Management, Society and Communication.
"They communicate it internally via intranets, via workshops. Surprisingly, a few corporations do a very good in terms of communication. I always, sometimes talk to people about the UN global compact. I ask people, any organizations do you know that your company is actually a signatory? Surprisingly a few employees know about their corporations good deeds. There's a certain communication failure here.

And then of course, there's external communication towards stakeholders, towards academics. This happens quite a lot through reporting I would say. CSR reporting, sustainability reporting; it is also sometimes called. This type of reporting is framed for legal frameworks in quite a lot of countries, so it's not voluntary, but it's mandatory.

Denmark for instance, has a law for CSR reporting in the sense that big companies have to report on CSR. This type of reporting is an important channel.

You also have this social media engagement, where companies engage with particularly, the young generation where they try to ... also get feedback from them."

Petter A. Stordalen, Founder and owner of Nordic Choice Hotels.
"So pay attention to your people, the planet, and profit. I always talk about those three, and in Nordic Choice, my company and the whole group is always, people, planet, and profit, in that order.

We will never have the same earnings like some of our competitors because we are giving back to the society. So we will never reach EBITDA at 12%. But we do it. We are happy with nine. Because the money we earn is money earned on a good way.

So I think social responsibility will be way more important. You need to be transparent in the future. The guests will, or customers will always find out what you're doing."

Business innovation.

Innovation is the process of making something new or doing something in a new way.

In business, innovation includes the concept of improvement. Business innovation involves developing new products or improving existing technologies, processes, designs and marketing to solve problems and reach new customers.

A few classic definitions are:

"Business innovation is the creation of new value and wealth for stakeholders to increase economic prospects" (Lorente et al., 1999; Miller, 1995).

Like IT innovation, business innovation should enable the achievement of goals across the entire organization. Innovation often begins with idea generation or brainstorm, followed by an evaluation of each idea based on business viability, feasibility and desirability.

Henry Ford, founder of Ford Motor Company has been attributed the famous phrase:

"If I had asked people what they wanted, they would have said faster horses."
Henry Ford, founder of Ford Motor Company.

A quote that seem to focus on solving a need rather than listening to the target group.[69] Henry Ford's initial advantage came from his creation of a virtuous circle that underpinned his vision for the first durable mass-market automobile. He adapted the moving assembly line process for the manufacture of automobiles, which allowed him to manufacture, market and sell the Model T at a significantly lower price than his competition, creating a new growing market.

Interviewees.

Henrik Fisker, Automotive designer and entrepreneur (BMW Z8, Aston Martin DB9, V8 Vantage, Fisker Karma, Mustang Rocket, VLF Force 1, Destino V8).

"It's interesting with the corporate world, innovation is more difficult because it's seen as... when you as an entrepreneur go out, you take a risk. It's you, an individual, taking a risk, at least in the beginning. In a corporation, if you're a CEO of a corporation, or a high level manager that can make decisions in innovation, you're taking a risk involving everybody else and their jobs and their future and the business of the company. The risk can seem much bigger when you make innovative ideas or have to make decisions on innovation in the corporation.

But I think that true leaders in the corporate leader do understand that you can't live with a status quo because your competition, sooner or later, is going to start moving the bar up. They're going to innovate

---

[69] Vlaskovits, Patrick (2011). Henry Ford, Innovation, and That "Faster Horse" Quote. August 29. Harvard Business Review.

sooner or later. There is people out there that will take some risk. For a corporate leader, it's very important I think, to try to find that balance of taking enough risk to really innovate but not so much risk that you put everybody in danger."

Dr. Kate Stone, Director Novalia.

"So, what we're trying to do is add interactivity and a deeper experience to every day objects. Those every day objects are things that have been around what feels like forever. If forever is a lifetime, then they certainly have been forever and forever and forever. But many of those things that sort of like have been decimated by what we can now do in the digital world. What we can do in the digital world has created an expectation of how everything should be.

So, like the cat's out of the bag or Pandora's box has been opened. We expect to touch things and have some sort of interactivity with them and have things be connected or update-able. Like we already have that expectation and all the beautiful things are around us are things that we love and things we feel familiar with and they're things that do not alienate us. So, what we're trying to do is to meet the expectations that people now have of an object but put them into things that we're familiar with and not alienated by."

Mikkel Borg Bjergsø Founder and CEO Mikkeller brewery, bars and restaurants.

"That's a good question. I think it's really hard to answer because ... I don't sit down on Wednesday morning with my crew and say, "Now we have to innovate. We have to find something new to do or come up with

some ideas." It's not how we do things. It just happens. It happens because we're interested in what we do, because we meet interesting people that we work with. The whole idea about if you're a company having an innovation department, it's not something that I believe in, because you cannot force people to be innovative, in my opinion. I'm sure a lot of people will disagree with that, but I don't think you get the same result if you force people into thinking and into coming up with new ideas.

I don't know where it comes from, but I have a huge interest in what I do, and I think if you have that, you will always look for something interesting to do and some interesting way to develop what you do already. For example, people ask me, I've done maybe a thousand different beers, recipes and beers, and people ask, "How can you come up with all these beers?" I'm like, "How can you not if you're interested in beer, and if you taste stuff, and if you travel a lot, and you taste a lot of ingredients and meet people that roast coffee or play music, or do something, how can you not be inspired? How can you go back and do the same three beer styles you've done all your life?"

I don't understand that part. I wish I knew what to answer, how to make people more innovative."

Henrik Fisker, Automotive designer and entrepreneur (BMW Z8, Aston Martin DB9, V8 Vantage, Fisker Karma, Mustang Rocket, VLF Force 1, Destino V8).

"Now, a good example where a risk was taken and didn't work in the corporate world was Coca-Cola. They made, some years ago, a new Coca-

Cola called New Coke. People may not remember that because a big failure, a big flop. They put it in the market, they probably spent hundreds and millions marketing it. A few years later, they eliminated it. That was a big corporate risk but they also did it in a smart enough way that if it would have been extremely successful, it was Coke, still because it was called New Coke. If it was a fiasco, then nobody will remember because it was called New Coke."

Lars Seier Christensen, Founder and owner Seier Capital, Co-founder and fmr. CEO Saxo Bank.

"I think you should not structure things too much. You should tell people this is what we're trying to do. We're trying to have a world class platform with tools that enable people to make sure informed decisions and make them be able to risk manage and be able to trade different products in a intuitive and easily understandable way. Now, you go and tell me how you're going to do that, right? You do that of course by speaking to your customers, by analyzing whatever else is in the market, and trying to better that.

I think again, you need to foster an environment where people are allowed to form their own opinions and allowed to get their own ideas, and allowed to fail also sometimes, with things that they think will work, because there's no way, again, we have ... Saxo Bank's not a huge business, but we have about 1500 employees, and for sure, those 1500 employees get a lot more ideas and probably also very often better ideas than my partner Kim and myself.

You need to make it part of the spirit, to try things and to think of new ideas and leave people a lot of room inside some overall framework for them to innovate. I don't think you really can put it in through a tough structure. Now, you have to innovate and now you have to do this and that."

Dr. Kate Stone, Director Novalia.

"I know for me, I've been really innovative with technology. But I also know that from the beginning I've said that the greatest piece of innovation that we need to discover is our business model. That's been the greatest challenge ... it's been the greatest challenge of all. Because, we've managed to create things that can connect with a lot of people and make a lot of people smile and have emotional ... emotional reactions. What we haven't been able to make people give us money or give us enough money. That's been a huge challenge for us.

So, it's been kind of like recognizing how to be innovate and how do we find a business model. As a team of people who develop technology, it's really important to ask ourselves, "Why do we create that technology? What is it that we're actually trying to do?" It's recognizing that it's not about the technology at all. What I've started to tell some of my colleagues is, "What we do isn't a technology, it's a philosophy." I think really the challenge is trying to see beyond what you think you create and what you think you do and see beyond that and understand more the philosophy of who you are and what you do and why you do it.

And when you can understand that, I think then you can be innovative towards furthering that goal rather than just doing more of the thing

377

that you do or creating more of the things that you create. Because you might actually realize if you understand the philosophy of what you do, that the next thing you do might look nothing like what you create and might also be nothing for the people who you create it for."

Henrik Fisker, Automotive designer and entrepreneur (BMW Z8, Aston Martin DB9, V8 Vantage, Fisker Karma, Mustang Rocket, VLF Force 1, Destino V8).

"Of course, there is the classic example of the iPhone from Apple, where for the first time, somebody made first of all, the phone that had no buttons, which seemed really strange. It cost about 20 times as much as the best Nokia phone. Of course, marketing probably told Steve Jobs, "Hold on a minute. How do you know that we can sell any of those? It doesn't make any sense." There was obviously a vision about if you put this out, there will be some people who is going to like and pay extra for it. That's of course the very classic example that you can use. You can see it in many other areas of design and for instance right now, I'm working on an electric car company, Fisker Inc. where I'm creating two vehicles.

One is the first vehicle which is a higher end luxury vehicle where yes, we had some experience with Fisker, earlier Fisker Automotive where put out the Fisker Karma, so there is some experience a little bit about what people like in that segment and why they bought it. Of course, then the only comparable is Tesla where you also see, yes, there is people there buying these cars and why, but it's still not a hundred percent sure exactly because there is so many different people. Now, I'm coming out with a vehicle which is much more extreme where I'm breaking away from some traditional means that I've often used in my designs which I know works.

I've stepped out on a risky thin ice, if you want and said, "Well, because we have an electric car, we don't have an engine. We don't have a gas tank." Why do we have to have the big hood and the big trunk when we don't have these two things in terms of the visual aspect? I've decided to really change that. For the first time, we have a four-door sedan which has extremely flat front end because there is no hood there. There is no engine. We have moved a lot of electronics into the front and we don't really use as a trunk, as some cars are doing it. We are still putting this other electronics in there. Then we are freeing up the trunk to make a large trunk. I've stretched the whole greenhouse to give it much more interior space than any other car in that type of car. I've done a lot of stuff that's really innovative and new. When you speak about it, it makes a lot of sense. The question is, is that going to resonate emotionally with the consumer?

Now, I believe it is. I'm right now, working on some really interesting, I would say sensual sculpture on this vehicle. I'm trying to spend everyday figuring out and changing it slightly with whatever knowledge I have, to bring that emotion out of that car which is why call it as actually Fisker E-Motion, it can be electric motion or emotion. I'm trying to extract that feel that I want people to feel in the design. But I have to do it without using traditional means. What I mean by that, traditional means to make a car look good is a very long hood. The cars we really admire like a Jaguar E-type, Ferrari 275GTB. Those cars have very long hoods."

Johan Boserup, Global CEO of Trading at WPP's GroupM.

"Business innovation can come from a number of different things. I think, primarily, it will come from two different places. One is, "Necessity is the mother of invention." I think if the industry changes; if you're competitive set changes; or your clients change; or the way you operate you have to change and you have to innovate the way you do it. Our industry, the media industry, has been through a digitalization through the last 10 years and we've had to innovate. We have a new competitive set rather than just going up against other media agencies without going up against big media companies and cross-over companies like Google and Facebook and data companies and all sorts of different... and we've had to innovate to keep up with them and to make sure that we have an offering that either complements or competes with them.

Also, our clients have demanded that we change and therefore we've had to innovate in order to keep winning clients and to retain the clients we have. But, I think more importantly, business innovation can come from individuals in the organization. I think that's actually a much more healthy route to business innovation. I think it's more long-term to have the right people in the right roles and allowing them and supporting them in being innovative. I think if you do that you're ahead of the curve. You have a more long-term strategy and you're moving the company and the people with it, rather than trying to push the people or pull the people behind some sort of official and necessity of invention."

Part VIII. Entrepreneurship.

Personal branding.

Personal branding is the practice of people marketing themselves and their careers as brands. It's the process of developing a "mark" that is created around your personal name or your career. You use this "mark" to express and communicate your skills, personality and values. The end goal is that the personal brand that you develop will build your reputation and help you to grow your network in a way that interests others. We often associate personal branding with musicians, actors and reality stars as they battle for media publicity. However, personal branding has been around for a while and really caught on when Tom Peters authored an article called "The Brand Called You" in a 1997 issue of Fast Company magazine.[70]

"Today brands are everything, and all kinds of products and services, from accounting firms to sneaker makers to restaurants, are figuring out how to transcend the narrow boundaries of their categories and become a brand surrounded by a Tommy Hilfiger-like buzz.

"Regardless of age, regardless of position, regardless of the business we happen to be in, all of us need to understand the importance of branding.

---

[70] Peters, Tom (1997) "The Brand Called You". Fast Company magazine.

We are CEOs of our own companies: me inc. To be in business today, our most important job is to be head marketer for the brand called You."
Tom Peters

If you understand your strengths, skills, passions, and values, you can use this information to separate yourself from your competitors and really stand out.

One example of a corporate leader known for his personal branding is Lee Iacocca. Lee Iacocca engineered the Ford Mustang and later became president and CEO of Chrysler. Throughout the 1980s, he appeared in a series of commercials for Chrysler's vehicles, employing the ad campaign, "The pride is back," to denote the turnaround of the corporation.

Figure 36.

Another example is Richard Branson. Branson is clear about being a risk taker using his endeavors as personal and corporate branding. He has taken on world record attempts in hot air balloons and a speedboat, and challenged both British Airways with Virgin Airlines and Coke with Virgin Cola. In that sense he is a master at creating an image for himself and his Virgin brand.

According to the acclaimed author Jim Collins, excessive self-promotion or personal branding may have negative consequences for a firm as it leaves the successor in a bad position. Brand value should be based on the firm and not just the current CEO.[71]

Interviewees.

Ole Henriksen, Founder and Creative Director, Ole Henriksen Skin Care Brand.

"I love being associated with my brand, I really do, because not alone has it clearly made me go out there in the world and connect with people. They know who this Ole guys is, they know what Ole Henriksen represent when they are first familiarized with the brand. So the personal branding has actually been a plus for me. And I think it began by being in the service business, because I began as a skin care expert, treating skin, getting to know skin intimately. But when you treat your clients in a one-

---

[71] Collins, James C. (2001). Good to Great: Why Some Companies Make the Leap...and Others Don't. Originally published: October 16, 2001. ISBN: 978-0-06-662099-2. LC Class: HD57.7.C645 2001. Page count: 320. Publisher: William Collins.

on-one basis, you obviously establish amazing relationships. It's about making it personalized.

So the way I have grown the brand is really on a very personal level. I like to say that every jar of cream has been "Olenized"- there's a little bit of Ole love in every jar and that I love this very day travelling the world non-stop, whether it is meeting with clients, or the people that sell the products, or... whoever it is. And are there drawbacks to that? Not at all, because I actually believe that for the longevity of the brand, the day I'm no longer with the brand, that brand has a stronger identity. There's a lot more to work with as well, because those people that go on with the brand, they need to have things to... the archives.

Chanel is a good example. Chanel was revitalized. First it sort of took a nosedive when she died, and now again it's a mega brand. As is Dior. Those are two examples of luxury brands. So for me, the day I'm no longer there, they can still play those dance videos of me, they can still see me in action, talking about life and beauty."

Kaspar Basse, Founder, CEO Joe & The Juice.

"If you ask me, I would argue I don't do any at all. We've never engaged in advertising really, except for our stores. You could argue that everything we do is advertising because of the experience in the stores. We always looked at our high rents as our marketing budget. I was actually a little afraid about all this public approach. I don't know how to control it. I think I could have been a lot better at it. As you say, the reason you may feel that it is very aligned with me as a person is, I think a reason from the fact that it's a company where our entire top

management has been here ten, twelve years, and we've just engaged on this journey together where it is, it fills a lot in all of our lives. Therefore there is an authenticity and a very honest approach to our interest and our enthusiasm about the company and the brand and the journey that we're on.

This probably, hopefully, people can feel all though the company. Whether they have direct contact to me or one of the managers. Everybody's concerned about it and everybody's interested in it. It's very difficult to be part of us if you are flat lining. That's probably why you end up seeing some kind of profiling connection to me. I honestly don't feel that I'm doing anything except taking care of my close partners and managers."

Asger Leth, Director & Screenwriter, DGA award winner. (Ghosts of Cité Soleil, Man on a Ledge, Five Obstructions, Move on (Telekom)).

"That's a good question. There's no doubt that we see a lot of personal branding within the tribe of directors. That's for sure. I don't think there's a yes or no. Is it a good thing or a bad thing? Can you use it? Can you not use it? I think there are some people that can, and I notice that. I'm not personally very good at branding myself, but I am branding myself at the same time. We cannot not. I'm often wearing these black outfits and shit, whatever. I do use personal branding, but I think in a more subtle way. I think there are directors, and I'll just name a few, because they wouldn't be upset.

I think they know very well, Lars von Trier from Denmark, absolutely. He's a branding expert. He's branding himself as the provocateur, the guy who says all the politically incorrect things. He's always making a mess of things. That's his branding as an auteur. That's great. I love it. He's very effectful. And he does it much more than people think.

That's very interesting to watch. There's other guys like David Lynch. Everybody in the world knows what David Lynch looks like, with his big hair and all that stuff. That's a branding thing. That also makes it, are we going to go watch the new David Lynch movie? Yeah, we are. For sure. It works. It sells tickets. Also, when producers are setting out, they're thinking about, who should direct this script? They're like, David Lynch. The branding goes both out to the audience, but also back into the back of the kitchen where the soup is made, you know what I mean. That's great.

There's guys like Tarantino. He's a master brander. Everybody knows who Tarantino is, what he is. His brand also goes into his movies, his dialogue. Everybody knows what a Tarantino dialogue sounds like. It's a branding. You absolutely put a stamp on it. That, again, sells tickets.

Then there are guys like David Fincher, who doesn't really brand himself. That's the other end of the spectrum, but everybody also knows he only brands himself in the movies, in his language of the movies. That's a brand in its own right, and maybe a more longer lasting brand, in a way.

I definitely have nothing against von Trier, Lynch, Tarantino branding themselves as persons outside of the movies, but I must say I'm full of respect for a guy like Fincher, whose film language consistency is so David Fincher that you start recognizing it for that, and that becomes a brand."

Peter Ålbæk Jensen, Producer, Founder & fmr. CEO, Zentropa.

"First of all, it has to be however you are branding yourself. If you are the CEO of the biggest bank in the country or from my point of view, from a crazy film company, it's still branding. It's just different values, presented in different ways. Personally, I've never though about doing anything, but since it has been me and Lars (von Trier) who started and we are some kind of exceptionists and we are a odd couple almost like Laurel and Hardy, Gø and Gokke in Danish. We are a funny setup because he's a spoiled upper class kid fro the rich areas of Copenhagen and I'm a redneck right wing countryside boy, with an IQ close to a mentally disabled person.

So it is fun just to let go and if you feel like lying on the table naked during an interview, do it. But I have never done it because I thought it would smart in order to do something, but why not? It costs nothing except for a little bit of pride, you can say. But first of all, it's meant to be fun, and it's meant to be funny activities that we think of hilarious and in my old age I'm not concerned about what all the people think about it. But at least it's memorable, and here in this company people always say it would be impossible then to be the successor. I stepped down as the head of the company August of last year and a group of five younger employees took over and there has been no problem. They're extremely serious, none of them is naked and running around bragging. They are positioning them in their way, in another way."

Peter Holten Mühlmann, Founder and CEO, Trustpilot.

"The way I'm thinking about personal branding is that it can be very beneficial for the business. You, as a person, can get a lot of attention. That then translates into more attention for the company. It can help the company to recruit. If there is this publicly... If there's a public person that people can relate to, people can see and if you can articulate values where people say, "Oh. I can identify myself with these values, that can really help your recruiting efforts. Then, finally, if you're considering whether or not you should do personal branding; I think it depends a lot on who are you? What do you want?

Fundamentally, I think you should do what makes you happy. If you're happy, you're usually successful. If you love all the glitz and attention, then do it. At the same time, just also know a company is very rarely won by you being a lot in the media, you going to a lot of the conferences and you doing a lot of the speeches. It's really won behind the computer screen or the desk, speaking with customers, in meetings or going fundraising. It's won with the work. I think, if you're really an iconic leader, go for it. Don't think you have to. Many great companies are just built by people who didn't need to have that big profile."

Benjamin Holk Henriksen, Strategic planning & branding.
Lecturer DIS and Copenhagen Business School, Author, Filmmaker
"The Mind of a Leader", "Holk Master-class".

"Personal branding is a most interesting concept, and I am really grateful for all the extremely interesting interviewees that are contributing to this episode. First of all I believe the term, and as we have

witnessed, the term is too broad to classify as an advantage or disadvantage. It depends on the situation. Are we talking about a small business, a thought of one man band, or a larger organization. Some people like reality stars and bloggers and so forth, personal branding is part of their game and they could not live without it. Same goes for some creative industries. I have been fortunate to talk to people like Philippe Stark and also Tony Visconti, who produced a lot of David Bowies albums, and they both stress the importance of personal branding, so definitely there are cases where it's most beneficial. Also if you are an entrepreneur, as we have witnessed with Ole Henriksen in this episode, bringing your own values and aspects into the company culture, can actually be a motivational factor.

But it becomes delicate when you talk about larger organizations, are you then doing it for your own good or for the benefit or the organization. It's questionable whether amazing people like Jack Welch from General Electric or Lee Iacocca, actually ended up having a bad impact on the organization because they left too big of a mark and that can be difficult to deal with later on in terms of financial benefits, but also the whole image."

Entrepreneurship: From idea to action 1.

If you look up the word entrepreneur in a dictionary one of the definitions you will find is:[72]

"A person who organizes and manages any enterprise, especially a business, usually with considerable initiative and risk."

What does it take to become a successful entrepreneur... is it really that difficult and does it require management skills, initiative, boldness or energy?

Let's start this episode with a few quotes from memorable entrepreneurs:

"Entrepreneurship is neither a science nor an art. It is a practice."
Peter Drucker, management consultant, educator, and author.

"When everything seems to be going against you, remember that the airplane takes off against the wind, not with it."
Henry Ford, founder of Ford Motor Company.

"Watch, listen, and learn. You can't know it all yourself. Anyone who thinks they do is destined for mediocrity."
Donald Trump, president of the United States of America.

---

[72] http://www.dictionary.com/browse/entrepreneur

Interviewees.

Mikkel Borg Bjergsø Founder and CEO Mikkeller brewery, bars and restaurants.

"Denmark is known for being a beer country, which means that we have one huge brewery. Actually the third biggest brewery in the world, and we're one of the smallest countries, so we are a country of beer, but we have had a very long tradition but not very good tradition with beer. Which changed in the late 90's when we had the so called beer revolution and we got a lot of new breweries popping up. I think we went from ten breweries to about a hundred and forty in eight years.

This whole interest in beer and different beer styles and stuff, I caught on to that, and started drinking different beers than the normal pilsner. Then in 2003 I thought it would be fun to home brew it myself. It kind of became a thing to brew beer in your kitchen, and so I did, and got really, really good results with what I did. I liked it, and my friends liked it and, which friends often do if beer is involved, because then they know, more beer will come their way so they're very positive.

Then in 2005 I decided it would be fun to get a reaction from people that I didn't know, wasn't in my surroundings, so I decided to start brewing on a little bit bigger scale, and released my first beer official release in 2006. It pretty much blew up from then because there is a rating site for beer called "Rate Beer," which is kind of known as the unofficial world ranking of beer and in 2005, still being home brew, I was named the 5th best brewery in the world, so I got a lot of interest from the beginning.

That's how it started. I didn't start it because I wanted to build a big company and live off of making beer. I just started because I wanted to make good beer and show people that the beer that we got, these micro... new craft breweries we were doing were interesting, but there was a lot more to that, and for example in the states they are a lot more interesting and extreme, and I wanted to show that as well, so that's why I started it."

Klaus Riskaer Pedersen, Entrepreneur, Author, Founder of CyberCity and CopyGene. Fmr. member of the European Parliament (MEP).

"Being an entrepreneur is a fancy branding for being a business guy, being somebody who wants to do business. What I've always done, and what I'm specializing in is innovating. It's two different worlds. When you want to understand my drive, my drives are innovation and changes. The only way you can make innovation that matters is by introducing disruptive innovation, where you disrupt existing business trajectories and business models and enterprises and incompetence. That's where you make the changes.

When I say innovation and disruption, I am rejecting the... the whole notion of entrepreneurship, it's rubbish. I basically hate that expression. It's a fancy branding for something we've always had. People want to earn a fair buck, buy something for $1 and selling it for $1.10. These guys have not understood anything about where this world is moving. We are moving away from bottom lines and into total value creation."

Petter A. Stordalen, Founder and owner of Nordic Choice Hotels.

"I was born and raised in a small supermarket in a small town in Norway. I was the third generation, supposed to take over this supermarket, or small grocery store for my father. I loved to work with my father, but the thing I loved most was to sell strawberries at the local market.

And even though the competition was quite tough, and at that time I was 12 years old, sometimes I did like every business man: I started to complain. I did complain to my father about competition, my sales stand, which was much smaller than the other sale stands. It was like five competitors at that time. And one night before I went to bed, my father was sitting next to me, and I had been complaining a lot. And then he told me, "Peter, I'll teach you one thing: sell the strawberries you have, cause those are the only ones you can sell."

And that night before I put my head on the pillow and went to sleep, the last thing I was thinking about was, "My dad is a genius. And one day, I will take over the grocery store."

But it didn't happen because even though it was my father's dream that I should be the third generation to take over, it wasn't my dream. I wanted to do something on my own, to start my own business one day. And I had to give away my father's business to my younger brother. I went to the capital, but the thing I brought with me was the story about the strawberries. And I named it, "The Strawberry Philosophy." It's been a very important part of my life because the philosophy is about, do the best out of what you have. Don't look at your competitors. Don't think, "If I just had this money, this business, if I just had that one, or that education." Then you will never succeed. Make the most out of what you have."

Henrik Fisker, Automotive designer and entrepreneur (BMW Z8, Aston Martin DB9, V8 Vantage, Fisker Karma, Mustang Rocket, VLF Force 1, Destino V8).

"Well, I started as an entrepreneur by leaving the corporate world with an idea. Right when I did it, it didn't seem like as big a deal as I realized it was once I had done it. I guess sometimes it's better to just jump out and find out how deep the ocean really is. Part of it is when you come from a big corporation, that time, I'd been at BMW, Ford Motor Company and Aston Martin. Aston Martin was not big but within Aston Martin, we had the support network of Ford Motor Company. When I went out and started making some specialty cars with a friend of mine, suddenly, you realize that this entire support network that you were used to had disappeared. You had to do everything yourself.

That was a big change. However, to be an entrepreneur, I think you have to have, first of all, an idea. You have to be willing to do everything to get this idea forward. That means you have to do all aspects of what's necessary to bring this idea to market, to production, to reality. Usually, most of us, we have been used to do work only on a certain aspect of a product. You might be the one that calculates the price, so the accounting department. You might be the engineer that engineers certain things. You might the guy in the PR department that is writing up the great press release or you might be the designer who is doing the shape. There is people usually doing many different things to create an ultimate product. As an entrepreneur, when you start, you probably have to do all that."

Molly DeWolf Swenson Founding member / CMO of RYOT.

"That's a good question. My path into entrepreneurship was really circuitous. I graduated from university having no idea what I wanted to do. The only things I even thought that I could do were management consulting; e-banking; or Teach for America basically non-profit work; or become a paralegal. And of those four, the only one that was only sort of even remotely interesting was paralegal work.

I applied for a bunch of law firm jobs in New York and one unpaid internship at a start-up modeling agency doing assistant booking. Got all the law firm job offers, didn't get the unpaid internship offer and completely re-evaluated everything and made it my mission to get a job at that specific start-up. And so, ultimately, I convinced the CEO to bring me on as a business development intern to help him raise his Series A round of funding.

So, that was my first introduction to entrepreneurship was right out of college. But, I didn't start my own ventures until a number of years later when I met my co-founders of Riot."

Klaus Riskaer Pedersen, Entrepreneur, Author, Founder of CyberCity and CopyGene. Fmr. member of the European Parliament (MEP).

"In my case, I came out of the political youth movement in the 1970s, which was the disruption of the youth movement in 1968, 70, 72 the flower power movement, where I was a teenager. My key kick off was questioning society, and how society works, and how political system

395

works, and how power bases work. I matured and got into business, started doing business in the '80s, where we also started to ask the question, "Who is the power base behind money?" When I was a young kid, you had the old guys network sitting on it, controlling everything, banks and the close circle of power, power brokers. But as the '80s opened up, you got the globalization, you got monetization, liquidity in the market, I mean liquidity changed, the concept of monetary policy changed, with Reagan and Margaret Thatcher.

Everything became more liquid, more transparent and that was the kick off to being disruptive in the sense that you would try to do projects, you could do project where you were no longer dependent on signing on contributions, even support from the original power base, you actually attacking it. That fitted very beautifully with where I came from.

There is a consistency, it isn't anarchistic, a disruptive access to doing new things, which are disruptive in the environment, which is fascinating, and that's why I started back in the '80s. I started in finance doing creative finance solutions, shareholder values, it was a new thing in parts of old Europe those days, venture capital, I was the first one to introduce it in Denmark with specialized funds to do that. That was the money side because it was in the '80s, but then it changes to breaking the statement monopoly of state distributed air-born television and over the air radio, where I established... broke those monopolies, created these networks, sold them on.

Later on... I went on and on, in all sort of things I've been doing, from stem cells to sort of introducing one of the very large ISPs, internet service providers in Denmark. Right now I'm doing medical cannabis in Uruguay. So you can see I'm constantly trying to focus on the synchronicity field, the power field where you will spot developments. Those developments will dictate where you would actually have the next development cluster, where you can expand the membrane and change where we do business and how we do it. Business is only the toolbox to make sure you do it right."

Lars Seier Christensen, Founder and owner Seier Capital, Co-founder and fmr. CEO Saxo Bank.

"To be honest, all business is a process. It's not like you say now I want to do Saxo Bank with a great trading platform. You decide you want to have your own business. I was actually, when we started out, it was a very traditional, telephone based brokerage, and we happened to stumble over the internet in the mid '90s and thinking, maybe this could be used for more efficient form of communication. Then we naively hired a few IT people and started developing the platform thinking that once it was done, we could stop spending all this money on IT and get on with life.

Didn't work out that way, today, we have about 700 IT people, I think. Really, we didn't have a very strong idea that that's where we're going to go. We had an idea that we can make life easier and make trading more accessible to our clients and that's what we did. It worked out, and we tried many things, some of them failed, some of them succeeded. That's one thing I think we've always been fairly good at, stopping things that are going wrong and focusing on what's going well.

It's not that you have a blueprint for everything you do. Hit and miss, and get some good ideas along the way. If you get a really good one, make sure you pursue that and discard some of the worst ones."

Entrepreneurship: From idea to action 2.

If you look up the word entrepreneur in a dictionary one of the definitions you will find is:[73]

"A person who organizes and manages any enterprise, especially a business, usually with considerable initiative and risk."

What does it take to become a successful entrepreneur... is it really that difficult and does it require management skills, initiative, boldness or energy?

Let's start this episode with a few quotes from memorable entrepreneurs:

"Risk more than others think is safe. Dream more than others think is practical."
Howard Schultz, CEO of Starbucks.

"I have not failed. I've just found 10,000 ways that won't work."
Thomas Edison, inventor.

"I'm convinced that about half of what separates the successful entrepreneurs from the non-successful ones is pure perseverance."
Steve Jobs, co-founder and CEO of Apple.

---

[73] http://www.dictionary.com/browse/entrepreneur

Interviewees.

Steffen Hjaltelin, Founder & Partner at Hjaltelin Stahl.

"When it comes to entrepreneurship, I got my best piece of advice when I attended INSEAD many, many years ago. We were in a class of 80 young leaders. Dominique, who was the strategic consultant for IBM, Professor, and an extremely smart guy... he asked into the classroom: "How many of you have considered starting your own company?" Every single hand in the room came up in the air. Everybody considered it. "How many are waiting for a unique idea to base it on?" Every single hand came up, everybody thought that.

He said, "I'm going to show you a concept that made the inventors billionaires." And then he reached under the desk and he opened a cheeseburger from McDonald's. And then we came up with the numbers as to how much that cheeseburger made for those guys. And then he said, "It's not about being unique; it's about being 10 percent better than your competition." And that just opened my mind completely, because it's true.

So for entrepreneurship, I can just advise: Find a place where you think you can become 10 percent better than the competition. And from there on, it is just 100 percent drive, drive, drive, drive, drive. And you are going to fail, and fail, and fail, and then just forward, forward, forward."

Petter A. Stordalen, Founder and owner of Nordic Choice Hotels.

"I started on a kind of education, but it was not really some super serious education. Then I ended up, a couple of years later, on Norwegian school on marketing, nearly by accident. Then I was reading this magazine, a

financial magazine, and there I saw an ad. They were looking, a head hunting company, and they were looking for a manager at the new shopping mall. The first really American shopping mall ever in Norway. You can read in the ad that they were looking for a person like, age 40-45, extensive experience, and all these things. I was 24. I was still not finished with school. I had never had a job before without the one I had, selling strawberries and working with my father in the grocery store.

But I thought that I was perfect fit for the job. And I did send my first and only job application in my life. I only had one thing that I could send, and that was one letter from my father, literally telling, "My son is a very good boy and he knows everything about what you need to know about supermarket business." And of course, nothing happened. I didn't hear anything from the company. So I just, one day, I decided to go to the address, which was in the ad. And I knocked the door and I said, "Something has happened because I've not been called or gotten an invitation for an interview." And they said, "No, that's correct because you are the least one to have this job." And I said, "But I'm perfect for the job."

Later on this guy told, in a magazine in Norway that I used two hours to convince him to send me to this town, it was the third biggest town in Norway, Trondheim. I'd never been there before. I had to pay the flight to get myself. But he accepted that I could be like ... he had two candidates already, both more than four years old. And I was a new potential, in the future guy, maybe I could work with some marketing.

So I took the first flight in the morning, because I needed to learn everything about what's going on in the town. This was the most important job in retail, in the property industry, in that town that year. So I remember, I still remember everything I was wearing that day. I had boots, a Levis 501, a white t-shirt, and a Marlboro coat. No, in fact, a fake Marlboro coat. I was walking around the city, stopped outside a shoe store. Then this old man came up next to me, it's like 7:30, 8:00 o'clock in the morning, and we started to talk. He did tell me a lot about what was going on in town. And then after twenty minutes he asked me, "So, what are you doing here?" And I said, "I'm here because I will be the new CEO of City Syd," which was the name of this new mall which was under construction at that time. This is back in '87. And he wished me good luck.

Three o'clock in the evening I went to this hotel, and this secretary guided me in the conference room and twelve men were sitting in a horseshoe. 11 serious faces and one smiling. One was smiling to me, the old man.

It turned out that he was one of the founding fathers of the project, City Syd. He was also controlling 50% of the shoe market in that part of Norway, and he liked me. So always be nice to strangers. Always be open-minded. They might help you one day. And the next. And that's important in business. The most important thing in business is actually execution. Don't only think about it. Do it.

It was, I did apply for the job. I did go to this head hunter company. I did take my time to learn about this new town. And I got the job. I was the youngest manager ever in Norway of a shopping mall. It turned out to be a huge success. So that was the start of my career. But I still had the dream. I wanted to do something on my own. But it was a good beginning."

Klaus Riskaer Pedersen, Entrepreneur, Author, Founder of CyberCity and CopyGene. Fmr. member of the European Parliament (MEP).

"Innovation is, in my understanding, something which is more than incremental. That is business development. Incrementalism is business development. Innovation is innovation.

Now, how do you do innovation? That is a very interesting topic. First of all, never invent anything. You are sure to be a loser. Don't invent anything. Don't even contemplate figuring out something nobody else has figured out, because you can be quite sure something is wrong. You are probably not the smartest guy on Earth, there are probably a lot of other smart guys, and if it's not there, there's probably a reason why it's not around. That is one way the invention track, you know, that is over 150 years ago. You had inventions. We have left the invention path, we are going into the application path, and conceptualization... you cannot invent anything, really. What you have to do is constantly figure out what are we doing right now, which can be done in a much smarter way? Very different. And what would that resolve in.

Here we are working with the idea of synchronicity, synchronicity space. Synchronicity is when you have developments, non-causal developments, which are not inter-related happening. Non-causality. Those different developments, which are not inter-related, however, seems to be going in a particular direction altogether, which is establishing the synchronicity track. Synchronicity is basically physics, mathematics, you know vectors. You put on vectors in different directions and you would have a median vector power going then you can establish a median path for the vector play. It is mathematics in the sense that you would have different things going on.

By your ability to see different things going on, you will see a new development track gaining it's traction, it's force. You would most likely see what's going on and recombine it, in a way nobody else did, in a smart way. You say, "Wow, if you do this, turn those things around a bit, we would actually strengthen the synchronicity track." The diffusivity of the vectors, you would actually try to align them, you would re-position some of the elements in the vector play and reposition them in the game field. By repositioning in the game field you would start to optimize your trajectory for the synchronicity track and essentially you will say, "Wow, this is smart. Can we really do this?"

When you hit that development track, that's where you go up and you hit the membrane of the existing business environment and the existing market and what is being done. When you hit that membrane and push on it, your development cluster becomes strong and pushes on the development of the whole membrane, then you will expand the conception of business and how it's done. You will have other peoples doing the same at the same time, that's very important. By being together, you will have... I mean I believe when we started internet there was only 50 internet service providers, something like that. It was nothing. It was early '95, so it was also very early. When we did stem cells, collection of cord blood stem cells for therapy, therapeutic use. When I looked it up there was about 13 or 15 that did that around the world."

Mikkel Borg Bjergsø Founder and CEO Mikkeller brewery, bars and restaurants.

"I was working as a school teacher when I started the company and actually worked as a school teacher until 2010, so for the first four years while running the company, I loved being a teacher, I love teaching, so it's not that I wanted to get away from teaching. I just started the company and then it grew.

I have no business education at all. I have no brewing education, so I had to learn everything from scratch, from zero. How to run a company, how to file taxes, and everything, I had to learn on my own, because I didn't have any employees for the first couple years. Obviously it took a tremendous amount of time. I mean, I worked, and I still work a lot, but I think the first six years at Mikkeller I worked at least 16 hours a day, seven days a week, every day, all year.

I think it takes that in order to build a company, to become successful at what you do. You have to acknowledge that it will take a lot of time, a lot of energy, and a lot of work. Otherwise, you can't succeed. I don't think so. I mean, you can probably do good, but you won't get out as much as I have if you don't work hard, and if you don't put a hundred percent of your energy into it.

405

That's something that I always tell people. I would advise people not to start if they're not ready for that, because if you're not ready to throw you whole life into it, it's not going to work. Building a business is not a nine to four job. It's fun, and that's another thing. You have to do it if you're interested in what you're doing. Brewing for me was a hobby that turned into a business, and I love beer, I love brewing, I love everything around it. You shouldn't do it because you think you can make money. Then you should just find something else. You should just start something that you're interested in, and then build that from scratch. Not because you think you can make a lot of money, because if you don't enjoy what you do, it's not going to work out."

Entrepreneurship: From idea to action 3.

If you look up the word entrepreneur in a dictionary one of the definitions you will find is:[74]

"A person who organizes and manages any enterprise, especially a business, usually with considerable initiative and risk."

What does it take to become a successful entrepreneur... is it really that difficult and does it require management skills, initiative, boldness or energy?

Interviewees.

Petter A. Stordalen, Founder and owner of Nordic Choice Hotels.
"No, no, no. I stayed very, very short. They raised my salary from 20,000 euro, or nearly the same as $20,000, it's a bit less but still, and they raised it to more than 100,000 in twelve months. And they thought it was because of me, that this was a huge success, but everything was right with that project. Even if you or anybody else could do the job I did, and I knew it. So I wanted to go to Oslo, the capital. I wanted some new challenge, some bigger challenge. So I was working for different companies, but it was very hard to start on my own because I had zero money. And cash is important. And it's hard to get in the beginning.

---

[74] http://www.dictionary.com/browse/entrepreneur

So, I ended up actually working for a bank controlled company dealing with bad bank business, like shopping centers, hotels. Then I was given this huge opportunity when the last big department store in Oslo, the capital of Norway, go into bankruptcy in 1992. This was big crisis, the biggest crisis we had in Norway. It was the same crisis you had in the States, it was saving in loans I think. This was a huge financial and property crisis in Norway. Most of the banks actually needed help from the government to survive, and then this department store, they were actually running out of cash. But the property still had a huge value. So that's another lesson to learn: never run out of cash. When bad times, when crisis comes, always have cash. Because cash flow and cash is the two most single important things to survive in business. And you will never go down if you have cash, so cash is important.

So I was the only one that wanted to take over this department store. The competition was, everybody in Norway was looking at this thing because it was a huge property. 250,000 square feet of property, AAA location Oslo. But again, I was putting together a good team. We worked hard for 48 hours. We were there, we were the last one, we were the underdog. And we won. And we did turn Steen & Strøm from losing four or five million dollars a year, to profit in less than six months. The idea we had was simple, to convert this department store into a shopping center. And we did it in a super short period of time. And that was the beginning of the biggest shopping center company ever in the Nordics.

We grew, we had the best people, we earned tons of money, and in 1996 we were a listed company. Strong balance sheet, a lot of cash. Strong cash flow. We had thousands of shareholders, but one guy had bought a lot of shares. And he didn't like me. In 1996 in June, I was fired. I went from hero to zero in a split second. I was in all the newspapers. I was on TV, humiliated. And then Mike Tyson, he said, maybe he hasn't said very many smart thing but once he said something like, "They all had a strategy until they were knocked down." And I was knocked down. But the only thing to do is to raise up again and think, "Okay. I will prove that I can do it again." And at that time, because I had some stock options, some carried interest, so I had some money and then I decided I wanted to do hotels. Why hotels? I love people. Hotel is a people business."

Henrik Fisker, Automotive designer and entrepreneur (BMW Z8, Aston Martin DB9, V8 Vantage, Fisker Karma, Mustang Rocket, VLF Force 1, Destino V8).

"Usually, when you start as an entrepreneur, you have some sort of innovative idea. I had some ideas about changing the way you create cars and how you built them, how you designed them. Of course, that means when you create something new, means really every time you open a door, you have no idea what's behind it. You get used to that every plan you create will never be the actual plan because you're going in the unknown because you're inventing something new. You're starting something new, whether that's a process or software, a product. You're going into something where you don't exactly know what's going to happen. That also changes the way you have to make decisions. It changes the way a product gets developed because you're inventing things as you go along. It's very hard to make a plan. You have to make a plan. That plan, there is a lot of ifs.

My experience is that you are finding yourself in situations many times where you open that door and thought something was going to be there and it's not. You have to make a gut feel, quick decision. Some of the things that you have in big organizations is before you make a decision, you usually have a lot of references. People who made a report and tells you, "Here is why we think this decision is good. We have all this knowledge." You have all this knowledge to review. After that, you can say yes or no. When you're an entrepreneur, a lot of times, you have nothing. You're just standing in front of something, time is running. Usually, time is money and you need to make a decision now. There is no time to ask for a report. There is nobody to make that report. It is about what you think is right. Should I do it or not? How do we do this? That is a totally different mindset of being an entrepreneur."

Klaus Riskaer Pedersen, Entrepreneur, Author, Founder of CyberCity and CopyGene. Fmr. member of the European Parliament (MEP).

"When you start off, you will probably be very few, and you will very, very quickly be a lot. That's the whole point in being first mover, that you come in. Don't be so much first mover that you will be alone, because you probably die. This is critical mass of development, you know? You need people who develop like yourself.

Let's take the internet, if somebody didn't make Netscape, or whatever, we didn't even have browsers or email clients when we started doing internet connectivity, people forget that. That came late '95, we didn't even have it. If nobody else had understood the internet, and we had been sitting coding trying to do connectivity, we would had been forced to do everything ourselves, we'd never been able to that, and never in a good quality.

Don't fear, and don't be afraid of being part of something, be happy that somebody are working, like you're doing, if they're doing 3D printing, everybody's doing that these days. You see it now with medical marijuana, I've been working with one and a half year now, we have been building up a substantial plantation in Uruguay, for raw material production one and a half year goes very early days. Now everybody want to do it, well they can't do it, but they will be able to in another year.

Still, it is the ability, in an almost autistic sense, to feel that what's going on, one two three four five, right now, that is odd, that is really changing something. It may very well be a technological change, it may very well be some entry-barriers which break down, it may very well be incumbent inactivity and passivity that is opening up this development space, and it may actually be very often some new ideas coming into the scene, which will be integrated into this sinography. From there on, it depends on execution, execution, and execution. And execution and execution and execution, that's where everything is. Forget about the ideas. Forget about sitting on a bar with your friends and discussing it and making nice plans and writing memos, it doesn't mean anything. From there on, when you have identified this development field, this game field, and you have repositioned the bricks, and you have established you're now hitting the development track, the synchronicity track, together with a lot of smart folks around the world, and you begin to hook up with these folks because you've seen it and somebody else has seen it, you will figure out where they are, because you will find them. I mean, you will hook up. Then, you know, everything is where you have to kick it at running, and then we get into execution. That's what it's all about."

Petter A. Stordalen, Founder and owner of Nordic Choice Hotels.

"I was finished with shopping centers, I had done that. Two times actually. I wanted something new. And this time I had money. So I bought a small hotel out of bankruptcy again and I started to go to a big conference. I was supposed to, I was invited to talk about shopping centers, but I was finished with that, so I told the audience that I will talk about my new business, hotels.

And then I told them that I will start hotels, and I will build the biggest and best hotel chain ever in Norway. And the people started to laugh. And I said, "I know why you're laughing, because of course like with the shopping centers, I will be the best one. I will be the number one in the Nordics." And in the Q&A session, one journalist had a question. "So Peter, how many hotels do you have?"

"One." They were laughing so much that they literally had to be carried out of the conference room. But from that day we grew with one hotel every second week. Fifty new employees came into the company every ten days. We went from one to 100 hotels. From a few employees to 5,000. And today, we are 190 hotels. We have three standardized chains, or brands, and then we have 21 independent hotels.

It's been some tough times. We have been gone through the crisis in 1998. That was Asia. And then the dot com crisis in 2002, 2003. And not to forget the big crisis after Lehman Brothers went bankrupt in 2008, 2009, which was pretty tough.

So that's a third thing to learn: always be prepared for crisis. It's like the Olympics, but they come not only every fourth year, they come every seven, six, seven years. It's like a cycle. And you need to be prepared. I don't know the name of the next crisis, but I'm prepared because I know it will come. Probably in the next twenty four months. I don't know if it will be because of some financial things, China, I don't know. But it will come. And every time some people tell you, "It's different this time," it's not. Crisis will come. But it's everything the same. In every crisis, it's a huge opportunity. My biggest growth has always been under and after this huge crisis. We did grow a lot after and under 2003 and 2008. We had the biggest expansion, took most new positions in 2009. Because we were literally alone and the world will only go under one time, according to the Bible. It will not happen in the next crisis, or the next one, and I will probably at least have five, six, seven crises for the rest of my business life. I'm already preparing for the next one."

The basis for entrepreneurship.

Interviewees.

Klaus Riskaer Pedersen, Entrepreneur, Author, Founder of CyberCity and CopyGene. Fmr. member of the European Parliament (MEP).

"I'm making a big distinction being an entrepreneur, which as a business guy and being an innovator, which is changing this world. Innovators, I've met quite a few of them actually, they are unpretentious. They are very, very bright. They don't give a shit about money. They are most probably quite academic actually, most of them, very well educated. We are very, very educated. It is sort of the academic kind of people, you would normally meet in the academic environment. Many of these guys, they're very smart, you cannot fool them, they know what goes on. You know, when you talk with these people just for a few minutes, you know, forget it. I mean, he or she knows what he is doing or she is doing.

If you talk about business people, I make an analogy between being an entrepreneur and being a business guy, which is different. They just want to earn some money, make profits. Those people you can always figure out, they are very driven by the basics of why you want to be a businessman and that is driven by greed, that's how it works."

"So can you recognize people who are business folks? Yes. You would normally recognize them because of the focus of the conversation, their desires and how they see life. Can you see a differentiation between people who are just going for business and people who want to do the

414

other stuff? Yes you can, because the innovation guys can be very quickly put in the mold, academics, politicians, that kind of stuff. Very similar kind of people interacting. That's the difference, in my view there's a difference, as I have spotted in all the years."

Henrik Fisker, Automotive designer and entrepreneur (BMW Z8, Aston Martin DB9, V8 Vantage, Fisker Karma, Mustang Rocket, VLF Force 1, Destino V8).

"Yeah. When you leave a large corporation, you have a very safe environment, at least you feel you're safe. Reality is maybe you of course can always get fired at one point in time. You feel you're safe. You have a constant paycheck, maybe a really good paycheck so you've created a life around you that fits that paycheck, whether that's your mortgage on your house or your car or your vacations etc.

Sometimes it may be good that you're not really aware what that means because if you think too much about it, you may never leave that environment because it's clear that there will be a change as you go out on yourself because suddenly you realize nobody is paying for your vacation. Nobody pays for you when you're sick etc. etc. That is going to become something that changes your life until you become very successful as an entrepreneur.

I would say when I left Aston Martin at that time, that was my last corporate job, people thought I was crazy. I had journalists saying, "You have the best design job in the world. You sit on the board. Why would you leave?" My answer was, "I felt I had reached the ceiling of the corporate world where I could go." I was in my late 30s. I thought I can't

415

sit on a beach and drink margaritas for the rest of my life and just sit on my laurels and think, "Wow. I did all this great stuff."

It was just too early for me. I wasn't in that mode that I could just move along in a soft pace and do what I needed to do. It was too young for me. I needed to do more stuff. I think that drove partly that risk appetite in me that I thought if I can do so well in the corporate world, maybe I can do better as an entrepreneur."

Klaus Riskaer Pedersen, Entrepreneur, Author, Founder of CyberCity and CopyGene. Fmr. member of the European Parliament (MEP).

"Everybody can learn to play piano, but very, very few do it well. This is how it basically is, so in order to do some of these things well, you will need to have a very basic DNA propensity to do these things in a style, way, or manner, which would be successful. That will also include certain personality traces on how you behave as a person, because you cannot disintegrate these things from how you do and work as a person. You have to be quite ruthless actually, you have to be very commanding, but at the same time also inclusive and social. It takes quite a lot. That is probably quite influenced by the way you have been brought up, the environment in which you've grown up. Si I'm afraid there is something here about environment and your basic DNA actually."

"Lots of people can be business people, you don't have to be very well educated, or very well brought up, or very talented actually, to make a successful business. Actually, you have to be stupid enough sometimes, to

416

make some business. Some business is so goddamn dumb, that you really have to be an idiot to do it, but you can earn lots of money."

"You have to understand, if you're are a business guy, bottom line profit guy, and you want to be part of the establishment, being a successful businessman, you don't want to have any problems with anybody. Then you are finished, you are dead. You're not invited anymore for the lunches, you are being kicked out of the clubs, you are depending on bank loans. You will be part of a fabric where you will be excluding yourself if you are in any way shape or form intimidating the establishment way of doing business, the incumbent way of doing business.

If you in your life are working on making innovation and understanding innovation is disruptive, and is "red ocean", and you are attacking incompetence. Then you will also know that you are basically and constantly at war. You are not at cozy meetings with fellow business guys, because all those fellow business guys, you've basically gone and fucked them in another three months, or 12 months or two years because they may do some business where you really want to go in."

Petter A. Stordalen, Founder and owner of Nordic Choice Hotels.

"Success is just based on a number of failings. I have failed, personally and in business. I was divorced but I did never lose my belief that I could marry again. That I could find another, a new love in my life. I was fired. I survived crisis. So failings, you must accept failings if you want to succeed. Most people, they tend to stop, to give up, just before the success is there. So you have not failed before you stop. Always try again. Always try to motivate other people to try. Hang in there. I was close in 2003, but

we never stopped believing. We will find a way out of this. It is tough right now, but the crisis will go over and we will survive. And we did. Many of our competitors, they didn't. They gave up. So never give up."

Klaus Riskaer Pedersen, Entrepreneur, Author, Founder of CyberCity and CopyGene. Fmr. member of the European Parliament (MEP).

"Everything you do is disruption a lot of people, a lot of business models are being disrupted by what you do. At some point in time you will make a mistake. Everybody makes mistakes, and everybody will really kick you very hard if they can. You meet all of them on the way down. They will all give you another kick in the ass on the ladder, so you get down very far, very fast.

You have to understand the nature of losing a battle. Losing a battle is not actually losing a war. Even if you lost a war at some point in time, you may actually survive yourself anyway. It may not necessarily impact what you have been able to achieve. Napoleon lost lots of battles, he won a war, he lost also a war, but he's still Napoleon. One of the brightest politicians we have seen in Europe any time. Created huge changes in the way of civic society and it's interaction with a society as such, the penal code, the way military was managed. He abstained from doing horrible mistakes, we had actually being doing later on in the European Union he didn't do. Very, very, very smart guy lots of things lost, came back again. He lost eventually. But not in the realm of history, he has not lost. I believe no person on which there have been written more biographies, I think it's about 1,000. This is pretty crazy.

Everything starts with your own understanding of what did I do wrong myself? You will always do something wrong yourself, you have to understand that to start with. That takes some time. And you say, "This is where I busted up." From there on, you can understand it, "That's a part of the bill I'm willing to pick up, now what about the rest of the bill?" Then you will be able to understand what happened and how you can integrate it.

Desert walks going into monetary. Whatever you do can be very productive for your way of thinking and your self confidence and your personality. It takes some pressure to create a diamond, as you say, and you need to have something that goes wrong to be really good. You cannot be really good until you've been through that pain. It doesn't matter, if you are a bit isolated. You have to understand that the loneliness is part of that you can do something which is really, really fantastic because you are lonely or isolated, because you're not depending. In philosophy and literature, dependence is a bad thing, even on friendships. I mean Proust he made his Disputably literature work rejecting friendship as a value. He said Friendship is not a value it is a dependency, and it restrains you from doing what you should do. It's memory in it's wrong sense. It's tradition in it's wrong sense. You have to be free, you have to be inspired. Basically the same when you do projects.

Projects are creative, it's a creative process. It's not bookkeeping, it's not lawyers work, it's creative. It's very sense of the matter."

Henrik Fisker, Automotive designer and entrepreneur (BMW Z8, Aston Martin DB9, V8 Vantage, Fisker Karma, Mustang Rocket, VLF Force 1, Destino V8).

"I will say, honestly, jumping out and becoming an entrepreneur was a lot tougher than I expected. It's tough when you are getting ... You're looking at your income and you suddenly realize, "If I don't make anymore money or if I haven't raised another funding in two months, I can't pay the rent." You got kids in school etc. and you can't pay. There is no backup. Now, this is America. You don't have a very strong social network that's going to save you if you're suddenly out of a job. Specifically if you have a high paying job which is you have all these amenities that you were used to, of course you can survive but surviving is tough if it means getting rid of your house, getting rid of your cars and everything else. By the way, I hadn't taken anywhere on vacation since I became an entrepreneur for many years. I was in a situation where it was so tight that it was a few weeks away and I really didn't know how I was going to pay the rent. In the last moment, we got a job in that we had worked for a long time, to get a design job in that saved us and got us over that hump. What would I have done if that didn't come in? Not sure. Maybe I had to borrow some money. I already had maxed out my credit cards just paying for food and everything else. Those are the moments that you normally don't experience when you're in a stable job. That's also why specifically if you have a family, especially if you have a family that's depending on you as your own income, it becomes even more difficult.

Today, my wife and I are working together. We are supporting each other. She is not depending on me. I'm not depending on her. We have now, with all the experience, laid out our business in a different way, where we don't put all the eggs in one basket, which is something that is tough to do when you just have one idea in the beginning. Later, you realize that is a good way to diversify it but it's really not something you can do when you go out the first time as an entrepreneur. You do have to take that risk. It is a risk. That's also why the reward can be big. Without risk, there is no big reward."

Klaus Riskaer Pedersen, Entrepreneur, Author, Founder of CyberCity and CopyGene. Fmr. member of the European Parliament (MEP).

"It's a very, very dangerous, extreme sport, to do innovative business projects yeah".

Strategic management for entrepreneurs.

Strategic management is the management of an organization's resources in order to achieve its objectives.

"Strategic management is not a box of tricks or a bundle of techniques. It is analytical thinking and commitment of resources to action. But quantification alone is not planning. Some of the most important issues in strategic management cannot be quantified at all".
Peter Drucker, management consultant, educator, and author.

"Greater is an army of sheep led by a lion, than an army of lions led by a sheep".
Alexander the Great.

Strategic management involves setting goals, analyzing the competitive environment, analyzing the internal organization, evaluating strategies and ensuring that management implements the strategies across the organization. Let's take a closer look at how successful modern entrepreneurs conduct strategic management and scale their business

Interviewees.

Klaus Riskaer Pedersen, Entrepreneur, Author, Founder of CyberCity and CopyGene. Fmr. member of the European Parliament (MEP).

"Well, first of all, the notion of making companies, businesses, in the 21st century, has dramatically changed. How I did business in the '70s, '80s, '90s and the '00s, you can forget about it. It's all gone, you can put it right away, you cannot do it anymore.

You cannot today make business on your own. If you are a gigantic company with gigantic resources, you're not even able to do it because you're not having the development capabilities and the creative capabilities. Even the biggest companies on this globe are integrating on the external borders, special capabilities, and open source environments where they integrate development capabilities, because they realize they cannot do it themselves. We are talking about the IBMs of this world, and Google have done it, I mean everybody. I don't know Apple actually, probably not. Quite a lot of people are realizing they have to integrate."

Lars Seier Christensen, Founder and owner Seier Capital, Co-founder and fmr. CEO Saxo Bank.

"I think it's actually very important not to be stuck with a blueprint or plan, because you cannot plan for everything, and you'll very often have to do a pivot, as you call it, to change your plan along the way, because something doesn't work or you get a better idea. You shouldn't be too stocked in what you really want to do. You need to listen to your clients, you need to provide what they want rather than what you think is a brilliant idea. Be very open to that.

Define as early on as possible, a set of values that you want to build the company around, so you're sure you get the right kind of people on board and they have the right understanding of what you expect from them. I think it's very important to build the structure of the company in a right way from the outset. A company will always have values, sometimes good, sometimes bad, but the more explicit you can be from the outset about that is what I expect from you, this is what I want you to pursue, these are the values that I want you to adhere to and that I expect that we agree upon, that's very important because really, the product will be very difficult to predict what it's going to end up with 10 years later. But the principles and the values and the way that you interact with your clients and the way that you listen to your clients will be very important during that process. I would say in a way, that's the most important thing, to make sure that you have the right people on board and you have the right attitude toward your customers, which is listening to them."

Klaus Riskaer Pedersen, Entrepreneur, Author, Founder of CyberCity and CopyGene. Fmr. member of the European Parliament (MEP).

"Everybody who thinks that business is about buying cheap and selling expensive, I mean this is sort of Trump logic. They would lose it, because this is not just about transacting and getting bottom lines profits anymore, it's about total value creation, and how you distribute that value creation between different stakeholders. All that is leaving the basic, old fashioned idea and style of being a business guy, I want to do some business, I want to scale, I want to be successful. Yeah, but you will not be successful anymore doing that, you'll be a loser basically, you haven't figured out what's going on.

You have to understand, whatever you do, you do not necessarily have to make innovation and disruption, not necessarily, but you have to *understand what you do is value creation in a broader sense, and how you distribute it is how you create the network group that can support you to be successful, and you can attach, on the periphery of your contact base, other people who has knowledge and can impact it and accelerate it. It doesn't help today to pick up the phone and say, "Hey, I've got a great idea, we can earn $100,000." Fine, get lost. Who would bother about that? Answering your question about where you start and how you begin, it's a type of person which are engaged in innovation and disruption, working in the Red Ocean, and building your projects on network situations. You will come from a background that can be basically everything, which is in the same category."*

Petter A. Stordalen, Founder and owner of Nordic Choice Hotels.

"Don't spend too much time on strategies. Strategies can be bought. You can even buy a market position. And a market position can be changed overnight. But the only thing that never can be copied is the culture. Culture is the magic things because people are the most important that you have in your company. Doesn't matter if you're Apple or Nordic Choice. It's a people thing. Wise people standing in a line for two nights to wait for the new iPhone. I have an iPhone, even though people tell me that Samsung is a better, smarter, faster, better camera, than iPhone. I love the storytelling. And I believe in the storytelling. Business is very much storytelling as well. It's not the most advanced mobile phone that will become the biggest success."

Klaus Riskaer Pedersen, Entrepreneur, Author, Founder of CyberCity and CopyGene. Fmr. member of the European Parliament (MEP).

"This is something which is quite well known, and quite objective. Basically, when you pass 50 people, you are going from one type of organization to another type. It is roughly 50 people, give or take. Because when you pass 50 people you have to start much more to use middle managers, and you have to distribute decision making powers, or like you said, they kind of run it. You will be forced to that."

Henrik Fisker, Automotive designer and entrepreneur (BMW Z8, Aston Martin DB9, V8 Vantage, Fisker Karma, Mustang Rocket, VLF Force 1, Destino V8).

"I think it's very important, if you go out specifically as the first time to become an entrepreneur, that you try to think about all the aspects of your idea. Not only the actual idea, if it's some sort of idea of a product or a software or a service. But also, everything that comes around this idea. How do I bring it to people? Is it going to be sold? Is it going to be leased? Who is going to do it? How does the financing look like? So have some idea that goes way beyond just the idea. It's good to at least play that out, not only in your head but a little bit in a plan. You may see some things that you know you're not able to solve right now but at least you are aware that this issue will come up eventually. You don't get surprised when you go out and talk to the investors and somebody throws a question at you and you go, "Oh, I didn't even think about that." It's good to be aware of all the potential issues. It's okay to sometimes say, "I haven't solved that yet but I'm aware of it." I know that we have to create an infrastructure to sell this product. When time comes, we are planning to get advisers in and talk about and figure out how we do it, but you should be aware of it. I think that's an important thing.

The second for me is that when you go out as an entrepreneur, I think you should really think about if your idea is different enough and really make sure that you take a big risk in terms of saying, "I'm going to do something that's really different in the market, and not be afraid to try it." Sometimes what you're up against is existing brands in whatever you do. It's very rare that you invent something that there is nothing that compares to that. Usually, you invent something that's better than something that's existing. If there is something existing, then usually, there is a very strong brand behind it, big infrastructure, everything else. You have to convince a consumer to buy your invention instead of the existing stuff, whatever that might be. You really want to make sure there is as large a separation between existing and what you're offering. The more you can push your innovation, the better it is, the more you can differentiate yourself. That's important.

Finally, I think when you go as an entrepreneur and have an idea of starting something, sometimes it's good to bring in a few people that are opposite of yourself... not just surround yourself with people who is doing the same as you are.

If you're an engineer, you may not want to hire another five engineers and you guys start something, or if you're a designer, don't hire another five designers, or a software developer hire another five software guys. You may want to have somebody who complement what you're doing in other areas where you're not very strong, so it could be the financial, it can be the marketing aspect, whatever it might be."

Steffen Hjaltelin, Founder & Partner at Hjaltelin Stahl.

"You have to find an area where you think you can become 10 percent better than your competition. From there on it's all about finding the right guy or the right girl. Find the area, find someone who has drive, drive, drive, drive; and make them roll with it in that regard. And your role will be more and more to make people actually work together on the team. Those are, in my regard, from my perspective, the secrets about getting something to succeed just in the modest way we have succeeded."

Lars Seier Christensen, Founder and owner Seier Capital, Co-founder and fmr. CEO Saxo Bank.

"You actually asking about how to let go? I have never found that so difficult, because I think it's pretty evident that if you hire good people and they have the right attitude, and they focus 100% on one area, in all likelihood, they will do it better than if you spent 5% of your time on that area while you're dedicating 95% of your time for something else. Yes, particularly in the early years, we did follow quite closely the details of what was happening, but I still think that it's pretty evident that it'll be best for you also to let go and let other people do a lot of the innovation and heavy lifting on the projects that they happen to be assigned to."

Klaus Riskaer Pedersen, Entrepreneur, Author, Founder of CyberCity and CopyGene. Fmr. member of the European Parliament (MEP).

"I've said now and then to people that ask me about it, I say, "Well if you want to compare it to generals, I'm General Patton. I'm not General Eisenhower. Eisenhower became president, but General Patton, he won the war. He was there where you had all the bullets, and the tanks, and the battles."

You're on a battlefield, you have to understand you're on a battlefield. When I make a project and I work my teams, they understand, and I make them understand. Forget it, there's no coziness here, we are in war, we are working together, one by one. If somebody doing a mistake here, the rest of us will have to pay the price because we are so depending on all of us being very, very smart. It's not that if I do a project I am the one deciding, I am the one being the older patron of the whole thing. I am just sort of director, I am a director."

Petter A. Stordalen, Founder and owner of Nordic Choice Hotels.
"Always employ people that are better than yourself. That's the DNA in Nordic Choice. And if you do that, the company will always grow."

Managing investors and growth.

Interviewees.

Klaus Riskaer Pedersen, Entrepreneur, Author, Founder of CyberCity and CopyGene. Fmr. member of the European Parliament (MEP).

"If you start out today, you will be depending on ... You will have very, very short window to operate in. Provided you have identified a business opportunity, which must be innovation base, and which you may have found by making a synchronicity judgment of what's going on in the development field. You will have a window, which is for all purposes, very, very short. There's a lot of smart people around in this world. You may profit from being one of the first ones, being one of the first mover groups is fine, it doesn't really matter not to be first mover, you can be doing very fine coming in, in the follow-through group. You have to be very early on.

The whole issue is you have to integrate people who can kick some ass with you. Basically today, all ownership is non proprietary, it is distributed one way or the other. Okay, you can distribute it between a few people or a lot of people, that depends. If you make a platform product on the internet, you will make a very diversified distribution, you make open source maybe. Everybody owns it, it will be non profit or whatever. Everybody is totally diversified, it's all a Wikipedia kind of thing. You may also choose to make it diversified, but not very diversified. You will have to diversify and integrate the minimum resources.

It will be kind of network ownership situation. Even if one, two, three, four, not one but a few people around. Very unlikely one guy, very unlikely one guy. One other partner is for marriages or sex, it's not for business. You will have more people. Already having on guy and yourself, that's the wrong starting point, it would never work. At least include somebody else then you can start voting if something goes wrong, then you can solve most of these problems after personal inabilities or inefficiencies or in capabilities or un-willingness or un-adaptability.

Having these people, setting up a network that's part of the equation and that you will do in a balanced way so people can contribute, like yourself. You will most likely have some specific capabilities or resources that are very important, those should of course engage. Also, with today's projects, certainly have things where you need some other capabilities where you have to cover them by bringing in other people, and you cannot hire them anymore. The good guys you cannot hire, they say, "Well come on." If somebody called me I'd say, "Get lost." The good guys, they work together, they split it up, they own it. On that basis you can solve quite a few of these more tragic problems with a couple of partners that falls out.

You can also sort this by some sort of ownership model where you have some sort of remunerations committee set up between you where you would sort of have options that are listing, and on the way. If you do not perform some options to go into the ownership are not vesting, or expiring in one way or another. You can do options or warrants as a kind of financial instrument to control some of this stuff here. There are some very clear instruments you can use in a financial terms, to solve it. The best solution is political, that you have the right people and you can vote, and if somebody not moving you can vote them out or block some options so he's cut off in an early part of the project, and he will not expand as the milestones are being met. That's my personal suggestion for this, but you have to be networked one way or another. From that group you will then start doing your funding, and you will slice your finding into very small increments, so you will take in smaller seed rounds. In my view, a project will have a handful of seed rounds before you can think about going into the venture capital stage, typically. You want to slice it up so you have a higher valuation, avoid dilution, and establish trust with your funding base."

Henrik Fisker, Automotive designer and entrepreneur (BMW Z8, Aston Martin DB9, V8 Vantage, Fisker Karma, Mustang Rocket, VLF Force 1, Destino V8).

"It's good to have in the beginning, somebody else that can complement what you're doing because most entrepreneurs is going to need eventually money. Go out and get some capital. It's very important you are able to articulate your idea and explain it to people. That usually demands that they see the entire picture, not just, "This is the idea." It comes down to manufacturing, cost, distribution etc.

It's important that you have got your idea far enough also before you go out to somebody and ask for money because sometimes, or mostly, you only have one chance to go out. You can't go back to the same guy who already told you no. The more you can yourself mature your idea and your business plan before you go out, that's another important thing. Ultimately, it also means you're going to own more of the company because it's all about valuation. The more value you're able to create early on, the more you're going to own of that company as you go out and raise money because somebody is going to ask you for a chunk of your company and saying, "I want X percent if I fund you." The more you mature with the idea, the more you can argue that you should own a bigger part because you've already spent a lot of time, which equals to money, and who has de-risked the project. Investors is all about risk. How much risk do I have? That's why the later investors put money in, the less equity they get. The earlier they get in, the more equity but the more risk. You want to be able to almost say, "I've taken it this far so the risk is less. Therefore, I should keep more of the company."

Klaus Riskaer Pedersen, Entrepreneur, Author, Founder of CyberCity and CopyGene. Fmr. member of the European Parliament (MEP).

"Most projects doesn't need a lot of funding to start off. And for heaven's sake, don't go out and ask for a lot of funding, go out and ask for small slices with a milestone based, and then you also have the huge advantage by doing this when the price will go up. If there's something investors like, reduce my risk when the risk is biggest. Allow me to increase it as the milestone goes along, and then they love prices are actually going up, because they earned money on their first investment, and the second, and the third. They don't get angry when you say, "You bought for $1, and now it's $2.50, and now it's $3.75, and now it's 6." They don't matter, they don't mind, as long as you can show there's been a reason why the price is going up, and somebody else is going along, probably some new ones. Your ability to slice it and add new investors, and establish a trajectory of price increases and milestones that are completed, is success to

financing. That should bring you to a level where you can launch your products and begin to establish some sort of incoming cash flow, and at that level you can go and do some of the venture type of larger finance rounds where you can take in some serious money."

Lars Seier Christensen, Founder and owner Seier Capital, Co-founder and fmr. CEO Saxo Bank.

"We didn't actually have a lot of funding, because in those days, it was different to start a financial institution. We started Saxo Bank with $100,000, and that was what we had, and that was what we had to make due with. The downside of that is obviously that we really had to get it right quite quickly. The upside of it was that we didn't have other investors in there. At the end of the day, we had full control of the company and we could take the time that we wanted to take to reach the right results.

That is a very important message also, try to bootstrap as much as you can, because while it's very tempting to take other people's money, it does change your life. If you get very dependent on other people's money and you think that you can just spend without really caring about seeing an income side, you may very well find yourself in the minority at some point and if you then make a mistake, the Mackenzie guys will come in and kick you down stairs. I've seen that happen many times, and that's very sad for people that actually started out with a great idea, but they ended up being prisoners in their own company and ultimately were thrown out because a private equity fund thought that they could do better."

Klaus Riskaer Pedersen, Entrepreneur, Author, Founder of CyberCity and CopyGene. Fmr. member of the European Parliament (MEP).

"I've done a couple of projects in the last few years, and I started immediately to bring in the money people, very transparent system where we have actually changed the way we do projects, with an open board room, which is transparent. Everything is transparent, you're having the due diligence documents, which are in Dropbox and all the shareholders have direct access to them, they are signing in the NDA's of course, but they have access to all important documents. Of course, if there's something which are technologically important, it is protected in special folders, which cannot be accessed, but in general, all documents affecting the company can be accessed and read in its original form. We are constantly advertising what goes on, on a current basis on Slack, which allowing all investors to see what's going on and put in comments everybody else can see. We are having a high degree of involvement in whatever we decide. We are making a load of shareholder meetings in an electronic form, on DocuSign, where everything can be handled electronically. Just by adding platforms, which are already there, we are having basically shareholders, which are feeling they're in the board, and they're in the decision making process, and understand what's going on. It's transparent, and also the bad news, so they can be very involved.

They way I see it, if you go to people help, asking, "Will you help me to do a new project," to seed financing, you're not just selling an investment opportunity and an upside. This is a lifestyle. You are asking for help to do something which is magnificent and fantastic. People should be happy and joyful to be part of that, but you should also allow them to be part of it. That's what they are paying for. When you do these things you may actually not succeed. It's terribly important that people are in trusting you with their risk funds in a start up, and seed financing. They must understand where did it all go wrong, when I lost my money? Do you don't lose their confidence.

You can lose a project and get back to these people if they understand what they did was, "I agreed on the risk, I agreed with what's being done. I think they executed it correctly, I knew what was going on. And I knew there was these three reasons why it didn't work and that was just a shame, but nobody fooled around. These were very smart and very good people, you can come back. So you have to protect your brand with investors. You have to take them in because they can scale your business and in creating trust. When you eventually want to take in some money to scale your business, you have to take in money at a certain stage. You cannot scale your business on your own cash flows. It's not possible in this world today, it's ridiculous, doesn't work.

And about losing influence. Whatever I do, I'm proud in saying, whatever I do I certainly do not have influence to decide anything. I can only do something shared with someone else. I'm actually pulling it, I'm advancing it, as something which are very important to the project. Even in the projects that I'm doing, I am the one responsible for starting it up, and the strategic management, chasing business models and correcting the project as it goes along for errors. I'm having a very important position, like the CEO of all this stuff here, in a sense chairman of the board really, the way I work. I'm not the guy who can just say, "Do it."

And if it's not a good idea, it could be stopped, and it should be stopped.
That's how it works."

List of interviewees.

Thank you to all the interviewees:

Leaders, entrepreneurs and artists:

Asger Leth, Director & Screenwriter, DGA award winner. (Ghosts of Cité Soleil, Man on a Ledge, Five Obstructions, Move on (Telekom)).

Birgitte Mabeck, Head of fundraising and marketing Red Cross.

Christina Bilde, Spokes person Roskilde Festival.

David Angelo, Founder & Chairman, David & Goliath advertising agency.

Dennis Balslev, CEO IKEA Germany. Fmr. CEO IKEA Denmark.

Henrik Fisker, Automotive designer and entrepreneur (BMW Z8, Aston Martin DB9, V8 Vantage, Fisker Karma, Mustang Rocket, VLF Force 1, Destino V8).

Johan Boserup, Global CEO of Trading at WPP's GroupM.

Kaspar Basse, Founder, CEO Joe & The Juice.

Dr. Kate Stone, Director Novalia.

438

Klaus Nørskov, Head of communication Red Cross.

Klaus Riskaer Pedersen, Entrepreneur, Author, Founder of CyberCity and CopyGene. Fmr. member of the European Parliament (MEP).

Lars Liebst, CEO Tivoli.

Lars Seier Christensen, Founder and owner Seier Capital, Co-founder and fmr. CEO Saxo Bank.

Malin Gardeström, International Marketing Manager, Carlsberg & Tuborg.

Matthew Bagwell, Managing Director Naked Communications Europe.

Mikkel Borg Bjergsø Founder and CEO Mikkeller brewery, bars and restaurants.

Molly DeWolf Swenson Founding member / CMO of RYOT.

Ole Henriksen, Founder and Creative Director, Ole Henriksen Skin Care Brand.

Peter Giacomello, Sponsorship and Reputation Director, Marketing Carlsberg.

Peter Ålbæk Jensen, Producer, Founder & fmr. CEO, Zentropa.

Peter Holten Mühlmann, Founder and CEO, Trustpilot.

Petter A. Stordalen, Founder and owner of Nordic Choice Hotels.

Stefan Kehl, Market Director Nordics (Norway & Denmark), SET, AppNexus.

Steffen Hjaltelin, Founder & Partner at Hjaltelin Stahl.

Tue Walin Storm, Director, Screenwriter, Founder Storm/Hansen (Nielson, Ford, Pirelli, The Raveonettes).

Professors and lecturers:

Anders Kryger, Senior Business Strategist, Industrial PhD Fellow at MAN Diesel & Turbo.

Andreas Rasche, Professor at Copenhagen Business School. Department of Management, Society and Communication.

Anne Marie Bülow, Professor at Copenhagen Business School. Dept. of management, society and communication.

Benjamin Holk Henriksen, Strategic planning & branding. Lecturer DIS and Copenhagen Business School, Author, Filmmaker "The Mind of a Leader", "Holk Master-class".

Christer Karlsson, Professor CBS, Stockholm School of Economics, EIASM Brussels Accredited "This is Lean: Resolving the Efficiency Paradox", N. Modig & P. Ahlstrom "Research Methods for Operations Management".

Fumiko Kano Glückstad, Assistant Prof. PhD in Cross-Cultural Communication & Cognition.

Karim Jabbar. Entrepreneurship & Innovation specialist. Industrial PhD Fellow Lecturer, DIS – Study Abroad in Scandinavia.

Leif Rasmussen. Strategic Branding. Lecturer, DIS – Study Abroad in Scandinavia.

Malene Torp. Executive Director, DIS – Study Abroad in Scandinavia.

Seidi Suurmets, PhD Fellow at the department of Marketing, Copenhagen Business School.

References.

References presented by chapter in alphabetical order.

Part I. Strategic planning and branding.

Mission & Vision.

Campbell, A., Yeung, S. (1991). Brief case: Mission, vision and strategic intent. Pergamon Press plc.

Target group.

Avery, J., & Steenburgh, T. (2012). Target the Right Market. Harvard Business review, October ISSUE.

Caffarella, R. S. (1982). Identifying client needs. Journal of Extension, 20 (July -August), 5-11.

Simons, R. (2014). Choosing the Right Customer Harvard Business review, March issue.

Stakeholder & Issue management.

Dougall, E. (2008). Issues Management. Institute for Public Relations, December 12.

Freeman R. Edward and Evan William M. (1990). Corporate governance: A stakeholder interpretation. Journal of Behavioral Economics, vol. 19, issue 4, 337-359.

Positioning.

D'Aveni, R. A. (2007). Mapping Your Competitive Position. Harvard Business review, November issue.

Reflection on the Marketing Mix.

Borden, N. H. (1964). The Concept of the Marketing Mix, J. of Advertising Research, 2, 7-12.

Kotler, P., Armstrong, G., Cunningham, P.H. (2005). Principles of Marketing. Toronto: Pearson Education Canada. pp. 67-70.

McCarthy, E. J. (1971). Basic marketing; a managerial approach. Homewood, Ill, R.D. Irwin.

Fast Moving Consumer Goods.

Leahy, Rose (2011)."Relationships in fast moving consumer goods markets: The consumers' perspective", European Journal of Marketing, Vol. 45 Issue: 4, pp.651-672, https://doi.org/10.1108/03090561111111370

Steenkamp, J.B.E.M. & Dekimpe M.G. (2009). Marketing strategies for fast-moving consumer goods. Financial Times, February.

Part II. Strategic planning and branding.

Reflection on product portfolio management and the Boston Matrix.

Henderson, B.D. (1970). "The Product Portfolio". The Boston Consulting Group.

Product life cycle.

Kotler, P. (1967). "Marketing Management: Analysis, Planning, Implementation and Control", Prentice Hall, 12th edn, 2006.

Brand equity and Brand extension.

Belsky, G. (2012). Business Time. The 10 Best Brand Extensions Ever. March 13.

De Mooij, M. (2014). Global Marketing and Advertising. Fourth edition. Sage publications. 30-31.

Doorley, J. and Garcia, F. (2011). The key to successful Public Relations and Corporate Communication. 2nd edition, Routledge, London.

Lennox, A. (2014). Smart brand extension allows Virgin to keep up appearances. The Guardian., Thursday 23 October 10.42 BST

Reflections on the SWOT analysis.

HBR Tools: SWOT Analysis. Tool by Harvard Business Review, 2015.

Humphrey, A. (2005). "SWOT Analysis for Management Consulting".

Reflection on leadership and Michael Porter's value chain.

Porter, M. E. (1985). The Competitive Advantage: Creating and Sustaining Superior Performance. NY: Free Press (Republished with a new introduction, 1998.).

Reflection on Lean.

Krafcik, John F. (1988). "Triumph of the Lean Production System." Sloan Management Review, 41–52.

Strategic Planning.

Mintzberg, Henry, Ahlstrand, Bruce Lampel, Joseph B. (2008) Strategy Safari: Complete Guide Through the Wilds of Strategic Management, 2nd ed. 2nd Edition. Pearson Education Limited.

Peng, Mike W., Li Sun, Sunny, Pinkham, Brian, and Chen, Hao (2009). The Institution-Based View as a Third Leg for a Strategy Tripod.

Part III. Communication campaign development.

Agency positions and the creative brief.
Suggett, Paul (2018), The Structure of an Advertising Agency. Get to Know the Typical Make-Up of an Ad Agency.
http://www.adcracker.com/brief/Sample_Creative_Brief.htm
http://www.thehealthcompass.org/how-to-guides/how-write-creative-brief
https://www.upwork.com/hiring/design/how-to-create-an-effective-creative-brief/

Holk's Communication Platform model CPM.

Aristotle's Modes of persuasion.
Aristotle, "Rhetoric", 350 BCE.

Creative development, Tagline, Logline and structure.
De Mooij, M. (2014). Global Marketing and Advertising. Fourth edition. Sage publications.
Katz, S.D. (1991). Film directing "Shot by Shot" visualizing from concept to screen.
Mackendrick, A. (2005). On Film-making 'an introduction to the craft of the director'.
Rosenberg, J. (2010). The Healthy Edit. Focal Press.

Storytelling.

Katz, S.D. (1991). Film directing "Shot by Shot" visualizing from concept to screen.

Mackendrick, A. (2005). On Film-making 'an introduction to the craft of the director'.

Rosenberg, J. (2010). The Healthy Edit. Focal Press.

Part IV. Media activation.

Push Pull strategy.

Debasis Pradhan. (2011). To push or to pull: Dynamics of promotional strategies: Tale of three rural industries.

Hopp, Wallace J.; Spearman, Mark L. (2014). "To pull or not to pull: what is the question?". Manuf Serv Oper Manage. Retrieved 13 June.

Robertson, T. (2018). Difference Between Push & Pull Marketing, smallbusiness.chron January 31.

Community Marketing.

Faris, R. (2015). Market to Millennials by Getting Out of the Way. Harvard Business review, December 09.

Fournier, S. & Lee, L. (2009). Getting Brand Communities Right. Harvard Business review, April issue.

Print.

Eldesouky, D. F. B. (2013). Visual Hierarchy and Mind Motion in Advertising Design. The arts Journal.

https://webdesign.tutsplus.com/articles/understanding-the-f-layout-in-web-design--webdesign-687

http://linchpinseo.com/effective-print-advertising-design

Product Placement.

Buss, Dale: "A product placement hall of fame" Date 06/22/98 online original. www.businessweek.com/1998/25/b3583062.

Gene Emery, Reuters "What's in a name: Product Placement in games" www.usatoday.com/tech/techreviews/games/2002/1/30/spotlight.htm

Govani, Shinan. (1999). Product placement in movies – Is it really so bad? February 10, www.csmweb2.emcweb.com/durable/

Karrh, James A., McKee, Kathy Brittain, Pardun, Carol J., (2003). "Practitioners' Evolving Views on Product Placement Effectiveness". Journal of Advertising Research; Jun, Vol. 43 Issue 2, p138, 12p .

Kogtvedgaard, Mogens. (2002). The law of competition (konkurrenceret).

Peebles, M. Ellen. "And now a word from our sponsor". (2003). Harward Business Review, Oct, Vol. 81 Issue 10, p31, 9p, 2c, 4bw.

Russell, Cristel Antonia. (2002). Investigating the Effectiveness of the Product Placement in Television shows: The role of Modality and the Plot Connection Congruence on Brand Memory and Attitude. Journal of Consumer Research, Dec, Vol. 29 Issue 3.

Links:

"Coca-Cola revises its guidelines in school nutrition, commercialism" (Atlanta Business Chronicle)
www.atlanta.bizjournals.com/atlanta/stories/2003/11/17/daily3.html

"Gimme a Bud"! Promotion, www.Advertising.utexas.edu

Hip Hop: Are we selling the song or product? July 9, 2003
www.pub12.ezboard.com
"Pepsi adds splash of color" www.hollywoodproductplacement.com
"Product placement in movies"
www.propguys/htdocs/pages/product/
Product placement with a "twist" Hollywood takes a hit from the
internet & moves towards guerilla style "permission Marketing"
www.hollywoodproductplacement.com

Cross Promotion.
Gruner, S.L. (1997). The Secrets of Cross-Promotion. Different
entrepreneurs tell how they have found marketing partnerships to be
an effective way to stretch a budget.
Kumar, D.S. (2012). The Dark Side of Cross-Selling. Harvard Business
review, December issue.

PR and the art of writing a press release.
How to Write a Press Release.
https://www2.le.ac.uk/offices/external/news/publicising/how-to-
write-a-press-release
James, Geoffrey. (2016). "How To Write a Press Release, with
Examples". cbsnews.com. CBS News. Retrieved 19 May.
Press release template.
https://www2.le.ac.uk/offices/external/news/publicising/how-to-
write-a-press-release/template
What is a Press Release? Digital Media PR, Public Relations/April 7th,
2015.
http://www.5wpr.com/new/press-release/

Part V. Digital marketing and social media.

Customer journey mapping.

Compare: "Customer Experience Management: What it is and why it matters". SAS. (2015). Customer experience is defined as your customers' perceptions – both conscious and subconscious – of their relationship with your brand resulting from all their interactions with your brand during the customer life cycle.

Richardson, Adam. (2010). "Using Customer Journey Maps to Improve Customer Experience". Harvard Business Review, November 15.

Srivastava, Apigee, Kumar. "How Data Analysis Drives the Customer Journey".

https://www.wired.com/insights/2014/01/data-analysis-drives-customer-journey/

Thompson, Ed and Kolsky, Estaban. (2004). "How to Approach Customer Experience Management". Gartner.com. Retrieved 2016-07-15. Summary: Managing the detail of customer experiences is an important part of any customer relationship management strategy.

Big data (p146).

Boyd, Danah & Crawford, Kate. (2012). "Critical Questions for Big Data, Provocations for a cultural, technological, and scholarly phenomenon". Pages 662-679. | Received 10 Dec 2011, Accepted 20 Mar 2012, Published online: 10 May 2012.

Hellerstein, Joe. (2008). "Parallel Programming in the Age of Big Data". Gigaom Blog.

Social media & viral marketing.
Surowiecki, James (2016). What happened to the ice bucket challenge? Derided at the time as "slacktivism," the social-media campaign has had surprisingly long-lasting benefits. The New Yorker, The Financial Page July 25, 2016 ISSUE.
Worland, Justin (2014). ALS Ice Bucket Challenge Donations Just Topped $100 Million. Time, Aug 29.

Paid, owned, Earned media.
Ceren Demirci, Koen Pauwels, Shuba Srinivasan & Gokhan Yildirim (2014). Conditions for Owned, Paid, and Earned Media Impact and Synergy, Marketing Science Institute, 14-101.

Strategies in an ever-changing media landscape.

Part VI. Global management.

Reflection on business development and Ansoff's Product Market Growth Matrix.
Ansoff, Harry Igor (1957). "Strategies for Diversification". Harvard Business review.

Barriers to entry.
Barriers to entry, exit and mobility, The Economist, Jul 13th 2009.
Demsetz, Harold (1982). Barriers to Entry, The American Economic Review Vol. 72, No. 1, pp. 47-57.
Lazaroff, Daniel E. (2006). Entry Barriers and Contemporary Antitrust Litigation, Posted Monday, December 4.

Reflection on sustainable competitive advantage strategy tripod and PEST analysis.

Aguilar, Francis J. (1967). "Scanning the business environment". New York, Macmillan.

Barney, Jay (1991). Firm resources and sustained competitive advantage. Texas A&M University, Vol. 17, No. 1, 99-10.

Barney, Jay, Wright Mike, Ketchen, Jr. David J. (2001). The resource-based view

of the firm: Ten years after 1991. 20 September.

Peng, Mike W., Li Sun, Sunny, Pinkham, Brian, and Chen, Hao (2009). The Institution-Based View as a Third Leg for a Strategy Tripod.

Porter, Michael E. (1996) What is strategy? Harvard Business Review November issue.

Porter, Michael E. (1980) Competitive Strategy: Techniques for Analyzing Industries and Competitors. Chapter 1. The Structural analysis of industries. Chapter 2. Generic Competitive strategies. New York: Free Press. (Republished with a new introduction, 1998.)

http://www.businessballs.com/pestanalysisfreetemplate.htm

Reflection on strategic planning and Michael Porter's five forces.

Porter, Michael E. (1979). How Competitive Forces Shape Strategy. Harvard Business review, March Issue.

https://en.oxforddictionaries.com/definition/competitive_advantage

Centralization & Decentralization.

Gouda, Dr. Islam Gouda (2014). To Centralize or Decentralize your Marketing. American Marketing Association. Warton.

Hatch, Mary Jo and Schultz, Majken (2002). The dynamics of organizational identity. SAGE Publications.

Lassenius, Fredrik & Holk Henriksen, Benjamin (2011). The Mind of a Leader I based on Niccolò Machiavelli's 'The Prince'. Episode 3. Astromax Entertainment.

Lassenius, Fredrik & Holk Henriksen, Benjamin (2010). Sådan tænker ledere/The Mind of a Leader. L&R business. 2010.

Reflection on Hofstede's cultural dimensions and Hall's High- and low-context cultures.

De Mooij, Marieke (2016).Global Marketing and Advertising. Understanding Cultural Paradoxes (Fourth edition).

Hofstede, Geert (1980). Culture's Consequences: International Differences in Work-Related Values", Sage Publications.

Hofstede, Geert. Dimensionalizing Cultures (2011). The Hofstede Model in Context. Universities of Maastricht and Tilburg, The Netherlands.

Hofstede, Geert, Hofstede, Gert Jan, Minkov, Michael (1994). Cultures and Organisations: Software of the Mind", Profile Books, London, 1994; 2nd edn, McGraw-Hill, New York, 2005.

Hall, Edward T. (1976). Beyond Culture.

Part VII. HR management and innovation.

Reflection on mission, vision and the golden circle.

Campbell, A., Yeung, S. (1991). Brief case: Mission, vision and strategic intent. Pergamon Press plc.

Partridgeon, Andy (2014). Executive Summary: The Golden Circle with Simon Sinek. Written. http://enviableworkplace.com/executive-summary-golden-circle-simon-sinek/

Sinek, Simon (2011). Start with Why: How Great Leaders Inspire Everyone to Take Action. Penguin.

Career Planning.

Reflection on HR management and Maslow's hierarchy of needs.

Maslow, A. H. (1943). A theory of human motivation. Psychological Review, 50(4), 370-396.

Leadership & job motivation.

Code of conduct and CSR.

Fair Labor Association. Nike, Assessment for reaccreditation, October 2008.

Friedman, Milton (1970) "The Social Responsibility of Business is to Increase its Profits", The New York Times Magazine, September 13.

Friedman, Milton (1962). Capitalism and Freedom. The University of Chicago Press.

Locke, Richard M. and Romis, Monica (2010) 'The promise and perils of private voluntary regulation: Labor standards and work organization in two Mexican garment factories', Review of International Political Economy, 17:1, 45 – 74.

Business innovation.

Vlaskovits, Patrick (2011). Henry Ford, Innovation, and That "Faster Horse" Quote. August 29. Harvard Business Review.

Part VIII. Entrepreneurship.

Personal branding.
Collins, James C. (2001). Good to Great: Why Some Companies Make the Leap...and Others Don't. Originally published: October 16, 2001. ISBN: 978-0-06-662099-2. LC Class: HD57.7.C645 2001. Page count: 320. Publisher: William Collins.
Peters, Tom (1997) "The Brand Called You". Fast Company magazine.

Entrepreneurship: From idea to action 1.
http://www.dictionary.com/browse/entrepreneur

Entrepreneurship: From idea to action 2.
http://www.dictionary.com/browse/entrepreneur

Entrepreneurship: From idea to action 3.
http://www.dictionary.com/browse/entrepreneur

The basis for entrepreneurship.

Strategic management for entrepreneurs.

Managing investors and growth.